The Collected Works of
Marie-Louise von Franz

MLvF

Volume 10

General Editors
Steven Buser
Leonard Cruz

Marie-Louise von Franz
1915-1998

Volume 10

The Problem of the Puer Aeternus:

Eternal Youth and Creative Spirit

Marie–Louise von Franz

Adapted new English version
by Alison Kappes-Bates

CHIRON PUBLICATIONS • ASHEVILLE, NORTH CAROLINA

Logo of the Foundation of Jungian Psychology, Küsnacht Switzerland:
Fons mercurialis from Rosarium Philosophorum 1550 (Fountain of Life).

© 2002 Stiftung für Jung'sche Psychologie
First published by Spring Publications

Adapted new English version by Alison Kappes-Bates
Cover Image by Martina Ott
Interior and cover design by Danijela Mijailovic

ISBN 978-1-68503-247-0 paperback
ISBN 978-1-68503-248-7 hardcover
ISBN 978-1-68503-542-6 limited edition paperback
ISBN 978-1-68503-543-3 limited edition hardcover

◇

A Note on the Compilation of The Collected Works of Marie-Louise von Franz

Marie-Louise von Franz was blessed with a keen intellect and an outstanding memory. As a classical philologist with a doctorate in Latin and Greek, she was familiar with the writings of the ancient philosophers. She was exceptionally well read. Her private library alone contained over 8,000 books and writings. She was also both diligent and conscientious in her work. She met C.G. Jung in her youth and found him to be an excellent teacher and mentor. She went on to become a close confidant and collaborator, particularly in his work on alchemy. Jung's psychological observations and the conclusions and hypotheses he drew from them about the structures of the unconscious psyche increasingly coincided with her own observations. Marie-Louise von Franz was imbued with an inexhaustible creativity that inspired her well into her old age. She devoted her last lecture to the rehabilitation of the feeling function, a subject that was of great importance to her and to C.G. Jung. Her unconditional devotion to the manifestations of the unconscious psyche was exemplary for all who met her during her lifetime, and for many who came to know her from her writings or their own dreams.

Only a few of her works survived in the form of finished manuscripts. Many of her books derived from transcriptions of her lectures, some of which were delivered in German, though most were in English. The English transcriptions were later translated into her native German. Her primary focus was always on the psychological context and background of her books, and less on their linguistic delivery. Some publishers therefore took the liberty of adding or changing certain things in her texts to make it easier for the reader, as they thought. After realizing what they had done, Marie-Louise von Franz indignantly insisted on her original text being used, claiming that what she had written was what she had wanted to express. Since then, many of her works have been translated into 23 languages, with editions of varying quality being used as the basis for translations into local languages.

In addition to the publishing rights, Marie-Louise von Franz left to the Foundation for Jungian Psychology a handwritten list in which she noted which editions of her books she considered to be the best and most accurate. After her death in 1998, the members of the Foundation decided to republish all of her works in German in accordance with her list. We have respectfully endeavored to remain as close as possible to her original tone, to correct obvious audio or transcription errors, to add footnotes to facilitate understanding, and to supplement texts when written records or tape recordings of her lectures were available. In some instances, this has resulted in greatly altered and revised publications, which we consider to be the basis for all new translations.

For the publication of the Collected Works of Marie-Louise von Franz by Chiron Publications, the Stiftung commissioned Alison Kappes-Bates, Hirzel, a professional translator who knew Marie-Louise von Franz for over 30 years and was a close companion until her death, to translate into English the newly-revised texts in German. Mark Kyburz, Zürich, an experienced translator of Jungian texts, re-edited the first three English volumes of Archetypal Symbols in Fairytales, translated Volumes 4 and 5, and will translate further volumes. The Foundation for Jungian Psychology is responsible for the content and the design, the latter having been created in close consultation with Chiron Publication, Asheville.

On behalf of the Foundation for Jungian Psychology,
Küsnacht, April 24, 2023
PD Dr. Hansueli F. Etter

◆

Foreword

Marie-Louise von Franz writes in her Foreword: "To my astonishment, innumerable young people have meanwhile felt moved by this book, which shows that a time problem has obviously been touched by it." I remember an incident told to me by a friend who, together with two colleagues, attended a lecture by Marie-Louise von Franz on the *Puer aeternus*. On the way home, one of the friends said, "I can hardly believe it, but Dr. von Franz was talking about me." To which the second friend replied, "I felt the same, again and again." My friend then added, "I felt the same way, too!" Clearly, all three men were unconsciously living their lives according to the archetypal pattern of the *Puer aeternus*. Marie-Louise von Franz had the unusual talent of being able to describe the effects of an archetype in a way that could be both understood and felt. Only those who allow themselves to be touched, or simply are touched, by an archetype can experience the meaning inherent in an archetype.

Marie-Louise von Franz's description of the archetypal effect of the *Puer aeternus* is based upon two works of world literature: *The Little Prince* by Antoine de Saint-Exupéry (1943) and *The Kingdom without Space* by Bruno Goetz (1919). The former book is famous not only among French-speaking people, but worldwide. Marie-Louse von Franz's interpretation of *The Little Prince* has never been published in French up to now. The little prince is a mythical hero: he is an archetypal symbol, and the energy of this symbol is powerfully constellated in our time.

Bruno Goetz's novel *The Kingdom without Space* serves Marie-Louise von Franz as a base for further elucidation of the *Puer aeternus* archetype. Marie-Louise von Franz encouraged Lorenz Jung, an analytical psychologist, and a grandson of C. G. Jung, to interpret Neil M. Gunn's novel *The Green Isle of the Great* Deep (1944), to shine a light on the positive guiding role of the *puer* aeternus.[1] Clearly, this core psychological problem of our time was anticipated by poets and was of great importance to Marie-Louise von Franz.

The first edition of this book in English was published in 1970 with the title *The Problem of the Puer aeternus* by Spring Publications, Zürich/New York. This edition was based on a tape-recording of a series of lectures held at the C. G. Jung Institute in Zürich in the winter semester of 1959/60 by Marie-Louise von Franz. A further English edition was published in 2000 by Inner City Books, Toronto, Canada.

The first edition in German was published in 1987 by Kösel, Munich. The most recent edition in German was revised by Irene Gerber-Münch, Zürich.[2] This became the basis for the book in hand. In her usual sensitive and professional manner, Alison Kappes-Bates, Hirzel, prepared the present volume for publication, for which we owe her our warm thanks. The Foundation also thanks Livia Kott, Zürich, for her invaluable support in preparing the manuscript for publication.

On behalf of the Foundation for Jungian Psychology, Zürich
November 19, 2023
PD Dr. Hansueli F. Etter, President

---

[1]Lorenz Jung, Der Archetypus des Knaben in der heutigen Zeit, Die positive leitende Funktion des Puer-Archetypus aufgezeigt anhand des Romans von Neil M. Gunn: Das Grüne Eiland der Grossen Tiefe. Jungiana B/4, Beiträge zur Psychologie von C. G. Jung, Stiftung für Jung'sche Psychologie, Küsnacht 1995.
[2]Marie-Louise von Franz, Puer aeternus, Ewiger Jüngling und kreativer Genius, Stiftung für Jung'sche Psychologie, Küsnacht, 2002.

Table of Contents

Foreword by Marie–Louise von Franz
for the German edition of 1987

1   The "*puer aeternus*" and the divine child as mythological figures are so widespread that ten volumes would not suffice to describe them. As an image of the self and of the creative genius, and as an image of religious renewal, as C.G. Jung has described it, they play a tremendous role in literature. Peter Pan, Jonathan Livingston Seagull, or the little girl Momo and the young hero in Michael Ende's books are all impressive images of what this archetype can mean, and they are loved accordingly. In a "fatherless society,"[1] i.e., in a society in which traditional values are being called into question, this archetype comes particularly to the fore. The ancient alchemists called their sought-after philosopher's stone "*senex et pue*'" — old man and youth — which shows that it is a matter of a pair of opposites which do, in fact, belong together: the thousand-year-old wisdom of the unconscious and its eternal, youthful power of self-renewal.

2   In this book, only one aspect shall be emphasized, namely, the practical description of how this archetype is experienced by individuals, and how it can be the source of renewal, but also the cause of an early death. The entire ambivalence of the creative, and the subtlety that is required in dealing with this archetype, shall be illuminated. Part One emphasizes the problem of the mother-complex that is always tied up with the *puer aeternus* problem. Part Two is concerned with the question why a *puer aeternus* does not like to be bound to the earth by a woman. Part Three particularly illuminates the problem of the generations, and the problem of political and religious renewal.

Mitscherlich, *Auf dem Weg zur vaterlosen Gesellschaft.*

3   Of course, there is a feminine aspect to the *puer aeternus* problem. The father-bound daughter most often has a problem with her spiritual/mental creativity, and the *puer aeternus* embodies her creative élan that, like the masculine *puer aeternus*, must undergo a process of maturation to overcome its dangerous side-effects.

4   With this book, that evolved out of a series of lectures at the C.G. Jung Institute, I was able to write myself free of my own *puer aeternus* problem almost thirty years ago. While fundamentally revising it this spring for the German edition, I was somewhat amazed when I looked back at this work from such a great distance in time: to my astonishment, innumerable young people have meanwhile felt moved by this book, which shows that a time problem has obviously been touched by it. The more the senex — the traditional spirit — in our culture disintegrates, the more significant the *puer* becomes to the problem of creative renewal.

Küsnacht, May 1987   Marie-Louise von Franz

❖

Preface

⁵ *Puer aeternus* is the name of a god of antiquity. The words themselves come from Ovid's *Metamorphoses*[1] where they are applied to the child-god in the Eleusinian mysteries. Ovid addresses the child-god Iacchus as *puer aeternus*.[2] Later, this child-god was identified with Dionysus and the god Eros. He is the divine youth who, in the mother-cult mystery of Eleusis, is born in the holy night as a redeemer. He is a god of life, of death and resurrection — the divine youth, corresponding to such oriental gods as Tammuz, Attis, and Adonis. The title *puer aeternus* means "eternal youth," but today we also use it to indicate a certain type of young man who has an outstanding mother complex and who therefore behaves in certain typical ways which I would like to describe in what follows.

⁶ In general, a man who is identified with the archetype of the *puer aeternus* remains too long in adolescent psychology, i.e., all those characteristics that are normal in a youth of seventeen or eighteen are continued into later life, coupled in most cases with too great a dependence on the mother. The two typical disturbances of a man who has an outstanding mother complex are, as Jung points out, homosexuality and Don Juanism.[3] In the case of the latter, the image of the mother is sought after in every woman — the image of the quintessentially flawless woman who will give everything to a man. He is looking for a goddess, so in every relationship that he has with a woman, he is forced to discover that she is just an ordinary human being. After his first sexual contact with her, his whole fascination vanishes, and he turns away disappointed, only to project the image anew onto another woman. He constantly longs for the maternal

---

[1] Ovid, *Metamorphoses*.
[2] Ibid., IV, 18.
[3] Jung, *Archetypes and the Collective Unconscious*, vol. 9/I, *CW*, § 162.

woman who will enfold him in her arms and satisfy his every need. This is often accompanied by the romantic behavior of the adolescent.

7   Generally, a man like this has great difficulty adapting to society. In some instances, there is a kind of anti-social individualism: in his mind, because he is special, he has no need to adapt, for that would be too much to ask of such a hidden genius! The arrogance of this attitude is based upon false feelings of superiority and, simultaneously, upon an inferiority complex. Such people usually also have great difficulty in finding the right kind of job, for whatever they find is never quite right or quite what they wanted. There is always "a hair in the soup." The woman, too, is never quite the right woman: she is nice as a girlfriend, but … . There is always a "but" that prevents marriage or any kind of definite commitment.

8   This all leads to a form of neurosis that has been described as living a "provisional life."[4] This is concerned with the strange attitude or fantasy that the right thing will come along at some point in the future, for example, the right woman, or the fulfillment of what one really wants. This attitude reflects a constant inner refusal to commit oneself to the moment. To a greater or lesser degree, this attitude is often accompanied by a savior or Messiah complex, with the secret thought that one day, one will be able to save the world by being the last word in philosophy, or religion, or politics, or art, or something else. This can go so far as to be a pathological megalomania. A trace of it can be found in the idea that one's time "has not yet come." The constant dread of such a man is to be bound to anything whatsoever. He has a terrific fear of being pinned down, of completely entering space and time, and of being the singular human being that he is. There is always the fear of being caught in a situation from which it may be impossible to slip out again. Thus, every just-so situation is hell. In symbolic language, this need for freedom and to have distance from reality in the *puer aeternus* is often expressed in a fascination for dangerous sports — particularly flying and mountaineering — to get as high as possible, away from the mother,

---

[4] Cf. Baynes, *Analytical Psychology*.

from the earth and from ordinary life. If this type of complex is very pronounced, many such men die young in airplane crashes and mountaineering accidents. In this form, it is a matter of a spiritual longing being transferred onto the outside.

9   A dramatic depiction of what flying means to a Puer can be found in this poem by John Magee[5] who, incidentally, died in a plane crash shortly after writing the poem:

10   High Flight
Oh! I have slipped the surly bonds of earth,
And danced the skies on laughter-silvered wings;
Sunward I've climbed, and joined the tumbling mirth
Of sun-split clouds, - and done a hundred things
You have not dreamed of -
Wheeled and soared and swung
High in the sunlit silence. Hov'ring there
I've chased the shouting wind along, and flung
My eager craft through footless halls of air…
Up, up the long, delirious, burning blue
I've topped the wind-swept heights with easy grace
Where never lark or even eagle flew –
And, while with silent lifting mind I've trod
The high untrespassed sanctity of space,
Put out my hand, and touched the face of God.

11   The so-called *pueri* generally do not like sports that require patience and long training, for the *puer aeternus*, in the negative sense of the word, is usually very impatient by disposition. I knew a young mountain climber who was a classic example of the *puer aeternus*: he hated carrying a rucksack so much that he preferred to train himself to sleep in the rain or snow out of doors. To do this, he developed a kind of yoga breathing that enabled him to survive even the frostiest of nights in a snow-hole, wrapped only in a silk covering. To not have to carry any weight, he also trained himself

---

[5] Magee, "High Flight."

to go practically without food. He roamed about for years all over the mountains of Europe and other continents, free of any equipment. In a way, he led a heroic existence, to escape from being bound to a hut or to carrying a rucksack. Seen symbolically, this young man's goal was to avoid ordinary life and to not be burdened with any kind of weight. This represents an absolute refusal to take responsibility for anything, or to bear the burden of any given situation.

12　　The positive quality of such youths is a certain kind of spirituality that comes from a relatively close contact with the collective unconscious. They have the charm of youth and the stirring quality of a drink of champagne. *Pueri aeterni* are generally very agreeable to talk to for they usually have interesting things to talk about and have an invigorating effect upon one. They ask unconventional, deep questions and go straight for the truth for they are constantly searching for genuine religiosity, a search that is typical for people in their late teens. In the *puer aeternus*, these qualities are generally prolonged into the middle of life, sometimes even beyond.

13　　But there is another type of *puer* who does not display the charm of eternal youth, nor does the archetype of the divine youth shine through him. On the contrary, he lives in a continual sleepy daze, and that, too, is a typical adolescent characteristic: the sleepy, undisciplined, long-legged youth who merely hangs around, his mind wandering indiscriminately, so that sometimes one feels inclined to pour a bucket of cold water over his head. The sleepy daze is only an outer aspect, however, for if you can penetrate it, you will find that a lively fantasy life is being cherished within.

14　　With this description I have summarized the main features of certain young men who are caught up in the mother complex and are therefore identified with the archetype of the *puer aeternus*. If viewed superficially, they appear to be mostly negative. We will still have to explain what is really the matter: the question I would most like to pursue is why the problem of this mother-bound type of young man has become so pronounced in our time. We know that homosexuality is increasing more and more — Don Juanism seems to me to be less widespread — and therefore the problem of the *puer aeternus* is becoming increasingly pressing. Mothers have certainly always tried to keep their sons to themselves, and some sons have always had difficulty in getting free and have rather preferred to continue to enjoy the pleasures of the nest. But one does not quite see why this natural problem is threatening to become such a serious problem in our time. I think that is the more important and deeper question we must put to ourselves; the rest of the psychological connections are self-evident. A man who has a mother complex will always have to contend with his tendencies towards becoming a *puer aeternus*. What cure is there? What can a man do if he discovers he has a mother complex? He did not do that to himself: it happened to him. In *Symbols of Transformation*[6], Jung refers to work as being the cure, but then he hesitates for a moment and asks himself, "Is it as simple as all that? Is there just the one cure? Can I put it that way?" But "work" is the one disagreeable word that no *puer aeternus* likes to hear, and Jung concluded that it was the right answer. My experience has also been that if a man pulls out of this kind of youthful neurosis, then it is through work. We may not, however, misunderstand this problem, for the *puer aeternus* can work when he is fascinated or in a state of great enthusiasm. Then he can work twenty-four hours at a stretch or even longer, until he breaks down. But what he cannot do is to work on a dreary, rainy morning when work is boring. This is the one thing the *puer aeternus* usually cannot manage to do, and he will use any kind of excuse to avoid it. Any analysis of a *puer aeternus* always comes up against this problem sooner or later. It is only when the ego has become sufficiently strengthened that the problem can be overcome, and then there is the possibility of sticking to the work. I have found that it is not much good simply preaching to people that they should work, for then they simply get angry and walk away from the analysis.

15   As far as I have seen, the unconscious generally tries to produce a compromise by indicating the direction in which there might be some enthusiasm, or where the psychological energy would flow

---

[6] Jung, *Symbols of Transformation*, vol. 5, CW.

naturally, for it is of course easier to train oneself to work in a direction supported by one's instinct. That is not quite so hard as working completely against your own flow of energy. Therefore, it is usually advisable to wait a while and find out where one's interest and energy flows. Then one can try to motivate the man to work there. But in every field of work, there always comes a time when routine must be faced. Even creative work involves a certain amount of boring routine, and that is when the *puer aeternus* runs away. Once again, he concludes that "this is not for him!" In such moments, dreams often show how one can push through the obstacle, and then the battle is won.

16   In a letter, Jung says of the *puer aeternus*, "I consider the *puer aeternus* attitude an unavoidable evil. Identity with the *puer* signifies a psychological puerility that could do nothing better than outgrow itself. It always leads to external blows of fate which show the need for another attitude. But reason accomplishes nothing, because the *puer aeternus* is always an agent of destiny."[7]

17   To go more deeply into the background of this whole problem, I want to interpret *The Little Prince*[8] by Antoine de Saint-Exupéry in Part One that follows.

---

[7] Letter to Oscar Schmitz, 23.2.1931 in Jung, *Letters*, vol. 1, 82.
[8] The original French publication was published with the title *Le Petit Prince*.

Part 1

'The Little Prince' (Saint–Exupéry)

◇

Chapter One
The Tragic Beginning

18   We know that Saint-Exupéry died in an air battle in the Second World War. Even though he had all the typical characteristics of the *puer aeternus,* he was primarily a great writer and poet. His outer life was difficult to trace. This is typical, for, as we mentioned earlier, the *puer aeternus* never quite touches the earth, so one can only pick up a few traces here and there of his biography. The *puer aeternus* never quite commits himself to any mundane situation but rather hovers over the earth, touching it from time to time, alighting here and there, and these are the traces one has to follow. More information on him only became available years after Saint-Exupéry's death; it is well summarized in Curtis Cates's biography of Saint-Exupéry.[1]

19   Saint-Exupéry (born 1900) came from an old aristocratic French family and grew up in a beautiful country house with its traditional atmosphere. He chose to become a professional aviator and acted for a time as a pilot for the Compagnie Aeropostale, which ran a service between Europe and South America. Around 1929, he flew the Toulouse-Dakar-Buenos Aires route and was also a collaborator in establishing new lines in South America. Later he was in command of a completely isolated aerodrome in the North African desert — Cape Julie. His main duty there was to rescue pilots who had crashed in the desert from dying or from falling into the hands of rebel Arab tribes. That was the kind of life such a man would like, and Saint-Exupéry preferred this isolated desert post to any other. In 1939, at the beginning of the war, he fought for France as a captain

---

[1] Cate, *Antione de Saint-Exupéry.*

in the air force. After the collapse of France, he had intended to escape to Egypt, but for technical reasons that plan had to be abandoned. He was then demobilized and went to New York, where he finished his book *Flight to Arras.*[2] Later, when the Allies landed in Africa, he wanted to return to the air force, and though he was refused on account of his age, he used every conceivable ruse and trick to be able to fly again.

20   In July 1944, having left Algiers with his plane on a reconnaissance flight over France, he disappeared without leaving any trace, either of his plane or of himself. Later, after the war had ended, a young German reported that Saint-Exupéry had probably been shot down by a German Fokker-Wolff plane. One man said that out of a group of seven planes, a French machine had been shot down over the Mediterranean, and from the indications given, it would seem to have been Saint-Exupéry's plane.

21   Saint-Exupéry's marriage was not a very happy one. His wife seems to have been a very temperamental and difficult woman, and he usually did not stay with her for more than a week or two; he would then be on his way again. When he was not allowed to fly, he always became depressed and irritable and would walk up and down in his flat from morning till evening, desperate and irritated. Only when he could fly was he able to become his normal self again and to feel all right. Whenever he had to stay on the ground and be with his wife, or remain in some other situation, he fell back into these bad moods, so he always tried to get back into flying.

22   His other books show how much he was concerned with present-day problems and with the *Weltanschauung* of our time. Those who have read them will have noticed that like many people, especially those of the French nobility, he has quite a bit of Nazi psychology. The upper layers of French society are often of German stock who immigrated into France not so very long ago. From an historical point of view and therefore especially in military circles and among the nobility, they have quite an affinity with the Prussian mentality.

---

[2] Saint-Exupéry, *Flight to Arras.*

This comes out undeniably in figures in Saint-Exupéry's novels: For instance, in Rivière, (in *Night Flight*[3]) where he tries to outline the Führer type — the cold man who sends his young flyers to their death for a higher purpose. This is just a part of the local make-up in his milieu and not really relevant for his deeper problem, which is a search for....but what is he searching for? But for what is he searching? That is a question which I will not answer now but will try to find the answer to it with you.

23 One of his most popular works is *The Little Prince*. This book was a tremendous success, and many people made it their bible and worship it. But if you talk to them about it, they generally adopt a slightly defiant attitude, insisting that they think it is a marvelous book. I have wondered about this defiant attitude a lot and I think the only explanation can be that even those who like it so very much have a small question mark in their minds. There is one question which I think one is allowed to put — even to its worshippers — and that is about the slightly sentimental style, a sentimental touch which, although it causes a certain malaise, does not detract from its value in other ways, even if one enjoys the book very much. In general, where there is sentimentality there is also a certain amount of brutality. There are classic examples of this amongst the Nazi heavyweights. Goering, for example, was able to make brutal decisions without a qualm but would weep if one of his canary birds died. Or the leaders of the concentration camps who had no difficulty sending innocent people to their deaths as part of their daytime "work" and were tender fathers and dog-lovers of an evening.

24 When we have interpreted *The Little Prince*, we shall take some case material where this will become very clear, namely, we are dealing with the shadow problem of the *puer aeternus*. There is usually a very cold, brutal figure somewhere in the background, which compensates the too idealistic attitude of consciousness and which the *puer aeternus* cannot voluntarily assimilate. In the Don

---

[3] Saint-Exupéry, *Night Flight*.

Juan type, for example, this cold brutality comes out every time he leaves a woman. Once his feeling has gone, out comes an ice-cold brutality with no human feeling in it, and the whole sentimental enthusiasm is projected onto another woman. This brutality, or cold realistic attitude, very often also appears in matters to do with money. As the *puer* does not want to adapt socially, or take on some regular job and work, but must nevertheless get money somehow, he generally achieves his purpose behind his own back, with his left hand, so to speak: He gets the money, God knows from where, and in rather mean ways. If you touch this unconscious shadow problem, you get a complex-related reaction.

25   From the characteristics of the *puer* that are being discussed here, one might easily get the impression that we are dealing with psychopathic characteristics. But it pays to differentiate. There is, for instance, the case I shall present later of a schizoid borderline type, who is a different kind of beast. My experience is that besides the *puer aeternus,* there is the psychopath or the schizoid or the hysteric, or the just slightly neurotic man, depending on the case in hand and the form that his problems take. Let us say somebody has a religious problem. In addition, the person can be a psychopath, or schizoid, or hysterical about it. The same applies to the problem of homosexuality, which can be combined with, or free from, other neurotic characteristics, and can be closely tied to the time problem. This seems to me to be a more comprehensive problem than an individual neurosis.

26   Concerning homosexuality, Jung had the idea that perhaps it is an unconscious compensation for overpopulation: Nature pushes this tendency toward homosexuality to compensate overpopulation, so that a certain number of people refrain from producing children. Nature might possibly employ such a ruse. As there were no statistics in former times, it is difficult to prove this development. We only know that homosexuality is now tremendously widespread and, in contrast to how it used to be, nowadays in the military, particularly amongst airmen, it has become a real problem.

27   Because I have had several requests to discuss the problem of the *puer aeternus* as an animus figure in women, I shall do so briefly, even though I have no material other than a few dreams. I can say that the problem is the same in its basic structure, except that it lies on a deeper level within the unconscious. The animus of the woman always anticipates what she has to do later in reality. The problem of the *puer aeternus* is having to come down to earth, which is analogous to what the woman's mind has to do in life, but it is further removed from her ego. The *puer aeternus* problem is always connected to creativity, and if a woman has a *puer aeternus* animus, she generally has a creative problem. Thus, the cure for women is unfortunately the same as for men: It is also work, which can, however, involve different layers, for example, in a pregnancy, which is also a creative act.

28   I remember the case of a woman who did not want to have children. She often dreamt of *puer* animus figures, and of Mother Nature pinning her down to earth. The dreams tried to motivate her to have children because a pregnancy brings a woman down to earth. She then has a definite commitment and can no longer toy with this or that any longer. This applies especially to women who are more of the hetaerae type, who have a lot of affairs with men and do not want to be pinned down. The child makes the relationship more definite and earths the woman. Having children requires a lot of very regular and sometimes boring work.

29   Now we will turn to the interpretation of *The Little Prince*. The story falls into two clearly defined parts, beginning with an introduction which is told by Saint-Exupéry in the first person, as if it were part of a personal autobiography. It begins like this:

30   Once when I was six years old I saw a beautiful picture in a book about the primeval forest called *True Stories*. It showed a boa constrictor swallowing an animal. Here is a copy of the drawing.

31 The book stated: "Boa constrictors swallow their prey whole without chewing it whereupon they can no longer move and sleep for six months digesting it."

32 I then reflected deeply upon the adventures in the jungle and in turn succeeded in making my first drawing with a colour pencil. My Drawing No. 1 was like this:

33 I showed my masterpiece to the grown-ups and asked them if my drawing frightened them. They answered: "Why should anyone be frightened by a hat?" My drawing did not represent a hat. It was supposed to be a boa constrictor digesting an elephant. So I made another drawing of the inside of the boa constrictor to enable the grown-ups to understand. They always need explanations. My drawing No. 2 looked like this:

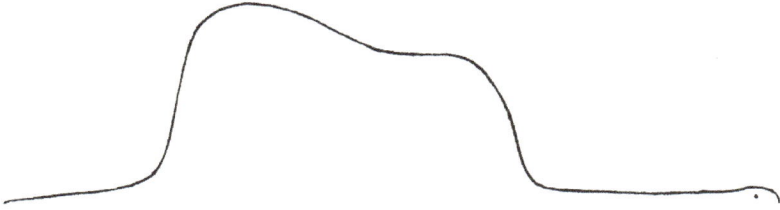

34   The grown-ups then advised me to give up my drawings of boa constrictors, whether from the inside or the outside, and to devote myself instead to geography, history, arithmetic and grammar. Thus it was that I gave up a magnificent career as a painter at the age of six. I had been disappointed by the lack of success of my drawing No. 1 and my drawing No. 2. Grown-ups never understand anything by themselves and it is rather tedious for children to have to explain things to them time and again.

35   So I had to choose another job and I learnt to pilot aeroplanes. I flew more or less all over the world. And indeed geography has been extremely useful to me. I am able to distinguish between China and Arizona at a glance. It is extremely helpful if one gets lost in the night.

36   As a result of which I have been in touch, throughout my life, with all kinds of serious people. I have spent a lot of time with grown-ups, I have seen them at very close quarters which I'm afraid has not greatly enhanced my opinion of them.

37   Whenever I met one who seemed reasonably clear-sighted to me, I showed them my drawing No. 1, which I had kept, as an experiment. I wanted to find out whether he or she was truly understanding. But the answer was always: "It is a hat." So I gave up mentioning boa constrictors or primeval forests or stars. I would bring myself down to his or her level and talk about bridge, golf, politics and neckties. And the grown-up would be very pleased to have met such a sensible person.

38   Thus I lived alone, with no one I could really talk to, until I had an accident in the Sahara Desert six years ago. Something

broke down in my engine. And since there was neither a mechanic nor a passenger with me, I prepared myself for a difficult but what I hoped would be a successful repair. It was a matter of life or death for me. I had scarcely enough drinking water for a week.

39   On the first night I fell asleep on the sand, a thousand miles from any human habitation. I was far more isolated than a shipwrecked sailor on a raft in the middle of the ocean. So you can imagine my surprise at sunrise when an odd little voice woke me up.

40   It said: "Please. . .draw me a sheep."

41   "What?"

42   Then he meets the little prince. But firstly, we need to draw our conclusions from this first part. It contains the whole problem in a nutshell.

43   We see here that he has never really got into the world of the adult. He speaks about its emptiness, its idiocy, and its meaningless-ness. There is talk about bridge and politics and neckties, which is the kind of adult world he is right to reject — it is persona emptiness. But he omits other aspects of adult life as well. We see in the feeling-tone of this first part that he thinks of childhood as the land of fantasy, the artist's life. He believes this childhood life is the true life and all the rest is empty persona, that is made up of running after money, making a prestige impression on other people — a life in which one has lost one's true nature. This is how he sees adult life, for he has not found a bridge over which he could take into adult life what we would call the true life. That is the great problem, I think, in a nutshell; namely, how can one pull out of this fantasy life of youth and youthfulness without losing its value? How can one grow up without losing the feeling of totality and the feeling of creativeness and of being really alive, which one had in one's youth? One can be cynical about it and say that one cannot have the penny *and* the cake — that it has to be sacrificed — but from my experience

I do not think that this is quite right. It is justifiable not to want to give up this other world. The question is a matter of how one can grow up and not lose it.

44　　Of course, you can drive people out of this childhood paradise and fantasy life in which they are in close connection with their true inner self on an infantile level, but then they are completely disillusioned and cynical. I remember once that I had an analysand who was a typical *puer aeternus* and wanted to become a writer, but he lived in a completely fantasy world. He came over from the States with a friend, and the two made up their minds that the friend should have a Freudian and he a Jungian analysis. They wanted to meet up again after a year and compare notes. They went to different countries and met as arranged, and the young man who had had the Freudian analysis said that he was cured of his problem and that he wanted to go home. Everything was all right, and he had understood his infantile attitude toward life; he had given up his mother complex and other nonsense. My analysand asked him what he was going to do, and the other said he did not know but that he must earn some money and find a wife. My analysand said that he was not cured at all: He still did not know where to go yet. He knew that he would become a writer and had started on that course, but he did not know where to settle, and so on. Then the one who had had the Freudian analysis said, "Well, it is strange; they have driven out my devils, but with them they have also driven out my angels!"

45　　That is just the problem! One can drive away devils *and* angels by saying that that is all infantile and part of the mother complex and, by undergoing a completely reductive analysis, put everything down to childhood sentimentality that must be sacrificed. There is something to be said for that. This man was in a way more cured than my analysand. On the other hand, it seems to me that such a terrific disillusionment makes one ask afterward whether it is worthwhile going on living? Is it worthwhile just to make money for the rest of one's life and get small bourgeois pleasures? It does not seem very satisfactory to me. At least the sadness with which the man who was cured remarked that with his devils his angels had also been driven out made me feel that he himself did not feel quite happy about his own cure. It had the tone of cynical disillusionment, which to my mind is no cure.

46   It must not be forgotten that the atmosphere of the milieu in which Saint-Exupéry grew up was very disillusioned and cynical. He usually moved in circles for whom bridge and money and such things were the only meaningful things. He was therefore right to protest, and to cling to his inner artistic and total view of life, and to revolt against such an adult life. One clearly sees how, in a subtle way, he mocks the adult world and how to the point that is. But at the same time, he does not know how to pull out of his childhood world without falling into the disillusionment of what he sees as the only value in adult life. If you combine this with the symbolism of the picture, it becomes even worse: The boa constrictor obviously is an image of the unconscious that suffocates life and prevents the human being from developing. It is the swallowing or the regressive aspect of the unconscious, the looking-backward tendency, that grips one when one is overwhelmed by the unconscious. You could even say that the boa constrictor represents a pull toward death. The boa is the monster of the night-sea journey, but in contrast to other mythological parallels, here the hero who has been devoured does not emerge from it again.

47   The animal that is swallowed by the boa is an elephant, so we should look into its symbolism. As the elephant was not known in European countries until late antiquity, there is not much mythological material. However, in late antiquity the elephant had great significance. When Alexander the Great went to India, he saw elephants and brought them to Europe. The Romans later used elephants to deliver supplies during their campaigns. If we read what has been written about them, we see that a great deal of mythological fantasy was spun around the elephant. It is said that "they are very chaste, that they only mate once in a lifetime and very secretly in order to produce their young and therefore," according to one medieval reporter, "they are an allegory of marital chastity. Like the unicorn, the elephant also loves a virgin and can only be tamed by

one, a motif which points to the incarnation of Christ." The elephant is said to represent invincible fortitude and to be an image of Christ. "In antiquity it was thought that elephants were terribly ambitious and that if they were not accorded the honour due to them, they would die from disappointment, for their feeling of honour was so great. Snakes love to drink the cool blood of elephants, and if an elephant suddenly breaks out, it is because it has seen a snake and it goes after it to trample it. In the Middle Ages, the elephant stood for a man who was generous but unstable and moody in character, for the elephant was said to be generous, intelligent and, therefore, taciturn, but when he once gets into a rage he cannot be appeased by any sensual pleasure other than music. . . . Elephants wash very often and use flowers to perfume themselves. Hence, they represent purification, chastity, and pious worship of God." This is all from the book *Polyhistor Symbolicus* by a Jesuit, Nikolaus Caussinus, who writes such funny stories about the elephant by summing up what the antique idiom says about it and then adding a little bit of medieval fantasy. This shows that the same thing happened to the Europeans that happened to the Africans when they met up with an elephant for the first time: They projected the archetype of the hero onto it. In Africa, it is considered a great honor if a person is given the title of lion, but the highest title anyone can be given is that of elephant. It is far above the lion, which is the image of a courageous man of the chieftain type, for the elephant is the archetype of the medicine man, who also has courage but, in addition, wisdom and secret knowledge.

48   Thus, from this standpoint, the elephant represents the individuated personality. Strangely enough, the European automatically projected the same thing onto the elephant and took him as the image of the divine hero, the image of Christ, outstanding in virtue, except for being moody and inclined to fits of rage. It is amazing, but Saint-Exupéry had precisely those two outstanding characteristics. Thus, one could say that the elephant is an exact picture of his character. He himself was subtle, chaste, and highly sensitive, along with being very ambitious and very sensitive about

everything that had to do with his own honor. He was continually on the search for religious satisfaction; he did not worship God, for he had not found Him, but he was always on the search. He was generous, intelligent, and taciturn, easily irritated and inclined to terrible moods and fits of rage. Thus, in the elephant there is an amazing self-portrait, and one sees the archetypal pattern illustrated in a single individual, without there even being much difference.

49   One could say that the elephant is the model fantasy of the grown-up hero. This model fantasy — the image in his soul of what he wanted to become — is, however, swallowed by the boa — the devouring mother — and this first drawing shows the whole tragedy. Very often childhood dreams anticipate the inner fate of a person twenty or thirty years ahead. The first picture shows that Saint-Exupéry had a hero aspect, alive and constellated, and that this aspect would never quite come through but would be swallowed back by the regressive tendencies of the unconscious and, as we know from later events, by death.

50   The devouring mother myth should naturally also be pinned down in connection with his own mother, but, as she is in a conspicuous position, I hesitate to comment on her too much. She was certainly a very powerful personage, a big, stout woman, who is said to have had a tremendous amount of energy, who was interested in all kinds of activities, and tried her hand at drawing, painting, and writing. She was a very dynamic person. It must have been very difficult for a sensitive boy to pull away from the influence of such a mother. It is also said that she always anticipated her son's death. Several times she thought he was dead and very dramatically dressed herself in large black veils such as French women like to wear when they become widows, and then had to take them off again as he was not yet dead. Thus, the archetypal pattern of what we call the death-mother was alive in her psyche.

51   The death-mother is not so openly acknowledged in our society, but I got the shock of my life when I had the following experience. I had to go somewhere to meet someone, and at that place the house-owner had a *puer aeternus* son who was completely under her spell.

They were very simple people. They had a bakery, and the son did no work at all but went about in riding-kit. He was a typical Don Juan type, very elegant, with a new girl about every four days. This young man once went bathing and carried his girlfriend out into the Lake of Zürich and, in the classical situation, *halb zog sie ihn, halb sank er hin* ("half drew she him, half sank he down") — as Goethe would have put it — and both went under. The girl was saved, but when he was brought out of the water, he was already dead. I read about it in the paper, but when I came back to this house, I bumped into the mother, who was a widow, and I expressed my condolences, saying how sorry I had been when I heard of the terrible accident. She invited me in and took me to the sitting-room where there was a very big photograph of her son on his deathbed, surrounded by flowers, set up like a hero's tomb, and she remarked, "Look at him! How beautiful he looks in death." I agreed, and then she smiled and said, "Well, I'd rather have him like that than give him away to another woman."

52 The Great Mother made a religious cult out of him, and then he becomes the dead Tammuz, Adonis, Attis, who replaces the image of God. He is also the crucified Christ, and she is the Virgin Mary, crying beside the Cross. There is great satisfaction in having such an archetypal meaning in one's life. One is not just So-and-So who has lost her son in an accident, but the Great Mother, the Virgin Mary, who weeps at the foot of the Cross — and that elevates the mother herself and gives her sorrow some deeper meaning. If she identifies with it in the wrong way, then it is like it is here. I was terribly shocked by what the woman said, but then I said to myself that this woman had had the naïveté to say what many others have thought. Being a simple woman, she said it right out: "It was better that way than to give him away to another woman." *She* was his wife! It seems to me that there must have been something similar in Saint-Exupéry's mother. Otherwise, why did she always anticipate his death and wear black veils ahead of time? It was as if she knew all along that it would end like that. We only know that this terrible impersonal pattern appears to have penetrated her personal life.

Consciously, Saint-Exupéry certainly had a positive mother complex, which always includes the danger of being devoured by the unconscious.

53   It is interesting that Saint-Exupéry says that he always goes around with this picture and tries it out on people to see if they understand. It seems he was not definitely doomed, as if his attempt to find some understanding gave him some hope. If only he could find somebody who would ask him what on earth he was drawing, that it was dangerous and meant such and such a thing! He wanted to be understood but he was not. I think that if he had got in touch with psychology — perhaps it is awfully optimistic of me to think so — something might have been done about him and his problem, because he was very near to finding the solution himself. But, tragically enough, he lived in the kind of French milieu where there was no psychological understanding, and in such an atmosphere, it is very difficult to get near to the unconscious. Modern French civilization, for different local and national reasons, is particularly cut off from the unconscious, so he probably never did meet anyone who could have given him a hint as to what was happening within his psyche.

54   The story then goes over to the *Little Prince*. We have already heard the part where Saint-Exupéry's airplane crashes in the Sahara, where he meets this little prince. I will go on with the text. The voice said:

55   "Draw me a sheep!"

56   I jumped up, completely thunderstruck. I rubbed my eyes, blinked hard and looked carefully around me. And I discovered an extraordinary little boy watching me gravely. Here is the best portrait I was able to draw of him later. [He drew him like a little Napoleon, by the way, which was a funny idea and typically French!] But of course, my drawing is not half as charming as its model. It is not my fault. I had been discouraged by grown-ups. . . [and then he goes off in the old way].

57 I therefore stared in total astonishment at this sudden apparition. Do not forget that I was a thousand miles away from any inhabited region.

58 But my little chap did not seem to be either lost or dead tired or dying of hunger, thirst or fear. He did not look like a child lost in the middle of the desert, a thousand miles from any inhabited region.

59 When I finally managed to speak, I said to him:

60 "But … what are you doing here?"

61 Whereupon he repeated softly and gravely: "Please draw me a sheep."

62 When a mystery is too overpowering, one dare not disobey. Absurd as it seemed to me a thousand miles from any human habitation and in danger of death, I took a sheet of paper and my fountain-pen out of my pocket. But I suddenly remembered that my studies had been concentrated on geography, history, arithmetic and grammar, so I told the little chap (a little crossly) that I did not know how to draw.

63 He replied: "That doesn't matter. Draw me a sheep."

64 Since I had never drawn a sheep I drew for him one of the two pictures I had drawn before. That of the boa constrictor from the outside. [His Number One drawing]. And I was astounded to hear the little fellow saying: "No! No! I don't want an elephant inside a boa. A boa constrictor is a very dangerous creature and an elephant is very cumbersome. Everything is very small where I live. I need a sheep. Draw me a sheep."

65 So I drew.

66 He looked at it carefully and said: "No. That one is already very sick. Draw me another one."

67 And I drew.

68   My little friend said gently and indulgently: "Don't you see that is not a sheep, it is a ram. It has horns..."

69   Once again I made another drawing. But it was rejected too, like the previous ones.

70   "This one is too old. I want a sheep that will live for a long time."

71   My patience had run out by then as I was in a hurry to start dismantling my engine as soon as possible, so I scribbled this drawing. And I explained: "That is only the box. The sheep you asked for is inside"

72   But I was very surprised to see the face of my young judge lighting up: "That is exactly the way I wanted it. Do you think this sheep will need a lot of grass?"

73   "Why?"

74   "Because where I live everything is so small . . ."

75   "There should be enough grass for him. I have given you a very small sheep."

76   He bent his head over the drawing: "Not so small that ... Look. He has gone to sleep."

77   And that is how I met the little prince.

78   Because the little prince only asks questions and does not give answers, it takes some time for Saint-Exupéry to find out that he has come down from the stars and that he lived on a very small planet.

79   This miraculous encounter in the desert is an echo of a real experience the author had. He once had an airplane crash in the Sahara Desert, but he was not alone as he is in this story, but was with his mechanic, Prevost. Because they had to walk very far from the site of the crash to the next oasis, they nearly died of thirst, and they were already hallucinating when an Arab found them and gave them some water out of his gourd. Later they were rescued by their comrades. In our story, Saint-Exupéry is alone; he is without his mechanic, who would have been a positive shadow figure, and

instead of being rescued as he was, he encounters something supernatural. Thus, an archetypal fantasy is added to the memory from real life, and this creates the hopeless situation with which most myths and fairytales begin, and which is the starting point for the supernatural and the numinous to appear. In fairytales, a man often gets lost in the woods or on the high seas. This suggests the psychological situation in which the conscious personality has come to the end of its tether. One feels completely disoriented, with neither goal nor outlook on life. In those moments, blocked energy piles up and, because it cannot flow into life, constellates unconscious contents that can manifest as supernatural apparitions. If the inner blockage becomes severe, hallucinations may arise; at the very least, one's dream life becomes highly activated to which one must pay attention; in other words, the numinous apparitions manifest within one's dreams. This often happens when the previous form of life has broken down and the conflict between one's conscious approach to life and one's unconscious goals needs to be resolved.

80　　When he had his actual crash in the desert, Saint-Exupéry was already in a life crisis. He was in his mid-thirties, and flying no longer completely satisfied him, but he could not switch over to any other occupation. He already had these spells of nervous irritability that he could only break through by taking on another flying job. Originally flying had been a real vocation for him, but slowly it had become an escape from something new and unknown that he could not face. This often happens in life. Our libido wants to be redirected toward another goal so it recedes from the old activity, and because we feel helpless, we persevere in the old activity perhaps for too long. This means regression and flight from our own inner feelings that are telling us we should now change to something else. If we do not follow this new flow of energy, often something happens either on the outside, for example Saint-Exupéry's air crash, or on the inside, that gives one a clear signal.

81　　There is a marked parallel in Islamic tradition to this meeting of the star prince. It is even possible that, having lived so long in the Sahara and having made friends with a number of Bedouins, Saint-

Exupéry might have heard about it. In the 18th Sutra of the Koran there is the famous story of Moses in the desert with his servant Joseph who is carrying a basket with a fish in it for their meal. At a certain place the fish disappears, and Moses says that they will stay there because something will happen. Suddenly, Khidr ("the verdant one") appears. He is believed to be the first angel of God, or the first servant of Allah. He is a kind of immortal companion of heroes who then goes along with Moses for some time but tells him that he (Moses) will not be able to stand him and will doubt his deeds. This does, indeed, happen even though Moses assures him that he has complete faith in him. Most people know the story of how they both come to a little village where Khidr makes boats in the water sink by drilling holes in them. Moses remonstrates, and Khidr reminds him that he had predicted that Moses would not understand. Later, he explains that robbers would have stolen the boats and that by bringing about this minor calamity, the fishermen will be able to use their boats again soon. Khidr had, in fact, done them a service, but naturally, Moses had been too simple-minded to understand. Once again, Moses promises that he will not doubt him and will not have such one-sided, rational reactions. Next, they meet a young man whom Khidr kills. Again, Moses explodes and asks how he could do such a thing. Khidr smiles and says that the young man had been on his way to murder his parents and that it was better for him to die and thereby save his soul, than to become a criminal. This time Moses is really willing to accept the explanation. But when, for a third time, something similar happens when Khidr causes a wall to collapse, only to uncover the hidden treasure belonging to two orphans, Moses once again rebels. Finally, Khidr must leave him.

82   This story, which Jung has interpreted in detail[4], illustrates the incompatibility of the conscious rational ego with the inner figure of the Self and its purposes. The rational ego, with its well-meaning intentions and thoughts, is absolutely off track in relation to the greater inner personality, Khidr. Naturally, this famous story serves to tell people that they should be able to doubt their conscious

---

[4] Jung, *Archetypes and the Collective Unconscious*, vol. 9/I, *CW*, §§ 243 ff.

attitude and should always expect the miraculous thing from the unconscious to happen. We have the same situation here, for something happens which is contrary to Saint-Exupéry's conscious ideas, which tell him that he wants to repair his engine and has no time. He wants to save himself with the old machine and is not willing to go on with the childish play with the little star prince. On the other hand, it is very significant that the little star prince is the only one who at once understands the drawing of the boa constrictor. Saint-Exupéry should be very pleased and see that it is his other side that really understands him, the first companion who belongs in *his* world — the world of his childhood that he misses so much. But he is impatient and just thinks it a nuisance and that he needs to get his engine in order. And then something classic happens, namely, this gesture of impatience that is so typical of the *puer aeternus*. When he must take something seriously, either in the outer or the inner world, he makes a few poor attempts and then impatiently gives up. My experience is that if you analyze a man of this type, it does not matter whether you force him to take the outer or the inner world seriously; that is unimportant, though perhaps it depends on the type. The only important thing is that he should stick with something. If it is analysis, then analyze seriously, take the dreams seriously, live according to them, or, if not, then take a job seriously and really live the outer life. The important thing is to do something thoroughly, whatever it is. But the great danger, or the neurotic problem, is that the *puer aeternus*, or the man caught in this problem, tends to do what Saint-Exupéry does here: just put it in a box and shut the lid on it in a gesture of sudden impatience. That is why such people tell you suddenly that they have another plan. This is not what they were looking for. And they always do it when things become difficult. It is not what they do, but the everlasting switching which is dangerous. Here, unfortunately though typically, Saint-Exupéry switches at this crucial moment.

83   Thus, in the little prince, Saint-Exupéry has found someone who understands his drawing of the boa constrictor and the elephant that has been swallowed by it. Since there is no lysis, no solution to the

conflict, this short introduction already indicates the tragic end of the book, as well as Saint-Exupéry's own death. In myths, the hero who has been swallowed by the dragon or the whale or a snake tries to get free. If then, in Saint-Exupéry's description of the drawing there is no lysis, it is a symbolic hint that there is something basically weak or broken in him from the very beginning. There is something in him that cannot escape the fatal aspect of the unconscious.

84   Saint-Exupéry speaks in a slightly ironical manner of the grown-up world and grown-up people who take themselves so seriously when, in fact, they are occupied with such trifles. That he himself had such attributes is shown quite clearly in the biographies. General Davet, one of his military superiors, says of him: "He was a man of integrity with a taste for childish pleasures which were sometimes surprising, and he had unaccountable fits of shyness when faced with administrative stubbornness; the latter always remained his *bête noir.*" Other biographies state that he was a little bit disappointing to people who met him because he was a bit of a poseur; he gave the impression of always acting and of not being a completely genuine personality. This tendency to go off into surprisingly childish pleasures is not only a symptom of the *puer aeternus* problem, but also belongs to the creative personality.

85   Creativeness presupposes a tremendous capacity for being genuine, for letting go, for if one cannot be spontaneous, one cannot really be creative, and that is why most artists and other creative people have a normal and genuine tendency to playfulness. That is also the great relaxation and means of recovery from an exhausting creative effort. Therefore, we cannot ascribe this trait only to Saint-Exupéry's *puer aeternus* nature; it might also belong to the fact that he was an artist.

86   General Davet's descriptions of Saint-Exupéry's inability to deal with public officials and his fear of those in administrative positions are important in connection with the motif of the sheep, which we now must discuss. To the man in an office, other people are sheep. As soon as we are faced with somebody in an official position, we become sheep. To him, we are just a number, and naturally officials

make one feel like that. It is the modern problem of the over-whelming power of the State, of the devaluation of the individual. The revolt which most people feel at being reduced to the level of a sheep in a flock is not confined to the *puer aeternus*, for there is something genuine and justifiable in it. Everyone who has not settled that problem within himself — namely, how far one must accept the fact of being just one of a number and how much one is an individual with the right to individual treatment — has this complex reaction against what Davet describes as military stubbornness.

87   Thus, this is not only Saint-Exupéry's problem, but is the great problem of the whole of Christian civilization. In France, however, it takes a specific turn, for the French tend to display exaggerated individualism, a kind of protest against all administration. Since the First World War there has been a tendency in France to revolt and be negative in connection with everything having to do with the pressure of the State. This even went so far that numbers of people voted for Communism, not because this really was their *Weltan-schauung*, but simply as a demonstration against the existing order. This shows an infantile attitude toward the problem of social and collective responsibility and brings to mind demonstrations by youths who resort to violence as a form of protest against society. In very young people who explode like this without any reflection, this is understandable. But when grown-ups behave similarly, when they vote for radical parties simply because they do not like those in the government, it is very immature. Nowadays, this is a very general complex and one which we all have in some form, for we have not yet decided how far we must accept being sheep shepherded by the State and how far we can reject such collective pressure. The *puer aeternus* has this problem in an even more pronounced form.

88   Before we go into the symbolism of the sheep, we should ask ourselves why Saint-Exupéry meets the little prince in the desert. In interpreting the story, we have taken the airplane crash as illustrating, in one way, an incident of Saint-Exupéry's personal life and, on the other hand, a symbolic or archetypal situation with which every encounter with the unconscious begins, namely, the

complete breakdown of former activities, of the goal in life and, in some form, of the flow of one's life energy. Suddenly everything gets stuck; we are blocked and stuck in a neurotic situation, and in this moment our life energy is dammed up, only to break through with the revelation of an archetypal image.

89   It is not inevitable that after such a collapse of one's conscious attitude a child is constellated in the unconscious. Any other kind of archetypal figure might turn up, for example, Khidr who appears after Moses lost his only nourishment in the desert. We should therefore go into the problem of the child-god. I want to discuss this, the greatest symbol in the book, in more detail only later when we know more of the story, for part of what the little prince really represents becomes clearer only then. For now, I would like to outline, what Jung says about the child-god:

90   This archetype of the 'child god' is extremely widespread and intimately bound up with all the other mythological aspects of the child motif. It is hardly necessary to allude to the still living 'Christ Child,' who, in the legend of Saint Christopher, also has the typical feature of being 'smaller than small and bigger than big.' In folklore the child motif appears in the guise of the *dwarf* or the *elf* as personifications of the hidden forces of nature. To this sphere also belongs the little metal man of late antiquity . . . who, till far into the Middle Ages, on the one hand inhabited the mine-shafts, and on the other represented the alchemical metals, above all Mercurius reborn in perfect form (as the hermaphrodite, *filius sapientiae*, or *infans noster*). Thanks to the religious interpretation of the 'child,' a fair amount of evidence has come down to us from the Middle Ages showing that the 'child' was not merely a traditional figure, but a vision spontaneously experienced (as a so-called 'irruption of the unconscious'). I would mention Meister Eckhart's vision of the 'naked boy' and the dream of Brother Eustachius. Interesting accounts of these spontaneous experiences are

also to be found in English ghost-stories, where we read of the vision of a 'Radiant Boy' said to have been seen in a place where there are Roman remains. This apparition was supposed to be of evil omen. It almost looks as though we are dealing with the figure of the *puer aeternus* who had become inauspicious through 'metamorphosis,' or in other words had shared the fate of the classical and the Germanic gods, who have all become bugbears. The mystical character of the experience is also confirmed in Part II of Goethe's *Faust*, where Faust himself is transformed into a boy and admitted into the 'choir of blessed youths,' this being the 'larval stage' of Doctor Marianus.[5] [...]

91   I do not know whether Goethe was referring, with this peculiar idea, to the *cupids* on antique grave-stones. It is not unthinkable. The figure of the *culcullatus* points to the hooded, that is, the *invisible* one, the genius of the departed, who reappears in the childlike frolics of a new life, surrounded by the sea-forms of dolphins and tritons.

92   *Culcullatus* means "one who wears a hood," who has a coat with a hood, and I think it highly symbolic that Jean Cocteau, who wore this sort of coat, thereby instituted the fashion of youths wearing these hooded coats. They are *pueri aeterni* and even wear that costume! I wonder if Cocteau knew about that.

93   The sea is the favourite symbol for the unconscious, the mother of all that lives. Just as the 'child' is, in certain circumstances (e.g., in the case of Hermes and the Dactyls), closely related to the phallus, symbol of the begetter, so it comes up again in the sepulchral phallus, symbol of a renewed begetting.[6]

---

[5] Ibid., §§ 268 ff.
[6] Ibid., §§ 298 ff.

94   The great problem with which we are confronted in this general outline by Jung is the double aspect of the child archetype. Just as in one way it means a renewal of life, spontaneity, and a new possibility suddenly appearing within or without and changing the whole life situation in a positive way, so also does the child-god have a negative aspect, a destructive one; namely, where Jung alludes to the apparitions of a "radiant boy" and says that this must have to do with a pagan child-god who has been condemned to appear only in a negative form. The negative child-god leads us into very deep waters, but it is safe to say that whenever the child motif appears, we are almost always confronted with the following problem.

95   The child motif when it turns up represents a bit of spontaneity, and the great problem — in each case an ethical, individual one — is to decide whether it is now an infantile shadow which needs to be educated, or something creative moving toward a future possibility of life. The child is always both: It is always behind and ahead of us. Behind us, it is the infantile shadow that we must leave behind and a childishness that must be sacrificed — that which always pulls us backward into being infantile and dependent, making us lazy and playful, thereby escaping problems and responsibility and life. On the other hand, if the child appears ahead of us, it means renewal, the possibility of eternal youth, of spontaneity and of new possibilities — the life flow toward the creative future. The great problem is always to make up one's mind in each instance whether it is an infantile impulse which only pulls backward, or an impulse which seems infantile to one's own consciousness, but which really should be accepted and lived because it leads forward.

96   Sometimes the answer to this dilemma is very apparent for the context of a dream can show very clearly what is meant. Let us say a *puer aeternus* type of man dreams about a little boy; then we can tell from the story of the dream if the apparition of the child has a fatal effect, in which case I treat it as the infantile shadow. But if the same figure appears to be positive, then you can say that it is something which looks very childish and silly, but which must be accepted because there is a possibility of new life in it. If it were always like

that, then the analysis of this kind of problem would be very simple. Unfortunately, like all products of the unconscious, the destructive side, and the constructive side — the pull backward and the pull forward — are very closely intertwined. Thus, when such figures appear, it is very difficult to decide, and sometimes it is practically impossible. That seems to me a part of the fatal situation with which we are confronted in this book and in Saint-Exupéry himself. One cannot (or at least I cannot) make up one's mind whether to treat the figure of the little prince as a destructive infantile shadow whose apparition is fatal and announces Saint-Exupéry's death, or to treat it as the divine spark of his creative genius.

97   A few years ago, one of our students at the C.G. Jung Institute evolved the idea that in certain people whose fate is very unfortunate there is something like a defective Self, that also appears as defective in symbolic form. This would mean that such people have no chance in life because the nucleus of their psyche is incomplete and defective, and therefore their individuation process cannot develop from this kernel. I do not agree with this idea because I have never seen such symbols of a defective Self without an accompanying defective attitude of the ego. Wherever you find such a defective symbol of the Self — where it is ambiguous, incomplete, and morbid — there is always at the same time, an incomplete and morbid attitude of the ego. Therefore, it cannot be scientifically asserted that the cause of the whole thing lies in a defective Self. It could just as well be said that it was because the ego had such a wrong attitude that the Self cannot come into play positively. If you eat completely wrongly and your stomach consequently does not react properly, you can react in one of two ways: You can decide that there is something wrong with your stomach. If you then consult numerous doctors without telling them that you are eating wrongly, the doctors will regretfully conclude that you have a defective stomach and that it is not possible to find the cause. If, on the other hand, you tell them from the outset that you eat all the wrong things, or that you do not eat at all, or eat irregularly, then you will be told that your symptoms have come about because of your poor eating habits, but that your

stomach is not the problem. Thus, this "defective" Self always goes hand in hand with an ego that does not function properly, and therefore, naturally, the Self cannot function properly either. If the ego is lazy, inflated, and not conscientious, and does not perform the duties of the ego-complex, then the Self cannot appear positively either.

98   One could object by saying that the ego cannot function properly if the Self is defective. Here we are confronted with the age-old philosophical problem of free will: Can I want the right thing? This is the problem that the *puer aeternus* man generally presents. He will say that he knows that everything goes wrong because he is lazy, but that he cannot want not to be lazy! Perhaps he may say that his neurosis is his inability, his inertia toward fighting his laziness. It is therefore useless to treat him as a rascal for whom everything would go right if he were not so lazy. This is an argument I have heard I don't know how many times! It is, to a certain extent, true, for the *puer* cannot make up his mind to work, so you can say that it is the defective Self. Something is wrong in the whole structure and so he cannot be saved.

99   This is a problem which comes up in many neuroses, not only in that of the *puer aeternus*. It goes very deep, and my attitude toward it is paradoxical: As long as I can, I behave as if the other person can make up his or her own mind because that is the only chance of salvation. If this proves impossible, then I turn around and say that it was not possible because of the way things developed. Otherwise, one falls into a wrong psychological superiority; namely, if a person goes wrong, or dies as the result of a disease or an accident, one might conclude that this occurred because he did not realize his problem — that it is his fault that he has this fate. I find this very distasteful. One does not have the right to decide that. If an individual cannot solve his problems, he generally gets horribly punished with hellish diseases or accidents. It is not, however, the business of others to point that out and to make it a moral issue. There I think one should stop short and take the other hypothesis — that the person could not do it, that the structure was defective

and therefore it was not possible. However, if the catastrophe has not taken place, it is better to take the more optimistic attitude: to try to create a hopeful atmosphere and believe in the possibility of a certain amount of free will. Experience shows that there are many cases where suddenly people can make up their minds to fight their neurosis and can pull themselves out of it. Then you can call it a miracle or that person's good deed, whichever you like, but it is also that which in theology is spoken of as an act of grace. Is it our good deeds that lead us to salvation, or is it by the grace of God? In my experience, we can only stay in the contradiction and stick to the paradox. Here, we are confronted with this problem in a specific form because, throughout the story, there is this tragic question in our minds. Something is constantly going wrong throughout the book, and one does not know whether it is Saint-Exupéry's fault or whether he could not help it. Was there some reason from the very beginning which prevented him from solving his problem?

100   Here, again, I must address the often-asked question as to whether it is possible that the Self, which is an archetype, can be defective? Quite rightly, one turns to Jung here who emphasized that there is nothing defective in the collective unconscious. I fully agree with him about this. I think that if the Self appears defective, it is because of a wrong attitude on the part of the ego. Objectively, it cannot be defective, which is why I cannot accept the idea of the defective Self. If the ego can change, something else changes; if the ego-attitude changes, then the symbols of the Self become positive. This is something we experience again and again: If the person in question can achieve a certain amount of insight, then the whole unconscious constellation changes. But my philosophical adversaries would say that the fact that one man can change and another cannot is due to the Self — and then one walks in a circle.

101   In this specific story, I shall therefore try to interpret the child figure in a double way — as the infantile shadow and the Self. Then we will try to find out which is which, i.e., we shall interpret all the material on a double rail to try to find out more about this problem. The thesis that the star child whom Saint-Exupéry meets is the

infantile shadow can very easily be proved, since he is the only one who understands the story of the boa constrictor and the elephant. That is a remnant of childhood. We have a letter from Saint-Exupéry to his mother written in 1935, shortly before his death, where he says that the only refreshing source he finds is in certain memories of his childhood, for instance, the smell of Christmas candles. Thus, his soul nowadays has completely dried up, and he is dying of thirst. There is his nostalgia for his childhood, and one can say that the little prince represents this world of childhood and is therefore the infantile shadow. It is typical that he writes in this way to his mother; one really sees that he is still involved in his mother complex.

102   On the other hand, it can be said that the fact that this child appears on earth is not only negative: It is not the apparition of just the infantile shadow, because, as we shall hear later, the little prince comes down from a star. This is an interesting parallel to Saint-Exupéry's plane crash that brought him down to earth, too. So, for the first time, two things meet on earth which hitherto were in the air: the star prince, who lived far away in the cosmos, and Saint-Exupéry, who was constantly flying in the air. From the moment the little prince lands on the earth, he is no longer only the infantile shadow because some part of him has touched reality. He is therefore now in an ambiguous position. If this could be realized, then he would become a part of the future, instead of being a pull backward. It is no longer only an infantile shadow but a form of self-realization that goes on and on. In practical terms, to become more conscious means to grow more and more into the reality of things — but this also means disillusionment.

103   The greatest difficulty we drag along with us from our childhood is the sack of illusions which we carry on our backs into adult life. The subtle problem consists in giving up certain illusions without becoming cynical. There are people who become disillusioned early in life. One sees this if you analyze so-called neglected children, i.e., those who either grew up in slums and had a terrible family life, or those from a wealthy background who suffered the same miseries except a lack of money but had divorced parents, a cold or tense

atmosphere at home. In both instances the feeling atmosphere was neglected. Such people very often grow up quicker than others because at a very early stage in their childhood they become very realistic, disillusioned, self-contained, and independent. The hardships of life have forced them to this, but you can generally tell that something went wrong from their rather bitter and falsely mature expression. They were pushed out of their childhood world too early and thrust into reality.

104   If you analyze such people, you find that they have not worked out the problem of childish illusions but have just cut it off. They have assured themselves that their desire for love and their ideals simply hamper them like a sack of stones carried on their backs. They feel they must get rid of it. But that is an ego decision that does not help at all, and a deeper analysis shows that they are completely caught up in childhood illusions: Their longing for a loving mother or for happiness is still there, but in a repressed state. They are much less grown-up than other people for they have simply pushed the problem into a corner. One then has the horrible task of reviving those illusions because life has got stuck there. Thus, the person in question has to be pushed back there, and one tries to help them reemerge properly. This is the problem one meets with in people who say that they can neither love nor trust anybody. For anyone stuck in this situation, life no longer has any meaning. Through the transference, they begin to hope that perhaps they might trust or love again, but you can be sure that the love that first comes up is completely childish. Very often the analysand knows what will happen — that it will just mean disappointment again. This is quite true, for such people bring out something so childish that it has to be rebuffed either by the analyst or by life itself. They are so immature that if, for instance, the analyst is in bed with flu, they experience it as a personal insult and a terrible let-down and disappointment. Quite grown-up people say that they know it to be unreasonable and idiotic but that that is how they feel, and they ask quite rightly what they can do about having such a child, such

incorrigible infantilism within themselves. Preaching helps them as little as it helps a small, furious child.

105   How can one meet this tremendous problem? If one shelves it as something hampering in life, as a source of illusion and trouble, then one is no longer spontaneous, but disillusioned and "grown-up" in a wrong way. But if one lives it, one is just impossible, and reality hits one over the head all the time. That is the problem. People who have shelved their feelings, or their demands on other people, or their capacity for trust, always feel not quite real, not quite spontaneous or really themselves. To shelve the divine child means not taking oneself completely seriously. One acts! One can adapt throughout life, but if one is honest with oneself, one knows that it is acting. Otherwise, one would behave in such an infantile way that nobody could stand one. What, then, can one do?

106   This is the problem of the divine child when it appears in this state that is somewhere between the true personality and infantility so that one just does not know what to do. Theoretically, the situation is clear: One should be able to cut away the childishness and leave the true personality. One should somehow be able to disentangle the two, and if an analysis goes right, that is what slowly happens. One succeeds in disentangling and destroying what is childish while saving one's creativity and future life. But, in practice, this is something which is immensely subtle and difficult to accomplish.

107   The divine child, or star prince, whom Saint-Exupéry meets in the desert, asks for a sheep, and we learn that he has come down to fetch a sheep to take back with him. Later in the story, it is said that on the planet there is an overgrowth of baobab trees that are continually sprouting. The star prince wants a sheep to eat the shoots as they appear so that he does not constantly have to work at cutting them off. But this he does not explain to Saint-Exupéry, and the real reason only comes out later.

108   Firstly, we must look at the symbolism of the sheep in the personal life of Saint-Exupéry and then also in general mythology. In one of his books, Saint-Exupéry says, "There is no bad outer fate,

only an inner one. There comes a moment when you are vulnerable and your own mistakes seize you and pull you down like a sort of whirlpool. [He naturally must be speaking with reference to flying. He means that there is no such thing as a chance crash: The one day you have an accident is the result of a whole inner and outer process.] It is not the big obstacles that count so much, but the little ones: three orange trees on the edge of an airfield, or thirty sheep which you fail to see in the grass and which suddenly emerge between the wheels of your plane." There was a time when flocks of sheep were used to keep down the grass on the airfields in many places, and it could happen that your plane by some mistake ran into them. One could say that he projects onto the sheep that fateful factor that one day will kill the *puer aeternus*. They are the fatal enemy.

109   The sheep has a very revealing name in Greek. It is called *probaton,* which comes from the verb "to walk forward." This is a marvelous name: The animal has no other choice and no other function than the capacity to walk forward! That is all it can do. The Greeks are even more witty, for they make the animal neuter and call it "the walking forward thing." This illustrates the most negative aspect of the sheep, which always follows the leading ram wherever it goes. You can read again and again in the papers that if a wolf or a dog chases the leading ram over a precipice, two hundred or three hundred sheep will jump over after him. This happened about ten years ago at Lenzerheide on an Alp when a wolf-hound chased the leading ram over the precipice, and afterward men had to go with their guns and knives and kill about two hundred sheep that were just piled up, one on top of the other. That is why one talks of a person as a "silly sheep." The instinct of walking and sticking together in the flock is so strong in them that they cannot pull out, even to save their own lives. In Walt Disney's film *The White Wilderness,* one can see the same thing with lemmings that wander into the sea. Once caught in such an instinctive move, the animal cannot pull out again.

110   The sheep tends to a similar instinctive behavior and therefore stands — when it appears in a negative connection in dreams — for that same thing in us: mass psychology, our tendency to be infected by mass movements and not to stand up for our own judgment and impulses. The sheep is the crowd-animal *par excellence*. Naturally, there is the crowd-man in each of us. For instance, you may hear that there are a lot of people at a lecture, and you say, "Then it must be good." Or you hear that someone has an exhibition at the main art gallery, and you go, but you do not have the courage to say that you think the pictures are horrible. You first look round and see others, whom you think ought to know, admiring them, and you dare not express your own opinion. Many people first look at the name of the artist before expressing an opinion. Such people are all sheep.

111   The sheep in mythology has a strange relationship to the world of the divine child. You all remember representations of the Madonna with her baby, Jesus, and St. John the Baptist playing with a lamb. Naturally the lamb is a representation of Christ himself, but in art it is exteriorized as something separate. He himself is the sacrificial lamb, the *agnus Dei*. In art, the sheep is shown as the playmate which naturally means (as always when a god is depicted with the animal) that it is his totem animal, what he is when he appears as an animal. In German folklore, there is a belief that the souls of children before they are born live as sheep in the realm of Mother Holle — a kind of earth-mother goddess — and those souls of unborn children are identical with what the Germans call *Lämmerwölkchen* (lamb-clouds) — in English, "fleecy clouds." The peasants thought these "fleecy clouds" were the souls of innocent children. There was the idea that if on Innocents' Day there were many such clouds in the sky, that predicted the death of many children. If you look up the traditional beliefs about sheep, you will find that they carry the symbolism of innocence, that they are easily influenced and affected by the evil eye and witchcraft. They can be bewitched more easily than almost any other animal and they can be killed by the evil eye. A sixth sense is also attributed to sheep for

it is said that their behavior often demonstrates foreknowledge. This sense is projected onto many domestic animals; horses and bees are also supposed to have a sixth sense. Having foreknowledge is not confined to sheep. But to be easily bewitched and persecuted by witches and wolves is specific to sheep in folklore tradition.

112   Because of its color, milk, like sheep, is also a symbol of innocence and purity that can be bewitched at any time. One of the chief activities of wizards and witches in peasant countries is to spoil the neighbor's milk. Innumerable precautions have therefore to be taken: Milk must not be carried across the street after seven o'clock in the evening; the bucket must be turned over before the cow is milked; three "Ave Marias" have to be said, and so on. Our hygienic precautions are nothing compared with the precautions against witchcraft taken in earlier times, that were infinitely more complicated: If, for example, a witch even walks past in the street, the milk in the bucket will turn sour, or blue, at once; if an evil eye is cast onto the cowshed, then the milk will be bluish from then on, and an exorcist must be found. It is interesting that symbols of something especially pure and innocent are particularly exposed to infection and to attack by evil. This is because the opposites attract each other, and innocence is a challenge to the powers of darkness.

113   In the practical life of the *puer aeternus*, that is, of the man who has not disentangled himself from the eternal youth archetype, one sees the same tendency — to be believing and naïve and idealistic. Therefore, he automatically attracts people who will deceive and cheat him. I have often noticed in analyzing this kind of man how they are attracted in a fatal way to rather dubious women or pick friends about whom one has not got a good feeling. It is as though their inexperienced naiveté and their wrong kind of idealism automatically call forth the opposite, but it is no use warning such people against such relationships. You will only be suspected of jealousy, and not be listened to. Such naiveté or childish innocence can only be cured of these illusions by passing through disappointment and bad experiences. Warnings are no good — such men must learn by experience, without which they will never wake

up from their "innocence." It is as if the wolves — namely, the crooks and destructive people — instinctively see such lambs as their legal prey. This naturally leads us much deeper into the whole problem of our religious tradition.

114   As you know, Christ is the good shepherd, and we are His sheep. This is a paramount image in our religious tradition and one which has created something very destructive, namely, that because Christ is the shepherd and we the sheep, we have been taught by the Church that we should not think or have our own opinions, but just believe. If we cannot believe in the resurrection of the body — such a mystery that nobody can understand it — then one *must* just accept it. Our whole religious tradition has worked in that direction, with the result that if now another system comes along, say Communism or Nazism, we are taught that we should simply shut our eyes and not think for ourselves, that we should just believe the Führer or the Kremlin. We are really trained to be sheep! If the leader is a responsible person, or the leading ideal is something good, then it is okay. The drawback of this religious education, however, is now coming out very badly, for Western individuals of the Christian civilization are much more easily infected by mass beliefs than the Eastern. They are predisposed to believe in slogans, having always been told that there are many things they cannot understand and must just believe to be saved. Thus, we are trained to have the psychology of sheep, which is a terrific shadow of our Christian education for which we are now paying.

115   Saint-Exupéry's work shows that he was possessed by this idea. He says in *The Wisdom of the Sands*[7]: "To build the peace is to build a stable big enough to embrace the whole flock, so that the whole flock can sleep in it. [What an ideal! Just to put mankind to sleep!] To build the peace is to borrow from God his shepherd's cloak so that all people can be accepted under it, under the divine cloak." We see here that he identifies with God. He is the Godhead who accepts mankind under his cloak — the religious megalomania of the *puer aeternus*.

---

[7] Saint-Exupéry, *Wisdom of the Sands*.

116   And now comes another complex: "It is just like a mother who loves her sons, and one son is timid and full of tenderness, another burning to live, and another is perhaps a hunchback, another perhaps delicate, but all of them in all their differences move the heart of the mother, and all, in the diversity of this love, serve glory."

117   There you see how the religious image of the divine shepherd and the sheep is mixed up with the mother-complex sentimentality in a very dangerous way. Suddenly it is the mother who is the shepherd and the children are the sheep. Along comes a wolf and eats the shepherd and takes the cloak, and then you will see what happens to the sheep! This is just what the wolf has been waiting for! In a religious or social context, the wolf may be the great dictators and leaders we have now, or any kind of person who lies and cheats in public life. In private life, it is the animus of the devouring mother who takes the lead for her sheep-son. And there are decent, devoted sons who believe that they have to honor and be chivalrous to their mother, the elderly lady. They do not see that the animus of their mother has eaten them and that it feeds on their innocence. The devouring animus of the mother feeds on the innocence and the best and most devoted feelings of the son; here, too, the sheep has been eaten by the shepherd.

118   Thus, the little star boy in our story wants a sheep. We learn that it is needed to eat up the overly-prolific trees, which are obviously a symbol of the devouring mother, so wanting a sheep seems at first sight to have a positive meaning, since the asteroid is threatened by an overgrowth — an overgrowth of the mother complex. I have just illustrated it the other way around, with the sheep as part of the mother complex, and not as the right remedy against that overgrowth. So here again it seems to me that we are confronted with complete ambiguity. In what way does the sheep help combat the mother complex? The story says that it bites off the new shoots, which are the overgrowth of the mother complex. But what does that mean psychologically? How much does the crowd-man within us help against the mother complex? Would the mother be somewhat less devouring if her son were to give in to her, or the wolf less

dangerous because it is well fed when the sheep willingly walk into the wolf's mouth? I do not think that a son who gives in to his mother's devouring desire has ever succeeded in improving matters. This has not been my experience for the devouring principle generally fattens and grows on every bite it gets.

119   What can help to free a man from his mother? If a man follows his predetermined pattern — namely, to free himself from his mother — he is doing the right thing. Let us say he hears a psychological maxim that everybody must free himself from the mother. If he does that, he really follows the sheep mentality: He does it because "one says so," and this frees him from his mother. That is quite correct. Very few young men normally have a strong enough individuality to pull away from their mother of their own accord; they do it via the collective. For instance, in our country, it is military service which helps young men to overcome their mother complexes. Many are improved or even cured of their attachment to their mother by military service. It is the sheep mentality, the crowd-man, which drives them into military service, but this collective adaptation can be a help to pull away from their mother. In the simpler layers of the population, military service largely still functions like the male initiation rituals in primitive tribes.

120   You can say that all kinds of very humble, not individualistic, collective adaptations help against the mother complex: as mentioned earlier, doing one's work, going to military service, trying to behave like everybody else, not having that kind of fancied individuality which is typical for the mother-complex man, and giving up the idea of being somebody special who is above having to make these humiliating adaptations. To accept being just somebody or nobody, in the crowd, is to a certain extent a cure, but only a temporary one and not the whole cure. Nevertheless, it is a first step in pulling away from the personal mother.

121   You see then — *similia similibus curantur* (like cures like). To become a crowd-man is psychologically a very dangerous thing, but it helps against the danger of the false individuality one develops within a mother complex. Then one is up against another danger —

the medicine used in such a case is dangerous. Nevertheless, that the star prince wants a sheep could be interpreted positively. In his ideal, divine isolation, he wants the company of the crowd-soul. That would enlarge the world of his little star. There are no animals up in his star world. If he brings one, that is a bit of an earthly instinct which he has brought up there, and this seems extremely positive. But you could interpret it negatively also, for it is not a conscious realization but only pitting one instinct against another. For this reason, I think we can arrive at a definite judgment and say that the sheep is rather more negative than positive.

122   Added to this is the fact that the sheep is in the box. I would say he would prefer to take the sheep up, instead of going down to it. He wants to pull the sheep up into the stars. But a sheep is something that belongs on earth. If, to have it, he were to stay on the earth, then it would be the thing that can pull him down into reality. In the same way, a man gets pulled down onto the earth if he goes through military service and a lot of other painful adaptations. But if you take the sheep up into the fantasy world of childhood, then it is not an adaptation to reality: It is more of a pseudo-adaptation. That is something very subtle and specific to Saint-Exupéry. It is particularly dangerous for him, to which he has a very strange reaction. He praises clinging to the earth, social adaptation, submission to the earthly principle, acceptance of the bonds of love, and so on, but he does not really stand by them. He assimilates the whole thing intellectually by taking it back into his imaginary world. This is a trick that many *pueri aeterni* perform: The realization that they should adapt to reality is an intellectual idea to them which they fulfill in fantasy but not in reality. The idea is executed only in reflection and on a philosophical level, but not on the level of action. It looks as though they have quite understood, as if they have the right attitude, as if they know what is important and right. But they do not *do* it. If you read Saint-Exupéry's work, you could attack me and say that he is not a *puer aeternus*. Look at the Sheikh in *The Wisdom of the Sands*[8], a mature man who would take responsibility

---

[8] Ibid.

on earth. Look at Riviere in *Night Flight*[9]; he is not a *puer aeternus* but a man who accepts his responsibilities. He is a grown-up, masculine man, not a mother-complex youth. It is all there in his ideas, but Saint-Exupéry never lived either the Sheikh or Riviere; he fantasized them, and the idea of the down-to-earth, grown-up man, but he never lived his fantasy. This, I think, is one of the trickiest problems in this specific neurotic constellation. The *puer aeternus* always tends to grasp at everything which would be the right thing to do and then to draw it back into his fantasy-theory world. He cannot cross the very simple border from fantasy to action. It is also the dangerous curve in the analysis of such people, for unless the analyst constantly watches this problem like an alert fox, the analysis will progress marvelously, the *puer aeternus* will understand everything, will integrate the shadow and the fact that he must work and come down to earth. But, unless you are like a devil's watchdog behind it, it is all a sham. The whole integration takes place up in the sky and not on the earth, not in reality. One must often play the governess and ask what time he gets up in the morning, how many hours have been worked in the day, and so on. It is a very tedious job, but that is what it boils down to because otherwise a fantastic self-deception occurs which can very easily catch the analyst.

123   We should now consider the sheep in the box. When you assimilate something intellectually, you put it into a box. A concept is a box. When Saint-Exupéry impatiently puts the sheep in a box, he accepts the idea, but *only* as an idea. It exists, but *only* in his brain-box. The little prince thinks the design is as good as a real sheep. Everything remains in the world of mental activity.

124   I have been asked whether Saint-Exupéry would have remained an artist if he had been cured of his *puer aeternus* personality. To be "cured" of being a *puer* does not imply being "cured of being an artist." If we consider Goethe, for example, we can see that in his early writing there is evidence of a mother complex, and he, too, felt that if he gave up the *puer* mentality, there would be nothing left. But he pulled through this crisis, and although the *puer* in his book

---

[9] Saint-Exupéry, *Night Flight*.

The Sorrows of Young Werther[10] shot himself, Goethe himself survived.

125   In the really great artist, there is always a *puer* at first, but it can go further. It is a question of the feeling judgment. If a man ceases to be an artist when he ceases to be a *puer,* then he was never really an artist. If analysis saves such pseudo-artists from being artists, then thank God! But we may not forget that Saint-Exupéry is not only writing about his personal problem: he is describing a collective neurosis. He has displayed the situation in literature so beautifully; he has raised the question. There is a type of artist who cannot make the switch that Goethe made, and therefore does not survive as an artist. One cannot say that they have not been artists, but that they did not grow beyond that switch-over. In *The Sorrows of Young Werther*, Goethe did not deal with the problem of the *puer* in a final way: It went on into other works. In *Torquato Tasso*[11], Goethe presents the next stage of the problem by objectifying the *puer* in Tasso and the adult in Antonio, the man who wants to live on earth, thereby detaching himself from the problem. It then becomes a conflict that goes even further in *Faust*. One's feeling tells one if the writer does — or does not — extricate himself from this problem. Objectifying the *puer* is only the first step.

126   I have found that, along with his other problems, a *puer aeternus* typically suffers from laziness. It is true that Saint-Exupéry and Goethe both worked hard. It must be said, however, that the *puer aeternus* must learn to carry on with work he does not like, not only with the work where he is carried away by great enthusiasm, which is something that everybody can do. Even primitive people, who are said to be lazy, can do that. As soon as they are gripped by something, they work, even to the point of exhaustion, but I would not evaluate that as work but rather as being carried away by a festival of work. The work which is the cure for the *puer aeternus* is where he needs to kick himself out of bed on a dreary morning and again and again take up the boring job, through sheer will power.

---

[10] Goethe, *Sorrows of Werther.*
[11] Goethe, *Torguato Tasso.*

Goethe took on a political position and served in Weimar; he sat in his office, reading little requests concerning taxation and so on. That is what he experienced in his work as Antonio, and this, too, somehow belonged to his life. Goethe lived what he wrote. He stayed in his office and gave his mind to the most boring questions when often he would have preferred to ride off somewhere. He somehow had a deep insight into the necessity of this part of life. As a feeling type, he thus developed his inferior thinking, which showed very much in the rather boring and unexciting side of his maxims (his conversations with Eckermann are most disappointing).

127   It is believed that Rousseau said that the greatest fault in his character was his laziness, even though it is well known that he worked from morning to night and read a great many books. But he must have escaped some other kind of work. People can cheat themselves by working themselves to death to avoid doing the work they should do. Rousseau had to keep his feet in a tub of water to get himself to work; he worked in a kind of trance with footbaths. His *Confessions*[12] might have been more to the point and less sentimental without these baths!

128   In this connection, I have been asked if an author can write out his neurosis. To do so has got nothing to do with talent — it is something we would all like to be able to do. I, at least, would very much like to make money out of my neurotic spots. I think the problem comes after the thing has been written. What one writes does concern one's own problem — otherwise the writing dries up. But when you have written out the problem, or while you are writing it, you have to live it. Whenever I have lectured on a problem, it has always come back on me afterward. I have observed that with sensation types it is the reverse: They live it first and then write it down. When you are writing on a problem, synchronistic events often happen to you at the same time, so that you have to live it concurrently. Jung told me that when he was writing on a special problem, he would get letters from all sorts of places — Australia, for example — in which the question he was writing on would be

---

[12] Rousseau, *Confessions*.

put to him. If you touch on an important and vital problem of your own, it generally happens this way, and this is the difference between only writing of your neurosis or going further. The problem will always tie in with you, and if you live it at the same time, then what you write afterward will be a step further on. Otherwise, you will again write of the same problem. Some writers always turn on the same gramophone record, whereas if you live it, the next thing will show progress. Goethe lived what he wrote, and what he next wrote was always a step further on. The Romantic poets repeated themselves much more for they went around in circles because they did not, or could not, live it at the same time. I do not mean to make accusations, but one should be prepared for what one writes to become constellated on the outside. So many artists do not want their work to be analyzed because they are afraid that then they would have to live it. This is the resistance that many of them have against psychoanalysis, for they say that their creativity would be analyzed away. But genuine creativeness is so terribly strong that not even the most gifted analyst in the world could wipe it out. This resistance to putting their work to the test is therefore very suspect.

129 You may have the impression that I have been too hard on Saint-Exupéry, who in his life showed courage and the capacity for substantial reaction, and one could not therefore accuse him of trying to escape reality.

130 Putting the sheep in a box is not a gesture of escape on the part of Saint-Exupéry, but springs from what one might call a certain nervous weakness to stand a conflict. Saint-Exupéry wants to get back to work on his engine. The star prince, instead of letting him quickly draw a sheep, bothers him, saying this drawing is not right, nor this, nor this, which means Saint-Exupéry is torn between the child — whose importance he completely realizes and who in a typically childlike way bothers him — and the machine. He feels sure that even if he were to draw another sheep it would not be right, or there would be a lot of questions, and, in fact, he urgently needs to repair his engine. If you take that symbolically, it means a conflict between the demands of the outer and the inner life which

establishes a tremendous tension. How can you comply with the demands of outer reality, which is right and reasonable, and those of the inner life at the same time? The difficulty is that the demands of the inner life need time. You cannot do active imagination for five minutes and then go off and do other things! If, for instance, one is in analysis, dreams must be written down, which is only the beginning, for one has not yet done any work. One should also meditate on them. It is a full-time job, but very often there are also the urgent necessities of outer life. This is one of the worst and most difficult tensions to stand — to be capable as far as possible of giving each claim what it needs. The weak personality — and I don't mean "weak" as a moral criticism — reacts accordingly with a short-cut reaction, making a definite decision to do one thing while putting aside the other. This demonstrates an incapacity for standing the tension beyond a certain point. A weak personality reacts with impatience, whereas a strong personality can bear the tension for longer. In our case, we see that, after the third attempt to draw the sheep, Saint-Exupéry gives up and devises a short-cut solution to get back to his engine. This is an indication of a weakness that shows up in certain other elements of the story, for instance, the star prince's planet is very tiny, he himself is very delicate, or, to take the first dream, the hero does not come out of the devouring snake, that is, the mother. If you look at photographs of Saint-Exupéry, you will see that he has a very strange "split" face: The lower part of it is like that of a boy of seven, the expression of his mouth is completely immature. It is a naïve little child's mouth, and there is a thin little chin, whereas the upper part of the face gives the impression of a very intelligent and mature man. Something is weak and just like a child. Therefore, there are certain tensions which he cannot stand. My commentary is not meant as a criticism, but rather as a statement of fact, such as a doctor might make, saying that the person is not strong and would probably not survive pneumonia. It is simply a statement of a tragic fact.

131   There are other men swallowed by the *puer aeternus* problem who would have the strength to stand more conflict, but who would

also react out of sheer impatience rather than from a tragic weakness. Those who suffer from their mother complex often do not want to stick with a situation. In *Aion*, Jung says, for instance:

132   'There is in him a desire to touch reality, to embrace the earth and fructify the field of the world. But he makes no more than a series of fitful starts, for his initiative as well as his staying power are crippled by the secret memory that the world and happiness may be had as a gift — from the mother. The fragment of world which he, like every man, must encounter again and again is never quite the right one, since it does not fall into his lap, does not meet him half way, but remains resistant, has to be conquered, and submits only to force. ... For this he would need a faithless Eros, one capable of forgetting his mother.'[13]

133 Thus, we see how impatience is sometimes an effect of the mother complex. I think this is true of Saint-Exupéry, too. But in addition, there is something tragic, namely an inborn weakness for which he cannot be held responsible. This means that his very vitality has somehow been weakened, and this is a tragic fate about which nothing can be done.

134   When, in this context, Jung refers to a "faithless Eros," he means the capacity to turn away from time to time from a relationship. This leads to another great problem: The *puer aeternus*, in the negative sense of the word, very often tends to be too impressed and too weak and too much of a "good boy" in his relationships, without a quick self-defense reaction where required. For instance, he takes much too much from the animi of the women around him: If one, for example, makes a scene, finding fault with him about this or that, he accepts too much of it at first. Then, one day, out of the blue, he has had enough and just walks out of the whole situation, in a completely cruel and reckless manner. You could say that consciously he is too weak and yielding, and the unconscious

---

[13] Jung, *Aion*, vol. 9/II, *CW*, § 22.

shadow is too cruel, reckless, and unfaithful. I have seen some who have taken practically everything from girlfriends (where one would have expected a woman to flare up long before), and then one day the *puer aeternus* just walks out on the situation and turns to another woman, not even giving the first one any answers. There is no transitional stage. The yielding "good boy," the man who gives in too much, is suddenly replaced by the cold gangster shadow, without any human relatedness whatsoever. The same thing happens in analysis: They accept everything, never come out with resistances, or assert their own standpoint against that of the analyst. Then, out of the blue, they say that they are going to another analyst, or are giving up analysis altogether, and if you have not happened to notice that this was coming, you fall out of the sky. There are no thanks, nothing at all. It is just finished. At first there was insufficient coldness and independence, or masculine aggressiveness, and afterward, too much in a negative, inhuman, and unrelated form. That is typical for many *pueri aeterni*. Much more strength would be required to have the thing out patiently with someone, rather than just giving in and walking away.

Chapter Two
The Encounter in the Desert

135 In our story, there now comes a long conversation in which Saint-Exupéry learns more about the little prince: He has fallen from heaven, from Asteroid B-612, and he wants the sheep so that it may eat up the baobab trees up there. I have never discovered what the association is for the number of the asteroid B-612. One can imagine from the way in which it is described that Saint-Exupéry is playing with his astronomical and mathematical knowledge and wants to express the idea of a little star X-Y. If there is a symbolic meaning, I do not know what it might be, or at least could not make a definite assertion.

136 The great danger comes from the baobab sprouts which grow into huge trees and whose roots, if allowed to grow, would split the planet. Thus, the little prince is kept constantly busy pulling up the little plants before they grow too big. That is his constant worry, and his idea is to get a sheep from earth which would eat the shoots to relieve him of the constant fight with the baobab trees.

137 Saint-Exupéry says that it would take a great many *elephants* to eat such trees. The little prince says that if he were to need a lot of elephants, he would have to put them one upon the other; they would not have space otherwise, and from such remarks, Saint-Exupéry constructs the situation. He makes a drawing to give his idea of what it would look like if the elephants were put one on top of the other. His sketch shows elephants standing one upon the other on all four sides of the planet: three elephants on one side, two on two other sides, standing upon each other, but the two elephants on the fourth side he draws from the back. Thus, the fourth function is

turned in another direction.[1] It is interesting that, without knowing anything about Jungian psychology, he makes the three developed functions alike and gives them a bit more importance, while the fourth function, by turning them in a different direction, appears to be inferior. Saint-Exupéry says:

138 'So, basing my work upon the descriptions of the little prince, I made the drawing you have just seen. I don't like to sound like a moralist. But the danger of baobabs is so little known and the rists are so considerable to whomever might get lost on an asteroid that, for once, I make an exception to my reserve. I say: "Children. Beware of baobabs!" It is in order to warn my friends of a danger of which they, like me, have been unaware for so long, that I have worked so hard over this drawing. My lesson was worth it. You may ask yourselves: Why are there no other drawings in this book as impressive as the drawing of baobabs?

139 The drawings in the book, which are by Saint-Exupéry himself, are very light both in color and drawing, but the one of the baobab trees has much deeper colors and is done with much more care and accuracy. He says himself that he has worked on it, and you see that at once, for not only are the colors strong but he has taken a lot of trouble to draw the details of the tree.

140 'The answer is quite simple: I have tried but with the others have not had the slightest success. When I drew the baobabs, I was driven by a feeling of urgency.'

141 Here we touch upon the main problem. Saint-Exupéry says that when he made this drawing of the baobabs, he felt the terrific danger. There are three big trees, but there is also a fourth figure, namely a small boy dressed in red with an axe in his hand. The little prince

---

[1] On the four functions of the conscious ego – thinking and feeling, sensation and intuition – see Jung, *Psychological Types*, vol. 6, *CW*. The two auxiliary functions are shown on each side of the main function, while opposite the latter is the fourth, the undifferentiated and so-called "inferior" function."

tells Saint-Exupéry that he had a neighbor on another asteroid who was too lazy to pull up the little roots of the baobab, so they grew to the size shown in the picture, and then it was too late. There he stands with his axe, but he cannot cut down the trees, and his asteroid perishes. The drawing shows the big trees and the helpless boy, and from the little axe and the size of the large trunks of the trees you see that there is no chance of cutting the trees down anymore. That is the "urgency" in the drawing, the one which Saint-Exupéry drew with an enormous effort.

142   As the star is very small, the elephants have to stand on top of each other and this expresses a particular difficulty which is where I am heading with this. For the problem is not that the elephants are too large, but rather that the earth is too small and not strong enough to carry them. There is not enough space for them. But what does that mean? Not that the ego is not strong enough. That is perhaps the result of the problem. We often say of people that they have not enough earth, and intuitively we are thereby saying either that they lack contact with reality — there is earth present, but they are not in touch with it — or that they are in touch with reality, but they have too little earth because there is not enough vitality. You could call earth psychological substance. And this brings us to one of the greatest problems in psychotherapy that one must deal with again and again: How much substance does the person in question have? How much can he carry? You can only guess that with your feeling — have a feeling impression about it. It cannot be measured scientifically, and sometimes one can misjudge the situation. Sometimes you think that a person does not have much substance, and when it comes to a vital conflict, suddenly, and surprisingly, a lot appears. Or you have the feeling that someone can carry a lot, but then, out of the blue, they break down. They have no strength, and this is only found out during the analysis. But if one has some experience of people, then one may be able to guess correctly how much carrying substance there is.

143   In his theory of schizophrenia, Jung makes a difference between what he calls the asthenic type and the strong type. In the strong

type, the problem is that there is an overwhelming wealth of strength and fantasy in the unconscious, confronted with a relatively weak ego. This may cause a split within the person. In the strong type it is really a plus which makes them ill. In the asthenic type, it is a minus that makes the person ill. Somehow neither the ego nor the unconscious has quite enough impetus. People in such a situation have no dreams. Where, in the greatest conflict, you would expect a vital reaction from the unconscious, the dreams are small and petty, or there are none. It is as though their inner nature does not react. It is very important to know that, because naturally, in the strong type one can risk a kind of reckless therapy. One can, for example, confront the person with the problem and risk a terrific crisis, a healing crisis, and they will come through it.

144   With the asthenic type, you can never do that. There one must adopt a nursing attitude, making constant blood transfusions, so to speak, never forcing the problem or pushing the person up against the wall because that would break them. One does not have to decide that oneself; in general, the unconscious decides. In the asthenic type, the dreams themselves do not push the problem. I have often been amazed when people of this type who have the most urgent problem have dreams which only talk about this or that detail, and do not poke into the main problem. Then I say to myself, "The confrontation is apparently not possible. The unconscious knows better than I do and says that this problem cannot be touched. It is too hot; it would explode the person." One has to go along with the seemingly little dreams there are and take the advice contained in them.

145   With the strong type, you generally see that the dreams hit directly at the core of the problem, with great dramatic structure. Then you see that the whole thing is driving to a climax and a healing crisis or a terrific conflict, after which the thing decides itself, either for good or for ill. It is similar on the physiological level. Sometimes — for example in the case of pneumonia — there can be a life-and-death fight with very high fever, but the patient gets through it and is cured. Others — and this is much stranger — do

not get any fever, only a little increased temperature. The illness drags on and does not come to a climax because the vital reaction in the body is not strong enough; there is not sufficient vitality. Sometimes there are combined cases. There may be strong people who have one weak spot, so the situation is mixed. Someone may have a vital make-up, belong to the plus type with which risks can be taken, but somewhere there is a minus, a split in the make-up. Here the situation becomes even more difficult as one must follow two lines, putting a lot of weight where it can be carried but never pressing on the weak spot which needs endless nursing, care, and patience. This combination is often found in very split personalities: on the one hand, there is an unusual capacity for life, but, on the other hand, they have an extremely vulnerable spot; this aspect has to be fenced off and especially cared for. Such mixed types are not difficult, for if one can get them to realize the situation themselves, they can take care of their weak spots. It simply means making them realize their dangerous corner, but also nursing them with patience, not force, paying constant attention to the weak spot so that it may slowly recover.

146   I think Saint-Exupéry is a mixed type, neither weak nor strong. He has tremendous strength, courage, vitality, and the capacity to change difficult situations, but one corner of his personality is extremely weak and lacking in vitality, and that is what this planet personifies. Naturally this one corner is the essential corner in his case, and these symptoms of not having vital reactions where they are important run through the whole book. We could say, therefore, that the will to live is too small in comparison with his genius and capacities. The earth signifies the will to live and the acceptance of life, and that is his weak spot. The incongruity of the personality is the problem. This does not so much illustrate the *puer aeternus* problem but is a specific problem in Saint-Exupéry; nevertheless, one often finds the one combined with the other. While the person who has too little earth may be able to assimilate everything psychologically, he will have great difficulty realizing things. Such people take everything in analysis quietly and honestly, but when

you press them to do something about it in outer reality, a terrific panic comes up. When the inner realization must be put into life, strength collapses, and you are confronted with a trembling child, who exclaims, "Oh no! I cannot do that!" This is an exaggerated illustration of the introvert's attitude in which there is great strength in accepting the inner truths, but very little when it comes to real life.

147   We have now looked at the only two elephant drawings in the whole book, and it is interesting to compare them. They represent reverse situations: In the first, the elephant is overwhelmed by the snake; in the second, the elephant is the overwhelming thing that does not have enough earth, which shows that the situation can be regarded from two angles: Namely, either that the greater personality, the hero, in Saint-Exupéry has been overwhelmed by the devouring unconscious — by the mother complex — or that the hero personality in Saint-Exupéry did not have enough foundation in order to become real. They are two aspects of the same tragedy. It is interesting that the little prince himself says that a boa constrictor is a very dangerous creature, and an elephant is very cumbersome. Saint-Exupéry is between the devil and the deep blue sea, for he does not know how to accept either his greatness or his weakness. He does not know how to get on with either of them.

148   The baobab trees in the drawing are enormous and give the impression of overrunning the whole star with their luxuriant growth, so you can say that Mother Nature is overwhelming the field of human culture and consciousness. If you look at the picture, you see that the roots of the trees are drawn exactly like snakes. I think, too, that it is not by chance that in the first drawing he chooses a *boa* and then calls these trees *bao*bab trees. There seems to be a play on the words. He seems to have associated the two factors: Both boa constrictor and trees are overwhelming. We should therefore amplify the trees rather on the negative side. How are we to interpret them in this drawing?

149   Gilgamesh comes to mind who had to cut down the cedar tree in Ishtar's forest. There, the tree represents the power of Ishtar who,

among other things, is the tree goddess who has appointed Humbaba as guardian to defend the tree. Here the tree is linked up with the negative mother. A further ready amplification is the tree as a symbol of life. In Jung's essay, *The Philosophical Tree*[2], the tree is generally interpreted as the symbol of life, of inner growth, of the process of individuation and of maturing. But this does not fit here. The tree is frequently connected with mother-goddesses, who are often even worshipped as a tree, not only with Ishtar, but also, in Germanic mythology, with Iduna, and in Greek mythology, with Demeter and other goddesses.

150   But there is an even closer relationship: for instance, Attis in the tree, or Osiris who hung in his coffin in a tree. There the tree is what one generally calls the death-mother in mythology. The coffin in the tree, and the dead person in the coffin, was interpreted as being given back to the mother, as being put back into the tree, the death-mother. At the Festival of Attis in Rome, a fir tree was carried with an image of Attis at the top of the tree, generally only the torso. In *Symbols of Transformation*[3], Jung quotes an old poem which says that the Christian cross has been looked upon as being the terrible stepmother who killed Christ. That would be the first association, namely, that the tree is the mother, the coffin, and has to do with the death of the *puer aeternus* god. How can we interpret that? We get into a contradiction: Symbolically the tree often clearly represents the process of individuation, but here this same symbol is identified with death, a destructive factor.

151   In the drawing, the tree is monstrous, much too big for the star, which indicates that the mother problem is too big and too devouring. How do we connect it with the process of individuation, a process of inner growth to which one is attached and from which one cannot get away. If you say no to it and do not accept it, it grows against you, and then it is your own inner growth that kills you. If you refuse the growth, then it kills you, which means that if a person is completely infantile and has no other possibility, then not much

---

[2] Jung, *Alchemical Studies*, vol. 13, *CW*, §§ 304 ff.
[3] Jung, *Symbols of Transformation*, vol. 5, *CW*, §§ 661 ff.

will happen. But if the person has a greater personality within — that is, a possibility of growth — then a psychological disturbance will occur. This is why we say that a neurosis is, in a way, a positive symptom. It shows that something wants to grow; it shows that that person is not right in his or her present state. If the growth is not accepted, it grows against you, at your own expense, and produces what might be called a negative individuation. The process of individuation, of inner maturing and growth, goes on unconsciously and ruins the personality instead of healing it. That is how the death-tree, the death-mother tree and the life-tree are essentially connected. The inner possibility of growth in a person is a dangerous thing because either you say yes to it and go ahead if you do not want to be killed by it. There is no other choice. It is a destiny that must be accepted.

152   If you look at the *puer aeternus* in the negative sense, you can say that he does not want to outgrow the mother problem. He wants to stay a youth, or in a youthful state, but the growth goes on all the same until it destroys him and then he is killed by the very factor in his soul by which he could have outgrown his problem. If, in actual life, you have to contend with such a problem, then you see how people refuse to grow and become mature and tackle the problem, and the unconscious becomes increasingly destructive. Then you have to say, "For God's sake, do something for the thing is growing against you and you will be hit over the head by it." But the moment may come, as the star prince says in the book, when it is too late, for the destructive growth has sucked up all the energy.

153   The luxuriant growth is also an image of a rich fantasy life, of an inner creative richness. Very often you find an image of a rich fantasy life, of an inner creative richness. Very often you find such a rich fantasy life in the *puer*, but that wealth of fantasy is dammed up and cannot flow into life because the *puer* refuses to accept reality as it is and thereby dams up his life. He gets up, for instance, at 10:30 a.m., hangs around till lunch time with a cigarette in his mouth, giving way to his emotions and fantasies. In the afternoon, he means to do some work, but first goes out with friends and then with a girl,

and the evening is spent in long discussion about the meaning of life. Then he goes to bed at 1, and the next day is a repetition of the one before. In this way, his capacity for life and his inner riches are wasted, for they cannot get into something meaningful but slowly overgrow the real personality. This kind of individual walks about in a cloud of fantasies, fantasies which, in themselves, are interesting and full of rich possibilities, full of unlived life. You feel that such a person has a tremendous wealth and capacity, but there is no possibility of finding a means of realization. Then the tree — the inner growth — becomes negative, and in the end kills the personality. That is why the tree is frequently linked up with the negative mother symbol, for the mother complex has this danger; because of it, the process of individuation can become negative.

154   There is a parallel in the Finnish epic *Kalevala*,[4] which describes the fight of the divine child and the tree:

155   Out of the sea a man rose
             a fellow came up from the billow:
             he was not big as big goes
             nor all that small as small goes
             but as tall as a man's thumb
             as high as a woman's span.
             Copper was the hat on his shoulders
             copper the boots on his feet
             copper mittens on his hands
             copper the patterns on the mittens.

156 [Väinämöinen asked the hero from the sea what he intended to do, and he replied,]

157   'I am quite a man, a small
             fellow of the water-folk.
             I have come to break the oak
             to shatter the brittle tree.'

---

[4] Lönnrot, *Kalevala*, 16 f.

Steady old Väinämöinen
put this into words:
'I do not think you were made
neither made nor appointed
to be the great oak's breaker
to be the grim tree's feller.

158 [But the little man took his axe.]

He struck the tree with his axe
bashed it with his even blade;
he struck once, struck twice
soon a third time tried:
fire flashed from the axe
and a blaze flew from the oak
and the oak wanted to tilt
the world-sallow to topple.
So at the third time
he could fell the oak
and shatter the world-sallow
and bring down the hundred-leaved.
The base he thrust to the east
the top he lowered north-west
the foliage to the great
south, the boughs half way northward.
[...]
When the oak had been broken
and felled the mean tree

159 [now comes the important part]

suns were free to shine
moons were free to gleam
clouds to scud along
and heaven's arches to curve
on the misty headland's tip
at the foggy island's end.

160   Here we see that after the wrong inner overgrowth of fantasy has
been pulled down and recognized as being simply the mother
complex, another dimension of consciousness appears — the sky is
seen again, the clouds can sail far, and the sun and the moon can
shine. There is not a narrowing of the horizon, for pulling down that
wrong growth of fantasy means a widening of the human horizon. I
think that it is an infinitely important text because one of the
objections which the *puer aeternus* always brings up when you want
to encourage him to fell the tree is that he does not want such a
narrowing of the horizon. I think that it is an infinitely important
text because one of the objections which the *puer aeternus* always
brings up when you want to encourage him to fell the tree is that he
does not want such a narrowing of the horizon. What would be left
if he had to give up his wishful fantasies, his masturbating, and such
stuff? He would be just a petty little bourgeois who goes to his office,
and so on. He could not stand such narrowing. But it is not true! If
one has the courage to cut down this wrong kind of inner greatness,
it comes again, but in a better form — the horizon and life are
widened and not narrowed. I think this myth should always be told
when the hero must cut the tree, because that is always what he does
not want to realize or believe. If he only knew how much wider life
would be if he could give up that wrong kind of inner life, then he
might perhaps do it.

161   The little prince's asteroid has not yet been destroyed by the
baobab tree, whose shoots he wants the sheep to eat, but his
neighbor's asteroid has been. How is this to be interpreted? The only
drawing about which Saint-Exupéry admits he was carried beyond
himself, "by a feeling of urgency," is the one which describes the lost
situation, where there is no more hope. Into that drawing he put his
whole love and energy. The doubling of the asteroids into the one
which is not yet lost and the other which is, can be interpreted
psychologically as the one being the other's shadow: The lazy fellow
who let the trees grow too big is a shadow of our little prince who
then also refers to him as a lazy neighbor.

162   But if it is the motif of the divine child that has doubled, that is falling apart into a "yes" and a "no," into a divine child and its shadow, this would mean for Saint-Exupéry that something that was previously unconscious has begun to touch the threshold of consciousness. Why does it then fall apart into the opposites? We could say that the figure of the star prince is both: an infantile shadow and a symbol of the Self. Up until now this figure has appeared double, which is why one did not know if it should be seen as positive or negative, whether the child reflected infantilism or the future life. It was both, and therein lies the great difficulty. In his essay *The Psychology of the Child Archetype*[5], Jung writes:

163   'The "child" is . . . *renatus in novam infantiam* [reborn into a new childhood]. It is thus both beginning and end, an initial and a terminal creature. The initial creature existed before man was, and the terminal creature will be when man is not. Psychologically speaking, this means that the "child" symbolizes the pre-conscious and the post-conscious essence of man. His pre-conscious essence is the unconscious state of earliest childhood; his post-conscious essence is an anticipation by analogy of life after death. In this idea the all-embracing nature of psychic wholeness is expressed. Wholeness is never comprised within the compass of the conscious mind – it includes the indefinite and indefinable extent of the unconscious as well.'

164 And now comes the important sentence:

'The "eternal child" in man is an indescribable experience, an incongruity, a handicap, and a divine prerogative [in more poetic and better language Jung is expressing what we are driving at: the incongruity or the handicap is the childish shadow and a divine prerogative]: an imponderable that determines the ultimate worth or worthlessness of a personality.'

---

[5] Jung and Kerényi, *Science of Mythology,* 97 f.

165 It is quite clear that Saint-Exupéry's genius is this divine child in him. He would not be such a genius or artist if he had not this capacity to be naïve and spontaneous. It is the source of his creativity, and at the same it is a little close to being something worthless, something that devalues his personality. Which is why I am always skating between a negative and a positive evaluation in my interpretation: It is both-in-one, and one does not quite know how to judge it. One cannot judge it but must simply take it as a contradictory factor, an imponderable thing. Here one could say that there is an attempt by the unconscious to disentangle the two motifs. The one would be the infantile shadow, the lazy one who just misses fighting the mother complex until it is too late; the other, the star prince, would be the Self, something that tries to flow toward the future, toward the possibility of being reborn, of finding a new possibility of life after a crisis, of finding a renewal. Here the unconscious attempts to show the two aspects separately so that consciousness can realize it, because consciousness is unable to conceive of a *mixtum compositum*. It generally needs to have it taken apart first so that it can be put together again, because our consciousness is made in such a way that it wants to separate things.

166 In Chapter One, I spoke of the neurosis of the provisional life, namely, that people live in the expectation of being creative *one day* (not yet, but one day), which is very often linked up with the savior complex. In his essay *Zum Gefühl der Ohnmacht*[6], Erich Fromm speaks of this problem in detail. He writes:

167 'If one believes in Time, then one has no possibility of sudden change, there is a constant expectation that "in time" everything will come all right. If one is not capable of solving a conflict one expects that "in time" conflicts will solve themselves, without one having to risk a decision. You find that very often, especially in believing in Time as far as one's own achievements are concerned. People comfort themselves, not only because they do not really do something

---

[6] Fromm and Funk, *Zum Gefühl der Ohnmacht*.

but also for not making any preparation for what they have to do, because for such things there is plenty of time and therefore there is no need to hurry. Such a mechanism is illustrated by the case of a very gifted writer who wanted to write a book which he thought would be the most important book in world literature, but he did not do more than have a few ideas as to what he would write and enjoy in fantasy what the effect of his book would be and tell his friends that he had nearly finished it. In reality he had not even written a single line, not a single word; though, according to him, he had already worked for seven years on it. The older such people get, the more they cling to the illusion that *one day* they will do it. In certain people, the reaching of a certain age, generally at the beginning of the forties, brings a sobering effect so that they then begin to use their own forces, or there is a neurotic breakdown which is based upon the fact that one cannot live if one does not have that comforting time illusion.'

168 This is a vivid description of what I tried to express. H.G. Baynes wrote about this long ago in his paper on the provisional life, as I have mentioned.

169 The next part of the book I am going to read in detail.

Ah, little prince! Bit by bit I came to understand your sad little life. . . . For a long time, your only entertainment had been the pleasure of watching sunsets. I learned that new detail on the morning of the fourth day, when you said to me,

170 'I am very fond of sunsets. Let us go and watch a sunset . . .'

171 'Wait for what?'

172 'Wait for the sun to set.'

173 You looked very surprised at first, and then you laughed to yourself and said to me,

174 'I keep on thinking I am at home.'

175   Yes indeed. When it is midday in the United States, the sun, as everyone knows, is setting in France. One would just have to travel in one minute to France to be able to watch the sun setting there. Unfortunately, France is too far away for that. But on your tiny little planet, all you needed to do was to move your chair a few steps. And you could watch the twilight falling whenever you felt like it...

176   'One day, I watched the sun setting forty-four times,' you told me. And a little later, you added,

177   'You know . . . when one is so terribly sad, one loves sunsets. . .'

178   'The day you watched those forty-four sunsets, were you that sad?' I asked.

179   But the little prince made no reply.

180   Is this a preview of his own early death? You could say so — with the symbolic 44 days. It is the romantic way of always thinking of death that is to be found in early youth. It is connected to the rest of the problem by there being nothing realistic about it. The thing keeps repeating itself: The sun sets over and over again. It is a form of egotism, of narcissism, and that is the kind of mood people get into when life is not flowing, when time is not filled out. When you are involved in inner or outer adventure, you have no time to look at the sunset, which might, however, be a restful momentary beautiful experience, after a full day — the moment when the peace of the evening comes to you. But then one does not generally feel sad; then the sunset is something beautiful and restful. If it makes you sad, it is because it has not been preceded by enough adventure.

181   Again, I think, it has to do with young people very often being tortured by a kind of boredom. I recall being often bored myself between 14 and 18, but since then, never. Outwardly it was because I had to stay for hours and hours in school instead of doing what I liked. As soon as I was able to do what I liked, the boredom disappeared. I have seen that, strangely enough, very often a neurosis

can be found among young people that lessens as they grow older. It has to do with the fact that they cannot yet do what they would really like to do, and therefore, they do not feel that they are in life. Boredom is simply a subjective feeling of not being in life. Actually, there is no real boredom. At university, I still had to take boring courses, but there I learned how to amuse myself at the same time. If you are inventive enough you can always avoid boredom; you just have to know how to put yourself into reality. One puts one's spontaneous fantasy into reality, and then boredom is gone forever. Then life can be agreeable or disagreeable, exciting or not, but it is certainly not boring any more. Thus, boredom is a symptom of life being dammed up; one does not know how to get what one has within oneself into reality. If one knows how to play, boredom goes. But there are children, and adults also, who do not know what to do or how to draw on their inner resources. In youth this is not so much a negative symptom because, to some extent, it is a part of the situation, for they cannot yet fulfil themselves.

182   The suffering of normal young people consists partly in the fact that inwardly they are already very efficient, intelligent, and grown-up, but outwardly, they are not given the opportunity to use these capacities. They are held back by society with the result that they are bored. I have taught in schools myself, with pupils mainly between 14 and 18 years old and I have often seen that many of the problems there were because many pupils were capable of reasonable judgment and were inwardly rich and intelligent, but in the outer situation, both at home and at school, they were treated as children. Naturally, life was then dammed up. This causes a kind of bored resistance against everything, with bad moods and poor work. If one succeeded in getting those students onto a higher level by giving them more intelligent work and more responsibility, the thing righted itself. They were artificially kept below their level, with the result that a sulky boredom came up. Thus, one should always say, "Just because you are bored, and just because you are lazy, now you have to do a double amount of work, but good stuff!" That puts an end to boredom.

183   It is well-known that between the ages of 16 and 20 suicide is very frequent: It is less common afterward. Young people at this age often have that strange kind of melancholy sadness about them. They feel like old people and have an expression on their faces as if they knew all about life and felt very, very old. What would be the use of playing about with the others, of dancing with girls or with boys. They retire into a kind of grandfatherly and grandmotherly attitude toward life. This is only a symptom and simply means that they have not found the clue to the water of life, where they could find an issue for themselves, so they drift on in this way. At that age it is technically difficult for people who are a bit different from others to find out what would be their possibilities in life, and then life gets dammed up. Obviously, we have the same situation here with the child who constantly looks sadly at the sunset.

184   We learn next that life on B-612 was not quite as boring as we had imagined, for Saint-Exupéry hears from the little prince that there is a rose on the planet: One day the seed of a rose came through space and landed on the little planet and has slowly grown, until a lovely rose has unfolded its beauty. Saint-Exupéry finds this out because the little prince is suddenly terribly upset and constantly asks him if a sheep will eat roses. If it does, then he cannot have a sheep because it must eat the baobab trees but not the rose. Thus, indirectly, through this anxiety, the little prince gives away the fact that he has such a rose on his planet. Then the description goes on:

185   But the plant soon stopped growing and started to develop a flower. The little prince, watching the growth of an enormous bud, sensed that this could well lead to a miraculous apparition, but the flower continued her preparations for her beauty in the shelter of her green chamber. She chose her colours with great care. She dressed slowly, carefully arranging her petals one by one. She didn't wish to appear all crumpled, like a poppy. She only wished to appear in the full glory of her beauty. Oh yes! She was very vain! Her mysterious preparations had lasted for days and days. And

then one morning when the sun was rising, she suddenly showed herself. And having worked so hard and taken such care, she yawned and said,

186 'Ah! I'm only half awake. . . Forgive me. . . I'm still quite dishevelled . . .'

187 But the little prince couldn't restrain his admiration and exclaimed,

188 'Oh! How beautiful you are!'

189 'Am I not?' the flower replied gently. 'And I was born at the same time as the sun.'

190 The little prince had to admit that she was not excessively modest but she was so enchanting!

191 'I believe it's time for breakfast,' she added a moment later. 'Would you be kind enough to attend to my needs. . .'

192 And the little prince, totally abashed, at once fetched a can of fresh water and sprinkled the flower.

193 Thus it was that she began from the outset to torment him with her demanding vanity. One day, for example, referring to her four thorns, she said to the little prince,

194 'Let them come, those tigers with their claws!'

195 'But there are no tigers on my planet,' objected the little prince, 'and anyway, tigers don't eat weeds.'

196 'But I am not a weed,' the flower replied sweetly.

197 'Please forgive me. . .'

198 'I am not afraid of tigers, but I hate draughts. You wouldn't have a screen for me, by any chance?'

199 'A horror of draughts . . . that's really bad luck for a plant,' remarked the little prince, thinking to himself, 'This flower is indeed a very complex creature. . .'

200 'In the evening I want you to put me under a glass dome. It is very cold where you live. And rather uncomfortable. Now where I come from . . .'

201 Too late she interrupted herself. She had arrived as a seed. She could not have known anything about other worlds. Embarrassed at having been discovered preparing such a naïve lie, she a couple of times so as to confuse the little prince.

202 'Where is the screen?'

203 'I was going to fetch it but you were talking to me!'

204 Whereupon she coughed a little more so that he should feel remorse.

205 So the little prince, in spite of the good will his love engendered towards her, came gradually to doubt her. He had taken words of no importance seriously and became very unhappy.

206 'I shouldn't have listened to her,' he confided to me one day, 'one should never listen to flowers. One must admire them and breathe their fragrance. Mine perfumed all my planet, but I did not know how to enjoy her. That tale of claws which irritated me so much should simply have touched my heart . . .'

207 And he confided further,

208 'At the time, I was unable to understand anything! I should have based my judgement upon deeds and not words. She cast her fragrance and her radiance over me. I should never have run away from her! I should have guessed at the affection behind her poor little tricks. Flowers are so inconsistent! But I was too young to know how to love her.'

209 Clearly, he alludes here to his experience of woman and of the first anima projection and how difficult it was for him. He gives away the fact that he was as little able to deal with the vanity and moods of women as he was with the charm and beauty of the rose. One of his wives' names was Rosa, and he married her in a very romantic mood. Because the little prince suffers too much from the

moodiness of the rose, he decides to leave the planet, and seeing the migration of a flock of wild birds, he decides to catch hold of one and let himself be carried away, which is how he came to earth. So now we suddenly learn that he came to earth because he could not stand the flower any longer. The moodiness and all the difficulties with the haughty princess in this rose drove him away from his planet. The rose is a bit sad too when he leaves, but she does not show it. The book says:

210   On the morning of his departure he put his planet in perfect order. He carefully swept his active volcanoes. He possessed two active volcanoes and they were very convenient for heating his breakfast in the morning. He also had a volcano which was extinct. But as he pointed out, 'You never know!' So he also cleaned out the extinct volcano. If they are properly swept, volcanoes burn gently and regularly, without any eruptions. Volcanic eruptions are like chimney fires. On earth, of course, we are far too small to sweep our volcanoes. That is why they cause us so much trouble.

211   The little prince tore up, not without a sense of sorrow, the last little baobab shoots. He believed that he would never have to return. But all these familiar activities seemed very precious to him on that last morning. And, when he watered the flower for the last time and prepared to place her under her glass dome, he felt like crying.

212   'Good-bye,' he said to the flower.

213   But she did not answer him.

214   'Good-bye,' he said again.

215   The flower coughed. But it was not because she had a cold.

216   'I have been silly,' she whispered at last. 'Please forgive me. Try to be happy.'

217   He was surprised by the absence of reproaches. He just stood there, quite bewildered, with the dome poised in mid-air. He did not understand this quiet sweetness.

218 'Of course, I love you,' the flower said to him. 'If you were not aware of it, it was my fault. That is not important. But you have been just as foolish. Try to be happy. . . Leave that dome alone. I don't want it any longer.'

219 'But the wind. . .'

220 'My cold is not that bad . . . The cool night air will do me good. I am a flower.'

221 'But what about animals . . .'

222 'I shall have to put up with a few caterpillars if I want to see butterflies. I understand they are very beautiful. Otherwise who will ever call upon me? You will be far away. As to large animals, I am not afraid of them. I have my claws.'

223 And, as naïve as ever, she showed her four thorns. Then she added,

224 'Don't hang about so, it's irritating. You have decided to leave, so leave.'

225 For she didn't want him to see her crying. She was a very proud flower . . .

226 That is a perfect description of a lover's relationship in which each one tortures the other. Both suffer in their inner hearts and are too proud to make a gesture of reconciliation, or do not know how to — animus and anima are in a negative way opposed to each other. Because of a lack of human feeling and a lack of life experience, young people often do not know how to bridge any momentary difficulty and run apart because of a quarrel. That is the fate of many early love affairs. It is also a magnificent description of the vanity and moodiness of the typical anima. The anima woman generally has a certain amount of infantile moodiness, this kind of irrational behavior, and particularly masculine men like this type of woman. She is a compensation for the logical continuity of their conscious life, but there is an intolerable kind of childishness in such behavior.

In her own way, the rose is as infantile as the little prince, which is why they must be apart.

227   In antiquity, the rose belonged to the cult of the goddess Venus and her divine child Eros. Roses were also used in the Dionysian mysteries, for Dionysus, too, is naturally an image of the early dying youth, and in the cult of Isis, roses also play a role. In Christianity, the symbol of the rose became split into two aspects: It became a symbol of the Virgin Mary and heavenly love and, on the other hand, of earthly lust — the Venus aspect. There is a medieval author who says of the thorns "thus the pleasures of love never lack a bitter sting." The Christian assimilation of antique symbolism generally runs like this: The symbol is cut into two, one part being ascribed to the devil and the negative aspect, and the other to the positive aspect. Whereas in antiquity and in pre-Christian times the positive and negative aspects were more closely linked together, in the light of Christian consciousness the two have been separated. This is why most symbols in medieval books are contradictory: The lion is a symbol of the devil, and a symbol of Christ; the rose is symbol of the Virgin Mary, and of earthly lust; the dove is a symbol of the Holy Ghost, and of lust, etc. We can go through a whole list of symbols and find the opposite in them all.

228   The rose has four thorns and is in the form of a mandala. It is, therefore, also a symbol of the Self and very often, in mythological symbolism, the place of an inner mystical transformation. But here, like the star child, the rose represents a too undeveloped and too infantile aspect of the anima, and therefore the two must be separated from each other to become mature. At present, they are only an anticipation of the inner totality, not yet its realization.

229   There are many fairytales in which a pair of children are persecuted by a stepmother. Generally, one of the two is killed or transformed by a spell and redeemed by the other partner. This same type of child-myth is also found in classical Greek mythology, for instance, in the story of the two children of Nephele (cloud). Mrs. Cloud has two children, Phrixos and Helle. Cloud's two children are persecuted by their stepmother, and they fly away through the air

on a golden ram, but Helle falls into the sea and dies. Her brother, Phrixos, escapes and later sacrifices the ram whose fleece is fastened to a tree. This is the original myth of the Golden Fleece: Nowadays, members of the Maltese Order wear the fleece as a golden chain around their necks. The golden ram whose fleece was nailed to a tree was compared to Christ, who was sacrificed and nailed to the cross. This explains why the Golden Fleece was looked on as a symbol of Christ and why it came to play such a special role in the Maltese Order. One could say that all these motifs of a couple of children, a little brother and sister, who are always partly killed and partly restored to life, are images of the inner totality of man which, in its infantile preformation, must be cut away so that ego consciousness may mature. The two are later reunited in a higher form. This explains why the rose drives the little prince away from the planet. If we look at it as a portrait of Saint-Exupéry, we can say that his inner genius (the little prince) was tormented by his anima moods, and that the aim of this suffering is to mature the too infantile nucleus of his personality. It could be put even more simply: If someone is infantile, he will suffer from terrific emotional moods — ups and down — and he will be constantly hurt. This is in order because if one is childish, there is only one cure, and that is suffering. When one has suffered long enough, one develops; there is no way around this problem. The childish personality nucleus is inevitably tortured.

230   If the rose had wept, instead of trying to hide her tears from him, if they could have talked over the trouble and exchanged their sorrow and not hidden it by a wrong kind of pride, then they could have matured together. But if you are not mature, you cannot talk about it. Again and again, one sees that every time the childish spot is touched, people begin to cry. They hide their childish spot in analysis for years. They do not do this out of dishonesty or because they repress it, but when, in the end, it comes out, they say that they knew they would start to cry, so what was the good of mentioning it because crying ends every conversation. Because they know this, they shelve the problem all the time, which means it does not

develop. That is the great difficulty, for the sore spot must come out, and has to be tortured; that is the only way for it to mature.

231   It is even more dangerous when the childish side is completely cut off. Such people do not show it, but you always have the feeling when with them that they are not quite genuine. Once you have established sufficient contact to talk to them and can tell them they are never quite themselves, that there is something not quite genuine, then come the tears! They do not know what to do about it because they would be genuine only if they cried, and they naturally do not want to cry. That is one form in which infantilism comes up; or the infantile shadow makes exaggerated feeling demands on the partner. Repression does not solve the problem, for the repressed child continues to cry or be angry in the corner and must be split off. One should keep close to it, however, for otherwise one loses contact with one's genuine personality, but one cannot simply let it out either. In my experience, it has simply to be tortured and suffer on and on until suddenly it grows up. If a man has an infantile anima, he must go through a tremendous amount of feeling trouble and disappointments. When he has gone through enough, he begins to know women and himself and then he is emotionally grown up. But if he pretends to be reasonable and represses his childish feelings, then there is no development. That is why it is better to behave like a child and be hit over the head by one's surroundings and those people with whom one is in touch all the time because then one suffers and the *prima materia* slowly transforms. That is the great problem which the infantile shadow — the divine child — puts upon one.

232   In *The Visions Seminar*[7], Jung expressed the same thing when he said that people who have difficulty in getting near their center only really experience themselves when they suffer, when they come to the experience of their real self, and it does not seem possible for them to get there any other way. I would therefore say that the child in the adult is the source of suffering. It is the child that suffers because with the grown-up part of oneself one can take life as it is

---

[7] Jung, *Visions*.

and therefore one does not suffer so much. The sufferings of childhood are the worst — that is the real suffering — though they may be over trifles, perhaps because the child must go to bed just when it wants to go on playing. We can all remember the catastrophic disappointments we had as a child. Looking back, they appear to be trifles, but in childhood, in that moment, it was an agony of suffering. This is because a child is whole, and total in its reactions, and therefore, even if it is only a toy that is being taken away, it is as though the whole world were being destroyed. Thank God, there is the compensation that five minutes later the child can be distracted and laugh again and has forgotten it all. But in childhood there are such terrific tragedies, which shows that the child within is the genuine part, and the genuine part is that thing which suffers, the thing that cannot take reality, or that still reacts in the grown-up person like a child, saying, "I want it all, and if I don't get it, then it is the end of the world. Everything is lost." The genuine kernel of the person has remained the same and it is the source of suffering. One could say that what is genuine in a person and what is naïve in them like a child is the source of suffering. Many grown-ups split off this part and thereby miss individuation, for only if one accepts it and the suffering it imposes on one can the process of individuation go on.

233   A little intermezzo gives us further information about Asteroid B-612: There are three volcanoes on the planet, two active and one extinct. Every morning when the little prince gets up, he cleans the three because, he says, "One never knows." In the picture he is cleaning one of the volcanoes, while on another he is cooking his breakfast in a pan with a handle. We see the flower under its glass, and on the extinct volcano there is a little cap, because it does not work. Thus, there are four landmarks on his asteroid: three volcanoes and a flower — it is a mandala.

234   How is the extinct volcano to be interpreted? Sometimes, we speak of a person as being like a volcano. This refers to a person who is inclined to have emotional eruptions, someone with a hot temperament and a lot of emotion which bursts out at any time.

What does it mean, then, if one of the volcanoes is extinct? It hardly means that he has overcome one corner of his emotions, for then it would not look like that. When a volcano becomes extinct, crust upon crust has formed within, so that the fiery kernel of the earth is covered over with material, and it is no longer active. It rather looks like the possibility of showing one's inner fire has become closed, as if in this corner the central fire of the asteroid has gone out. It is a rather catastrophic picture for this means that life has left — that there is no way out for the energy, not even through a negative eruption. If a volcano dies on a heavenly body, it means that the central fire slowly burns down and fades away, that the earth is in a process of dying or getting cooler, and that the inner process of transformation of the material which is within is slowing down and becoming less intense. We need to look at it in conjunction with the small size of the planet, with the smallness of the earth on which the elephants cannot stand. There is again a hint of vital weakness: In one corner the vitality is going out and with it, the capacity for a direct emotional reaction.

235   The image of an extinct volcano often appears in psychiatric material, illustrating what might be described as a postpsychotic state. People in a psychosis have tremendous emotional explosions after which there comes the regressive restoration of the persona[8], when such people are literally comparable to a burnt-out volcano. They are reasonable, adapted, back in life, but the fire has gone: Something has been burnt out by the previous destructive explosion. If you treat such postpsychotic cases, you notice that when certain important problems are touched upon, there is no reaction. Usually, if one gets close to a person's vital problem, things get hot. People get excited and nervous, and they begin to lie, to blush, or to become aggressive — there is some sort of emotional reaction. With a postpsychotic state, this is not so, for just when one might expect things to get hot, the patient simply says, "Yes, yes, I know!" There is no reaction exactly when it might be expected to be painful. This could be expressed by the simile of the burnt-out fire. The

---

[8] Jung, *Two Essays on Analytical Psychology,* vol. 7, CW, §§ 252 ff.

destruction has been so great that the fire has disappeared. The dreams then may show a burnt-out volcano as a symbolic image of the postdestruction condition. We have all probably experienced the awful after letting out a very strong affect: One feels only fatigue and indifference. All reaction has been exhausted and it is as if one is burnt out. Here the destruction is only partial, for only one of the four orientation points, one of the three volcanoes, is extinct. We might compare these with the four functions and then it would mean that one function has given out. The flower would probably stand for feelings, in which case the opposite would be thinking, where the volcano is the biggest and is well drawn. Then we must find out which of the other functions is burnt out. From his type, I would say that it is probably sensation and his connection with reality. However, I do not think that an explanation through the functions is very relevant. It probably alludes to another problem.

236   Saint-Exupéry had a little brother who was three years younger and of whom he was very fond and who died at the age of 14. His brother's death came as a great shock to him, and he never quite got over it. This little brother is very much mirrored in the whole story of the little prince, and I think that Saint-Exupéry consciously had him in mind when he wrote it. For him, the child who came to earth and then left it again was associated with the trauma of the death of the little brother, with whom he had a very good contact. I think this shock burnt out a part of his personality and he never quite recovered. It is as though a part of his infantile personality died at the same time as his brother. Afterward, Saint-Exupéry was only a half, so that the dead little brother is a picture, probably, of a part of his own person, of his capacity for reaction. The little prince would thus be an exterior image of what happened within himself, a projection of something which is dead and split off in Saint-Exupéry.

237   Saint-Exupéry was 17 when his brother, François, died at the age of 14[9] in 1917, so he was still a boy, but old enough to fully realize the catastrophe of the death of the child. Probably the child succumbed to the pressure of the unfavorable family situation, and

---

[9] Cate, *Antione de Saint-Exupéry*, 19-47.

from Saint-Exupéry's standpoint, he was the one who could not stand the atmosphere and had to leave the earth because he could not come down into this world. The fact that the little prince always cleans the dead volcano because "one never knows" indicates that there is a faint hope that it might become active again. I think this confirms our idea that there is a basic vital weakness, or destruction, in the deeper layers of the psychological earth in Saint-Exupéry, which ultimately was responsible for the fact that he could not get over his midlife crisis, a tragedy that is normal for the *puer aeternus*.

238   The little prince leaves Asteroid B-612 and, holding onto a flock of birds, travels through space. He does not come directly to earth but visits and explores six neighboring asteroids. This does not seem to me to be a very important part so I will only discuss it briefly. On the first asteroid there is a king who gives silly and completely ineffectual orders that nobody obeys. To save face, he finds out what is about to happen, such as when the sun is about to set and then orders the sun to set at that time. (I do the same thing with my dog, who never obeys me. If I want to show how obedient he is, I tell him to do something which he is going to do anyway. Then I say, "See how well he obeys me!") This king is very clever. Obviously, Saint-Exupéry is making fun of the inefficiency of the power complex here. On the next planet is a man who only wants admiration — he is a personification of vanity. On the third planet is a drunkard who drinks because he is so ashamed of being a drunkard. On the fourth asteroid is a businessman who does nothing but count his star coins; the stars represent coins to him, and he counts them all day long. The fifth is, to my mind, the most interesting. This asteroid is very small, and on it is a lamp-lighter who has to light his lamp every evening and put it out in the morning, as was formerly the case in big cities. By some unfortunate development, this planet has become much smaller and rotates much more quickly, which means he must light and extinguish his lamp once every minute. On the sixth planet is a geographer who tells the little prince about the earth and says he should visit it. These six figures which the little prince now meets on his journey through space could be called shadow figures, but

also some of Saint-Exupéry's inner possibilities of adaptation to reality, but we will go into this later.

239   The idea that the little prince should visit several planets before he goes down to earth is an interesting variation of an archetypal motif. In some gnostic philosophical systems influenced by Platonic ideas it was believed that the soul was a spark which lived in heaven. When born, it had to descend through all the planetary spheres, each of which invested it with some quality. Afterward, the soul was born in a human body on earth, where it lived an earthly life with the fortunate and unfortunate inherited dispositions which it had received on the way down. This idea is linked up with astrology: in heaven, the soul spark was beyond astrology, and it was only during the descent from heaven to earth that the human soul acquired its horoscope: from Venus, an attribute of Venus in a certain constellation, from Mars, a quality of that planet in a certain constellation, and so on. Thus, on reaching the earth, each human has a specific horoscope. On death, the soul returns upward, giving back the qualities (sometimes symbolized as clothes) which it had received on the way down, thereby arriving naked at the heavenly gates where it returns into the eternal light. Thus, after death, the soul rids itself of the planetary influences.

240   It can be said that the soul spark is a symbol of the Self; the different planetary qualities are the inherited psychological and instinctual disposition with which the human being is born, having received aggressive instincts from Mars and sexual instinct from Venus, in all their aspects and psychological qualities. Later, I shall bring material in which the same idea is seen in the dreams of a typical *puer aeternus* who must come down to earth and first goes through the realm of the stars. This illustrates the idea that Saint-Exupéry has not yet entered the just-so-ness of his personality, his earthly disposition, but keeps away from his own body and his own inner earth. In that way, he is not really himself; from a certain point of view, it is as if he was not completely born.

241   One could thus understand the king, the vain man, the drunkard, and the businessman in a parallel way and call them all

different possibilities of the future grown man. Saint-Exupéry describes them all in a rather mocking way, again making fun of adult life. He says that one prays to money, another to nonexistent power, and a third indulges in a quixotic activity, maintaining old values which are no longer valid. The king could be said to represent something that Saint-Exupéry could have lived. This is also true of the vain man, for Saint-Exupéry was not without a certain amount of self-reflective vanity, as has been confirmed by several reporters who met him and who said he was a bit of a poseur. He could also have taken to drink. The businessman I cannot quite imagine, but perhaps that, too, was possible. Thus, apart from the lamp-lighter, the different planet dwellers represent ordinary possibilities of becoming grown-up in a wrong way, or an endeavour to find a pseudostyle of grown-up existence.

242   I think the lamp-lighter is most interesting because, if Saint-Exupéry had followed the family tradition, he could have turned into such a Don Quixote personality. There are many such types in the upper French nobility. They simply live on the past glories of France, having got stuck in the 18th century with all the ideals of the gentleman and chivalry and they have a solid Catholic background. They are peculiarly out of step with present-day life. The poet Lavarande, a contemporary and colleague of Saint-Exupéry, obviously identified with this approach to life. He wrote novels in praise of the "good old times," of chivalry and nobility. But Saint-Exupéry was too sensitive and intelligent and, in a way, too much of a modern man to accept such a regressive form of life. As he shows in the lamp-lighter, the pace of life has accelerated too much and no longer permits the ideal of the gentleman-farmer or the nobility-officer; such roles have become ridiculous and illusory. This shows how difficult the position of the poet is, for he cannot find any given form of life which would suit him and offer him a collective pattern in which to fulfil himself.

243   Only the geographer is a more positive figure. Saint-Exupéry was very fond of geography, something which a pilot in earlier times had to know very well. This geographer could be interpreted as a

psychological function of orientation, a capacity for finding and mapping the way on earth. Power, money, public applause, and drink symbolize four things which Saint-Exupéry cannot make his god, or to which he cannot pray. This only leaves the lamp-lighter, of whom he says, "[That man] is the only one I could have made my friend. But his planet is too small. There is not enough room for two..." That was something which tempted him for a minute, but he rejected that also. Then comes the relatively positive figure of the geographer.

244   The story goes on:

> So the seventh planet was the Earth.
> The Earth is not just an ordinary planet! There are 111 kings (not to mention the Negro kings, of course), 7'000 geographers, 900'000 businessmen, 7'500'000 drunkards, 311'000'000 conceited individuals – in other words, approximately 2'000'000'000 grown-ups.

245   Here he states quite clearly what he thinks about grown-up people on the earth, where he now arrives. The first thing he meets is a snake.

246   So when the little prince arrived on the Earth, he was very surprised not to see any people. He was beginning to fear he had come to the wrong planet, when a coil, pale gold as the moon, moved in the sand.

247   'Good-evening,' said the little prince politely.

248   'Good-evening,' said the snake.

249   'What planet have I fallen on?' asked the little prince.

250   'On the planet Earth, in Africa,' replied the snake.

251   'Oh!. . . Then there are no people on the Earth?'

252   'This is the desert. There are no people in the desert. The Earth is big,' said the snake.

253 The little prince sat down on a stone, and looked up at the sky.

254 'I wonder,' he said, 'if the stars are lit up so that each one of us can find his own star again. Look at my planet. It is right above us. . . But how far away it is!'

255 'It is beautiful,' said the snake. 'Why have you come here?'

256 'I am having some difficulties with a flower,' the little prince replied.

257 'Oh!' said the snake.

258 And they remained silent.

259 'Where are the men?' said the little prince, at last resuming the conversation. 'One feels rather lonely in the desert.'

260 'It is just as lonely among men,' said the snake.

261 The little prince gazed at him for a long time.

262 'You're a strange animal,' he said at last. 'You are as thin as a finger . . .'

263 'But I am more powerful than a king's finger,' said the snake.

264 The little prince smiled. 'You do not look very powerful. . .you don't even have paws. . . you cannot even travel. . .'

265 'I can carry you farther than a ship,' said the snake.

266 He twined himself around the little prince's ankle, like a golden bracelet.

267 'Whomever I touch, I send back to the earth from which they came,' he added. 'But you are pure and innocent and come from a star.'

268 The little prince said nothing.

269 'I feel sorry for you, so weak on this Earth of granite. I may be able to help you one day, if you become too homesick for your own planet. I can . . .'

270 'Oh! I understand you perfectly,' said the little prince. 'But why do you talk in riddles all the time?'

271   'I solve them all,' said the snake.

272   And they both fell silent.

273   We should firstly interpret the golden-yellow snake. It offers to help the little prince in the form of offering to help him to commit suicide: the temptation to die. The snake says that he can send people back to the place from where they came. He suggests that the earth is too hard for the little prince, that he will not be able to stand it, but that he, the snake, can help, by bringing him back to where he came from. The snake also says that he can solve all riddles, for death solves all problems. It is a death temptation; an offer of a way to escape from life as an ultimate solution to an insoluble problem: The snake would kill him with its poison, which is what happens at the end of the book. Before we go into the specific quality of the snake here, namely, as the temptation of death or the helpfulness of death, we should see what it represents in general.

274   Like all animals, the snake represents a part of the instinctive psyche, but it is an instinct that is far removed from consciousness. Jung says about the snake: "The lower vertebrates have from earliest times been favourite symbols of the collective psychic substratum, which is localized anatomically in the sub-cortical centres, the cerebellum, and the spinal cord. These organs constitute the snake. Snake-dreams usually occur, therefore, when the conscious mind is deviating from its instinctual basis."[10]

275   When a snake dream occurs, it is a signal that consciousness is especially far away from instinct. It shows that the conscious attitude is not natural and that there is an artificial dual personality which appears to be in some ways too well adapted and too much fascinated by the outer world and, at the same time, inclined to fail hopelessly in decisive moments. In such a case, Jung continues, we find that there always exists a sort of secret attraction to the missing inner double, which one both fears and loves as the thing that could make one whole. That is why the snake in mythology is essentially

---

[10] Jung, *Archetypes and the Collective Unconscious*, vol. 9/I, CW, §§ 282 ff.

double: It is an enemy of light and at the same time a savior in animal form — a symbol of the Logos and of Christ. When it appears in the latter form, it represents the possibility of becoming conscious and whole. Instead of intellectual understanding, it promises knowledge born from immediate inner experience: insight and secret wisdom — gnosis.

276   We can see that the snake in our story has this same double role. It offers to kill the little prince and to free him from the weight of the earth, but this offer can be understood in two ways — as suicide, or the good fortune of getting rid of life. It is this ultimate philosophical attitude which says that death is not a catastrophe or a misfortune but an escape at last from an intolerable reality, which may be looked upon as something unimportant that yet hampers one's innermost being.

277   In ancient mythology, the snake very often appears in combination with the motif of the child. For instance, the mythical god of the Athenians was King Erechteus, who was the son of Athene who, as a little child, was kept in a basket into which one should not look, for one would have seen a child surrounded by snakes. Quite what it means one cannot be sure, but in southern France *coffrets gnostiques* have been found (probably from the Middle Ages and not earlier) in which naked children are playing with snakes. The child-god and the snake-god are often combined in this way.

278   Like the snake, the child-god is also the archetype of the poisoner. The Cupid of antiquity has a very poisonous arrow with which he can even subdue — as the poets say — the great god Zeus, for if Cupid shoots an arrow at him, Zeus may have to pursue without hope an earthly woman, even if he does not like the situation. In a light way, many late poems of antiquity, the so-called *anakreontika*, make fun of this little boy who, with his poisonous arrow, can subdue the whole world to his will. If Cupid shoots an arrow at you and you fall in love, it depends to a certain extent on your own reaction as to whether you like it or not. If you do, you will be happy and say that you have fallen in love. But if you do not, then you will say that you have been poisoned and have been made

to do something you do not like; you have been forced into a situation which to the ego feels like subjection or poison.

279   Thus, there is a secret connection between the snake and the eternal child. The snake is the shadow of the little prince himself, his dark side. If the snake offers to poison him, it could mean an integration of the shadow. Unfortunately, it takes place in the Self and not in Saint-Exupéry's ego, which means that the whole thing happens in the unconscious and the psychological nucleus moves away from reality again. It really should have been Saint-Exupéry who was poisoned; that would have detached him from the little prince. It is likely that when his little brother died, he was told that François was now an angel in heaven and quite happy not to have to live on this earth. Saint-Exupéry probably believed this more than others might have done. He took it in and realized that death was only partly a misfortune and that possibly created in him his very detached and philosophical attitude toward life.

280   The *puer aeterunus* very often has this mature, detached attitude toward life, which is normal for old people, but which he acquires prematurely: The idea that life is not everything, that the other side is valid too, that life is only a part of the whole of existence. Here the death-temptation prevents the little prince from coming right down onto the earth. Before he has even touched it, the snake comes along and says as much as, "If you don't like it, I know a way out." Thus, before he has even come down to earth, he already has the offer of death. I have met many people with a similar difficult constellation who do that: They live only "on condition," which means that they constantly flirt with the idea of suicide. At every step of their lives, they think they will try something or other and that if it does not work, they will kill themselves. The *puer aeternus* always keeps his revolver in his pocket and constantly plays with the idea of getting out of life if things get too hard. The disadvantage of this is that he is never quite committed to the situation as a human being. He always has the mental reservation, "I will go into this, but I reserve my right as a human being to kill myself if I can't stand it any longer. I shall not go through the whole experience to the bitter end if it

becomes too insufferable." If one cuts off the wholeness of the experience, one cuts oneself into bits and remains split. A transformation can only take place if one gives oneself completely to the situation.

281   On a minor scale, this can be found when people have been in analysis for years, but with a lot of mental reservations tucked away in some overcoat pocket which are never put on the table, never brought into the analytical process. Therefore, it remains always slightly conditional and not quite "it." You wonder why it does not go further. If there is such a sticking place, you generally find that in a woman it is made by the animus, and in a man by the anima. They just hold something back. For example, "Oh well, this is just analysis, but life is something different," or "This is an analytical relationship. One must stand by one's transference, but it does not quite count; it is different from other relationships," and so on. Such secret detaching thoughts prevent the whole thing from ever being quite whole. One plays the role of the analysand and goes through the process seemingly honestly. One secret, however, is not given up, and with some people, it is the idea of suicide. If this idea is held back through some inner process, nothing is quite real. If you live with the idea that you might escape life, then the possibility of total living is lamed, for one needs to be totally involved with all of one's feelings.

282   The snake is very clever, for just when the little prince arrives on earth and might get involved with reality, it sneaks up and says, "Oh, you see, life is hard, and it is very lonely on earth. I have a secret; I can help you out of it." It is very ambiguous. I think the most poisonous aspect of this problem is that one does not notice that one has such a mental reservation: It "has" one; one is possessed by it. Sometimes one can only notice it indirectly if one asks oneself why one is not living completely. "Why am I cut off from life? Why is everything not quite real all the time?" Then you can be pretty sure that either the animus or the anima has put something between you and reality in a very clever way. In a man, it is generally through the mother complex, for that is like a plastic envelope between him and reality so that he is never really in touch. This transparent envelope

constantly separates him from real life. Nothing in the present moment quite counts. With a woman, it is the animus who whispers something at the back of her mind, some kind of "nothing but" remark. Suppose, for example, as a man you get in touch with a woman toward whom you feel warmly, to which she seems to respond, but all the time you have the feeling that you cannot quite get through to her feeling and if it is not your fault, it is the animus's doing. It may happen that a woman with a positive attitude comes to me for analysis. She does not appear to lie but hands me her whole material and seems to have confidence in me. But all the time I have an uncanny impression that the thing is not sticking together somehow. I then feel that if a catastrophe were to happen, there would be a chance of this woman snapping or committing suicide, that — to express it symbolically — we are not attached to each other. A woman like this might suddenly write to say she is interrupting the analysis for some reason — because she is going away, or she lacks money, or some other reason, or pseudoreason — and then you are just left completely nonplussed.

283   It is the father complex that triggers an animus possession. I remember the case of a young girl with whom I had a very good contact, but one day she came and attacked me in a most horrible way. When I broke through it, she collapsed, and it came out that she had made up her mind to commit suicide and this was to be a goodbye quarrel. She wanted to kill her feeling for me so that she could commit suicide. That came absolutely out of the blue. The contact the day before had been very good, nothing had happened in our relationship, but for some reason, she had had enough of her difficulties in life and secretly made up her mind to commit suicide. But then she thought that her feeling for me was something which stood between her and suicide, so she made up her mind to behave so nastily to me that I would be fed up with her and then she would be free to go. That was an idea that had suddenly stung her like a snakebite. I had warned her. She had had a dream which said that an old man was rattling autonomously around on a child's red bicycle. This old man was a suicidal drunkard. In this way, I knew

she had a father-animus figure who was linked up with childish emotion — the child's red bicycle — that was rattling around autonomously at the back of her psyche. Though I interpreted the dream and told her that something in her was like that, she could not get it; she looked at me blankly, but then one day, it broke through. That is what happens when there are snake dreams. Then one must expect that people will act out of the blue.

284   After fifteen years of marriage, a man who had a lot of snake dreams suddenly made up his mind from one minute to the next to divorce his wife without even talking to her about it first. He might perhaps have done such a thing after one year's marriage, but not after fifteen! I had met him the week before when everything was okay, and the next week the whole thing was done and the lawyer was in charge! For fifteen years, he had lived with her, and apart from animus-anima trouble, which was not worse than in many other cases, it had been all right. But there was the snake in him! I had always warned him to watch out for either committing suicide or something else when such ideas got hold of him. The snake indicates the capacity for cold fits in which some instinctive action can be taken. I think that in that case the divorce was not wrong, or possibly not, or at least it was something to be seriously considered, but what was inhuman was the sudden cold fit. The idea had not occurred to him before, and then he made up his mind and arranged the whole thing with his lawyer within twenty-four hours! Naturally, his wife could rightly complain that this was inhuman, for it was. He could have discussed it with her, saying that their marriage had become a habit without any meaning in it anymore, or something like that, to prepare her emotionally for the shock. But he did not even do as much as that.

285   The girl who wanted to commit suicide did do something more, for she had at least wanted a goodbye quarrel. She was more related, for she did not just go and commit suicide but tried first to ruin our relationship; that was a gesture of relatedness. If someone rings up and says, "I am going to commit suicide, but I just wanted to say goodbye," that is human; one part of the personality is still outside

of the snake. She was possessed by the old man on the child's bicycle. That is why I said that the snake relates to the animus in women — in this instance, with the father-image, which was very negative. The old man showed how unrelated he was. He ran along autonomously, and she was caught by this as she was doing the same thing. I told her I thought that if she committed suicide, her ghost would hover over her corpse and be very sorry! It would have been a suicide motivated by an affect. It was not a situation in which she saw herself confronted with the problem of life and death, and it was up to her to make a conscious decision, and I did not tell her not to commit suicide; I told her not to do it so rashly and under the compulsion of an affect. It was not a mature decision. She should just think it over, and if she had really made up her mind to commit suicide, then it would not matter if she waited another week when she could do it after having come to a definite decision. She should not do it in the middle of an affect and then regret it afterward — if that is possible! The immaturity of the sudden decision for self-destruction was wrong; a week's delay would have caused her to question whether she really wanted to die or not. Many people live unconsciously and have never asked themselves about life and death. This is very dangerous. When you get in touch with such people, you realize they have a constant secret mental reservation. If you tell them, they do not understand and just shake their heads for it is completely autonomous. The person never seems to be quite present. There is always something evasive. In the case of the girl, when the crisis came, she and then I caught the man on the bicycle. He had always worked at the back of her mind, always making everything not quite true.

286   With men, the mother complex has the same effect, except that in a way it is even more difficult to catch because it does not form itself in the man's mind as an idea. The girl had the definite idea of killing herself because life was not worthwhile; it was a kind of reflection. But the mother complex form of that is manifested in a depressive mood, a "nothing but" mood, something completely vague and intangible. Men with a negative mother complex have it,

particularly when something goes well (say that they find a girlfriend who suits them or are successful in their professional life). You might expect them to look a bit happier; instead they look pale and say, "Yes, but…," and they cannot express the mood in words. There is a childish state of constant dissatisfaction with themselves and the whole of reality. That is something very difficult to catch, and it is very infectious; one gets depressed oneself by it and cannot even react.

287   Saint-Exupéry is an example of this kind of irritated bad mood. He had moods where he just paced up and down his flat the whole day, smoking one cigarette after another and just feeling annoyed, with himself and everything else in the world. This is how the mother complex comes out in a man, in these snarling, disagreeable moods, or in a flat depression. It is an antilife reaction that has to do with the mother. Saint-Exupéry also had the tendency to take opium. It has been pointed out to me that the whole psychology of the drug-taker relates to the idea of flirting with death, with getting away from reality and its hardships. Generally, people who take drugs have quite a lot of snake dreams. The poisonous snakes in their soul make them poison themselves because they do not know, or see, any other way of solving their inner conflict. Sometimes, alcohol also goes along with this problem for it, too, acts as a drug. For Saint-Exupéry, flying, or drugs, represented the two possibilities of getting rid of those irritated depressive moods. The problem was that he never worked his way through one of these moods. He tried to turn it off by flying, but he never got to the bottom of the trouble, namely, a suicidal tendency due to this deepest weakness which he could not overcome.

288   When the little prince goes on, he meets with several astonishing things. The first discovery that he makes on earth is that there are hundreds of roses that look exactly like his own.

289   And he was suddenly overcome with sadness. His flower had told him that she was the only one of her kind in the universe.

290 And here were five thousand of them, all alike, in one single garden!

291 'She would be rather resentful,' he thought to himself, 'if she could see this . . . she would cough and cough and pretend she was dying so as to avoid being thought ridiculous. And I would have to pretend to nurse her, for otherwise she would really let herself die . . .in order to humiliate me.'

292 And he said to himself once again: 'I thought I was rich, with a flower unique in all the world, whereas in fact all I had was a common rose. That, and my three volcanoes which came up to my knees, of which one is perhaps extinct forever . . . That doesn't make me a very great prince . . .'

293 And, lying in the grass, he cried.

294 You probably all know examples among the Romantic writers, such as, for instance, E.T.A. Hoffmann's *The Golden Pot*[11], about which Aniela Jaffé[12] has written a very good paper, or the novel *Aurelia* by Gerard de Nerval[13], who showed what a great problem it was, especially for the Romantic authors, to accept the paradox that the anima could be a goddess and, at the same time, "an ordinary person of our time." Gerard de Nerval fell in love with a little midinette in Paris. Perhaps his having some German blood in him was responsible for the fact that when he fell in love, he was carried away by deep and overwhelming romantic feelings. This girl seemed to him to be the goddess herself and meant at least as much to him as Beatrice had to Dante. He was completely overwhelmed by his feelings of romantic love. But his cynical French side, the Gaulois in him, could not stand it and spoke of her as *une femme ordinaire de notre siècle* — an ordinary woman of our time! The result was that he ran away from her and then had a very catastrophic dream: He came into a garden where there was the statue of a beautiful woman which had fallen from its pedestal and broken into two parts. The

---

[11] Hoffmann, Golden Pot.
[12] Jaffé, *Bilder und Symbole.*
[13] Nerval, "Aurelia."

dream says: If you judge her like that, you break your soul-image into two — an upper and a lower part. The upper part is the romantic goddess, and the other part is just an ordinary woman — any other girl would do — and she is a statue and no longer alive. Afterward came the whole catastrophic development of his schizophrenia which ended in his hanging himself by a canal in Paris.

295   The catastrophe was that he could not stand the paradox that to him this woman was divine and everything unique, while his reasonable personality told him she was just one pretty little midinette among hundreds in Paris, and he a young man who had fallen in love with her, and there were hundreds of others like him! It is the paradox of being human — that we are one specimen among billions of other specimens of the same kind — as well as the fact that each one of us is unique.

296   As Jung emphasises, to think of oneself in a statistical way is most destructive to the process of individuation for it makes everything relative. Jung said that communism is less dangerous than our habit of thinking statistically about ourselves. We believe in scientific statistics which say, for example, that in Switzerland so and so many couples marry per year and find no flat, or that such and such a percent of people in each town are psychologically disturbed. We do not realize what it does to us when we read statistics. It is completely destructive poison, and what is worse is that it is not true; it is a falsified image of reality. If we begin to think statistically, we begin to think against our own uniqueness. But it is not only thinking but a way of feeling. If you go up and down the main street, you will see all those stupid faces and then when look into a window, you will see that you look just as stupid as the others, if not worse! And then comes the thought that if an atom bomb were to destroy it all, who would regret it? Thank God all those lives have come to an end, including my own! In a statistical mood, one is overwhelmed by the ordinariness of life. This is wrong because statistics are built up on probability. But probability is only one way of explaining reality, and as we know, there is just as much uniqueness and irregularity. The fact this table does not levitate, but remains where it is, is only

because the billions of electrons that — statistically — constitute this table tend to behave like that. But each electron could do something else. Or imagine confronting a person with a lion. You put a lion into a room into which you introduce one person at a time. You would see that everyone would behave differently. One would stand petrified and exclaim, "Oh!" Another would dash out of the room. The third might not even be afraid; he may have a delayed reaction and afterward say he had not believed it. Each reaction would be its own unique type of reaction. As a test, it would be quite revealing, for each person would react typically and differently. But if you were to bring a lion into a lecture hall full of people, I bet that everyone would retire to the back of the room, for then the collective reaction prevails. That is why statistics are only half right. They give a false picture because they only give the average probability. When we walk through the woods, we step on a certain number of ants and snails and kill them, but if we could write the life history of each ant or snail, we would see that its death had been a very meaningful end at a typical moment of its life.

297   This was the basic philosophical problem Thornton Wilder raised when he wrote *The Bridge of San Luis Rey*. The bridge collapsed at a certain moment and some people drowned — you read of such things every day in the paper. But Thornton Wilder asked whether that was just chance, and he tried to show that each of these five people had undergone a certain inner development in their lives and that being drowned when the bridge collapsed was the finale to a very meaningful moment in the lives of each one. But the statistician would say that it was quite probable since every day two hundred people crossed the bridge, so anytime it fell there would be about five who would be drowned, and they would be there by chance. That is a falsified view of reality, but we are all poisoned through and through by it. Gerard de Neval, for instance, could not face the problem that the woman he loved was unique to him, for his statistical reasoning told him that she was just one of the many thousands, which, in a way, was true, too. But it was a half-truth, and a half-truth is, as Arnold Toynbee said, worse than an absolute

lie. This is what causes so much difficulty for the *puer aeternus*. This is why he does not want to go to an office and do some ordinary job or be with a woman. Inwardly, he is always toying with a thousand possibilities of life and cannot choose just one as he does not want to become a part of some statistically average situation. Recognition of the fact that one is one of thousands and that there is nothing special about that is an intellectual insight against which one's feeling function rails.

298   The inner battle between the feeling of uniqueness and statistical thinking is generally a battle between intellectualism and allowing feeling its own place in life. Feeling evaluates what is important to me, and my own importance is the counterbalance to intellect. If you have real feeling, you can say certainly that this is an ordinary woman (for if you see her walking along the street, she is not very different from any other), but to *me* she is of the highest value. That would mean the ego makes up its mind to defend and stand up for its own feeling without denying the other aspect. The solution would be to say, "Yes, that may be so from the statistical point of view, but in my life, there are certain values, and to *me* this woman is of special value." For this to happen, an act of loyalty is required toward one's own feeling; otherwise, one is split off from it by statistical thinking, which is why intellectual people tend toward communism and other "isms." They cut themselves off from the feeling function. The feeling function makes your life, your relationships, and deeds feel unique; it gives them a definite value.

299   When the statistical way of thinking gets people, it means they have no feeling, or weak feeling, or that they tend to betray their own feeling. We can say that a man who does not stand for his feelings is weak on the Eros side. He is the intellectual type with weak Eros, for he cannot accept his own feelings, or stand up for them and say, "This is how I intend to live, for this is the way I feel."

300   Admittedly, this is more difficult for a man than for a woman, which is expressed when we say that the man is weak on the Eros side. For example, if you say to a mother that her children are not unique, that there are such brats all over the place, she will reply that to *her* they are unique, for they are her children. A woman is more

likely to have a personal attitude. The man must think impersonally and objectively and, if he is a modern type, also statistically, and then it turns like a poison against him. This is especially true for men who have a military career and must sign papers which decide the life and death or fate of many people. A high-ranking officer must decide what battalion to send to which place, knowing that some of those men will probably not come back, that some must be sacrificed. He must detach his feeling to be able to act, for if at such a moment he were to think personally and with feeling about those men in the battalion whom he is sending to their death, he would not be able to do it. The same applies to a surgeon who, when he must perform an operation, may not reflect and remember that this is such and such a person. His task is to perform a technical operation which will result in life or death. This is why most surgeons do not operate on members of their own family. Experience has proved that it is much better not to do so. I know of many accidents that have happened through an awkwardness on the part of a surgeon who never makes a mistake, (but if it is his own wife or daughter, he may), so it is better that the operation should be performed by a colleague in whom he has the most confidence. To be able to detach from feelings is an essential part of a man's life, for he often needs to have a cold, scientific, objective standpoint. But if he does not relate to the anima and try to deal with his Eros problems, he cuts his soul in two. That is why men, in general, have more trouble accepting Jungian psychology than women do. Because of our insistence on the acceptance of the unconscious, men must accept feeling and relatedness — Eros — and to a man that is just disgusting; it is as if from now on, he must nurse babies. It feels like that to him — it is against nature. But if men wish to develop further — just as women must now learn to share the man's world by becoming more objective and less personal — they must make the countergesture of taking their own feelings and their own Eros problems more seriously. It is an unavoidable part of human development that we must integrate the other side — the un-developed side — and if we do not, then it catches us against our will. Indeed, the more a man takes his Eros problems seriously, the less effeminate he becomes, although it may look like the opposite to him. If he stiffens and does not take his feeling problems seriously, he will involuntarily become effeminate. In general, it can be said that the *puer*, who tends to become effeminate, has a better chance if only he will take his feeling seriously and not fall into the pitfall of statistical thinking — if he does not suddenly think, "Oh Lord! Hundreds and thousands! — and me, too!"

301 The story continues very logically; the next creature the little prince meets is a fox, who tells him that he wants the little prince to tame him.

302 It was then that the fox appeared.

303 'Good morning,' said the fox.

304 'Good morning,' the little prince replied politely, though when he turned around, he saw nothing.

305 'I am here,' said the voice, 'under the apple tree...'

306 'Who are you?' said the little prince. 'You are very pretty ...'

307 'I am a fox,' said the fox.

308 'Come and play with me,' suggested the little prince. 'I am so terribly sad...'

309 'I cannot play with you,' said the fox. 'I am not tame.'

310 'Oh! I'm so sorry,' said the little prince. But, after some thought, he asked, 'What does "tame" mean?'

311 'You do not live here,' said the fox, 'What are you looking for?'

312 'I am looking for men,' said the little prince. 'What does "tame" mean?'

313 'Men,' said the fox, 'have rifles and they hunt. It is a real nuisance. They also raise chickens. Those are the only activities they are interested in. Are you looking for chickens?'

314 'No,' said the little prince. 'I am looking for friends.'

315 [We see here that Saint-Exupéry knows what projection is!]

'What does "tame" mean?'

316   'It is something which is too often forgotten,' said the fox. 'It means to establish ties...'

317   '"To establish ties?"'

318   'That's right,' said the fox. 'To me, you are still just a little boy like a hundred thousand other little boys.'

319   [Now he is going to say how you get away from statistical thinking.]

'And I have no need of you. And you have no need of me, either. To you, I am just a fox like a hundred thousand other foxes. But if you tame me, we shall need one another. To me, you will be unique. And I shall be unique to you.'

320   'I'm beginning to understand,' said the little prince. 'There is a flower . . . I think she has tamed me. . . .'

321   'Possibly,' said the fox. 'One sees all sorts of things on Earth...'

322   'Oh! But this is not on Earth,' said the little prince.

323   The fox seemed puzzled.

324   'On another planet?'

325   'Yes.'

326   'Are there any hunters on that planet?'

327   'No.'

328   'That's interesting! And any chickens?'

329   'No.'

330   'Nowhere is perfect,' sighed the fox. Presently, he returned to his theme. 'My life is monotonous. I hunt chickens and men hunt me. All chickens are alike and all men are alike. So I get a little bored. But if you tame me, my life will be full of sunshine. I shall recognise the sound of a step different from all others. The other steps send me hurrying underground. Yours will call me out of my burrow like the sound of music. And look yonder! Do you see the cornfields? I do not eat

bread. Wheat is of no use to me. Those cornfields don't remind me of anything. And I find that rather sad! But you have hair the colour of gold. So it will be marvellous when you have tamed me! Wheat, which is also golden, will remind me of you. And I shall love the sound of the wind in the wheat. . .'

331   The fox became silent and gazed for a long time at the little prince.

332   'I beg of you...tame me!' he said.

333   'Willingly,' the little prince replied, 'but I haven't got much time. I have friends to discover and a lot of things to understand.'

334   'One can only understand the things one tames,' said the fox. 'Men have no more time to understand anything. They buy ready-made things in the shops. But since there are no shops where you can buy friends, men no longer have any friends. If you want a friend, tame me!'

335   'What should I do?' asked the little prince.

336   'You must be very patient,' replied the fox. 'First you will sit down at a little distance from me, like that, in the grass. I shall watch you out of the corner of my eye and you will say nothing. Words are a source of misunderstandings. But every day, you can sit a little closer to me. . .'

337   So, they become closer friends. When the hour for the little prince's departure arrives, the fox tells his secret, as he had promised he would.

338   'Now here is my secret. It is very simple. It is only with one's heart that one can see clearly. What is essential is invisible to the eye.'

339   'What is essential is invisible to the eye,' the little prince repeated, so as to be sure to remember.

340 'It is the time you have lavished on your rose which makes your rose so important.'

341 'It is the time that I lavished on my rose. . . ' said the little prince, so as to be sure to remember.

342 'Men have forgotten this basic truth,' said the fox. 'But you must not forget it. For what you have tamed, you become responsible forever. You are responsible for your rose. . .'

343 'I am responsible for my rose. . .' the little prince repeated, so as to be sure to remember.

344 It can be said that the fox teaches the little prince the essential value of the here-and-now and, with it, the value of feeling. Feeling gives value to the present, for without it, one has no relationship to the situation in the here-and-now. With feeling comes responsibility and, through that, the awareness of one's own individuality.

345 Here again is the common theme of the helpful animal that teaches man how to become human or, in other words, about the process of individuation.

346 In his article "The Primordial Child in Primordial Times,"[14] Professor Kerényi cites a Tarar poem which runs:

347 Once upon a time, long ago,
There lived an orphan boy,
Created of God,
Created of Pajana.
Without food to eat,
Without clothes to wear:
So he lived.
No woman to marry him.
A fox came;
The fox said to the youth:
'How will you get to be a man?' he said.
And the boy said:
'I don't know myself how I shall get to be a man!'

---

[14] Jung and Kerényi, *Science of Mythology*, 29; cited from Radloff, *Proben der Volksliteratur*, 271, 400.

348 And then, exactly like the fox in our story, this fox teaches the orphan boy how to become human. Like the snake, the fox represents an instinctual power in man himself which, though it is represented as an animal, really belongs to humanity. In mythology and in medieval allegories, the fox plays a very paradoxical role. In his *Mundus Symbolicus*[15], Picinellus says about this: "The fox represents sly cruelty; he is a bad flatterer. He represents lust. He is extremely cautious and moves along in crooked paths." Gregory the Great says, "Foxes are false animals; they always use crooked ways and therefore represent cunning, sly demons." This fits with the fact that in Southern Germany, Austria, and Switzerland, foxes are supposed to be the souls of witches. In our local stories, it is believed that when a witch goes out, her body lies in bed half dead while her soul goes out as a fox and causes damage. There are a lot of stories in which a hunter meets a fox who causes a storm, so that the hay, which has just been brought in, gets blown away — or something of that kind. Or there is a fox near an avalanche and the avalanche comes down, and then the hunter shoots but only wounds the fox. The next morning when he goes through the village, he sees an old woman limping, or with a bandaged arm, and he thinks, "Aha! That was the fox!"

349 Strangely enough, in China and Japan there is the same belief that a fox is the exteriorized soul of the witch or the hysterical woman and is also the cause of hysteria and psychological trouble in women. A German psychiatrist by the name of Erwin Baelz was in Tokyo around 1910 and he described such a fox case, without knowing any of the mythology that I have just mentioned. He was introduced to a Japanese peasant woman who had fits. When she was normal, she was stupid — a fat, unintelligent woman. Then she suffered what could be called "fox fits" and became quite different. She herself said that she felt a pain in her chest and then she had a nervous need to bark and would bark like a fox. Afterward, as Baelz says, she went into a trancelike state and became clairvoyant. She told the psychiatrists in the ward all about their private lives and

---

[15] Picinelli, *Mundus Symbolicus.*

their marriage problems and other things. In such moments, she was highly witty and intelligent and very uncanny. After a while, she would get tired and pale and would bark a little again before falling asleep. When she woke up, she would again be the stupid person with whom you could not do much. It was a typical case of a dual personality: She was either the fox-witch or a stupid peasant.

350   In medieval symbolism, the fox has not only this negative meaning but is also an animal of the god Dionysus, who has, among others, the name Bassareus — derived from the Greek word for fox! In Christian allegory, this idea continued. As Picinellus says, "The fox is a symbol of faith and foresight because a fox investigates things by his hearing, and thus also the Christian can perceive the divine mysteries only with his ears and not penetrate them with his eyes." Here the fox is the one who knows about what is invisible. This is interesting because in our story (quite independently, for I do not think Saint-Exupéry read anything as strange as Picinellus) the fox also says, "It is only with one's heart that one can see clearly. What is essential is invisible to the eye." The fox believes in that which is not obvious but is known to feeling — that which is opposed to statistical reality.

351   If the little prince had understood what the fox had said, if he had really understood it and had not just repeated it mechanically without apparently taking it in, what would have happened to him? He does suddenly understand why the rose back on his planet is meaningful, for he says something like, "Oh! I have wasted a lot of time. So that is why she is unique to me! And that is why I have to be responsible for her and not take her as one of the many." This realization makes it look as if he had understood the fox, but something is lacking. It does, indeed, help him to go back to the rose later, perhaps even to choose death. But what he does not notice is that he has one friend on the planet, the rose, and one friend down here, the fox! If he had really understood, he would not only have made up his mind to go back to the rose, but he would have fallen into a conflict and asked himself what he was going to do? The fox is here on earth and that friendship must last, for otherwise it is

meaningless. But now the fox makes him realize that at the same time he has an obligation to the rose. There is again a fatal constellation! He should not have concluded that he must go back to his rose; he should have fallen into a conflict because now he has a friend on each of the planets. But it does not even occur to him that through the fox he has got into a conflict! His only conclusion is that he must go back to his rose. Thus, the fox's teaching, which really would be something to tie him to the earth, operates just the opposite way in him: It liberates him from the earth and makes him long to go back to the asteroid. This shows how deep and fatal the death-pull is in Saint-Exupéry.

352   A conflict would have arisen if he had realized that he had to say yes to the fox here, and yes to the rose over there. Then he would have fallen into an adult psychological state where one is constantly in conflict because one has obligations to the figures of the beyond, that is, to the unconscious, and obligations to human reality on this side. For instance, if a man has an obligation to his anima and to the woman with whom he made friends or married, then he gets into the typical duality situation of life. One always has a real conflict and a double pull. One is always torn between obligations to this side of life and to the inner or other side. That would be the realization, or the crucifixion — the basic truth of life: that life is a double obligation and that life itself is a conflict because it always means the collision of two tendencies. That is what makes up life, but this realization escapes the little prince completely or he flees from the realization. It is one more of those little, but fatal, turns in the story which point toward the tragic end.

◆

Chapter Three
The Goodbye

353 After the fox had taught the little prince that the feeling function makes one's relationship unique and he is therefore responsible for his rose, the little prince at once made up his mind to go back to the rose. It never occurred to him that he has now also some tie to the fox. Later he says to Saint-Exupéry,

354   'You must get back to your engine. I shall wait for you here. Come back tomorrow evening....'
    'But I was not reassured. I remembered the fox. One runs the risk of crying a bit if one allows oneself to be tamed...'

355 We see that he only feels some slight sorrow at leaving the fox. As I mentioned earlier, it does not occur to him that he could get into a conflict and take that conflict seriously by asking himself to whom he is now bound. The decision is one-sidedly in favor of a return to the rose and the beyond.

356   Then follows one of the most poetic episodes of the book. Saint-Exupéry begins to suffer from thirst and walks into the desert. The little prince goes with him and suddenly causes him to find an imaginary well whose water refreshes him and fills him with joy — it is a *fata morgana*. They walk and walk, and the little prince always says that there is a well somewhere. And then they see one. Saint-Exupéry begins to doubt if this can be true, knowing that where there is a well in the desert there is also a village. With this well, there is no village. But the little prince runs toward it and tries to work the pulley, and the two drink from this imaginary well. In *Terre des Hommes*[1], Saint-Exupéry says of the water,

---

[1] Saint-Exupéry, *Terre des Hommes*.

357   'Oh water, thou hast no colour and no taste. Thou canst not be defined. One tasteth thee without knowing thee. Thou dost penetrate us with a joy which cannot be explained by the senses. Through thy blessing all the dried-up sources of our heart begin to flow afresh. Thou art the greatest treasure on earth. Thou dost not suffer any mixture or brook any alteration. Thou art a dark divinity but thou dost impart an infinitely simple joy.'

358   This episode in the book goes back to the time when he was lost with his mechanic, Prevost. They walked and walked and had the experience of a *fata morgana*. At the last minute they met a Bedouin who gave them a drink of water from his bottle and so rescued them. This is probably the experience that he describes in *Terre des Hommes*, and here he describes it again. It was one of his deepest experiences and therefore appears repeatedly in his books.

359   Since the divine child, whom the little prince represents, is a symbol of the Self, he is also the source of life. Like many mythological saviors, or child-gods, he *has* the source. This raises the question as to why the motif of the source of life, the water of life, is so often combined with the motif of the divine child: What are the practical links? He has the force of renewal and is a symbol of the self, and, as the child side, he represents the flow of life and the possibility of renewal because the child has a naïve view of life. If you recall your own childhood, then you remember how intensely alive you were. The child, if it is not already neurotic, is constantly interested in something new. Whatever else the child may suffer from, it does not suffer from remoteness from life — unless it has been thoroughly poisoned by the neuroses of its parents. Otherwise, it is fully alive, and that is why people, thinking back to their own childhood, long to have that naïve vitality which they have lost in becoming grown-up. The child is an inner possibility — of renewal. But the question is how this gets into the actual life of an adult. If an adult person dreams of a girl or a boy, in practical terms it means a new adventure or a new relationship, or more precisely, a new

adventure on the level of those functions that have remained naïve. It has to do with the inferior function which has remained childlike and completely naïve, and through which renewal comes. It is what conveys a new view and experience of life when the worn-out superior function comes to its end, and it is also what imparts all those naïve pleasures which one has lost since childhood. That is why we must learn to play again, but on the line of the fourth or inferior function. It does not help if, for instance, an intellectual person starts some kind of intellectual play. If a thinking type were to quote the Bible saying that unless you become like little children you will never enter the kingdom of heaven and were then to go to a club to play chess, that would not help at all, for it would again involve the main function. There is a great temptation to do that, namely, to accept the idea of play and of turning to something else, something noncommittal, but to do it within the field of the main function. I have often seen feeling types whose feeling function has run out. I tell them that they must do something which has no purpose, something playful, and then they propose going and working in a kindergarten, or something like that. But that is nonsense, for that would again be on the feeling side. It would be a half-way acceptance and an escape at the same time. The really difficult thing is to turn directly to the inferior function and to play there. This would mean that the ego must give up its control, for if you touch your inferior function, it will decide what it wants to play, not you. Like an obstinate child, it will say it wants to play this or that, even if you suggest it is not suitable and will not turn out well. In an intuitive, perhaps, the inferior function may want to play with clay and the person lives in a hotel room and would much prefer something clean because working with clay is too messy for a hotel room. But you cannot dictate to the inferior function! If you are an intuitive and your inferior function wants to play with stones or clay, then you must make the effort to find a place where that would be possible. That is exactly the difficulty; the ego always has thousands of objections to turning to the inferior side.

360   The inferior function is a real nuisance, just as children are, for you cannot put it in a box and take it out when it suits you. It is a living entity with its own demands, and it is a nuisance to the ego which wants to have its own way. The half concession of giving the enemy something so as to be left alone, which most people try when they see they have to turn to the inferior function, always reminds me of the Greeks who went about with their pockets full of honey-cakes: If one threw something to the dark powers, they would leave you alone, a kind of buying oneself off by throwing a sacrifice. When descending into the underworld, the Greek heroes always had honey-cakes to throw to Cerberus so that he fell asleep, and they could slip by. That can work sometimes, but for the main conflict it does not work. You cannot appease these demands by throwing them some little thing. But if you accept the humiliating experience which makes the ego submit to the demands of the inferior or childish part of the personality, then the divine child becomes a source of life and life has a new face. One discovers new experiences and everything changes.

361   Naturally, the child is also a uniting symbol for it brings together the separated or dissociated parts of the personality, which again has to do with the quality of being naïve. If I trust my naïve reaction, then I am whole; I am wholly in the situation and wholly in life. But most people do not dare do this because one exposes oneself too much. However, one just needs the courage, being somewhat shrewd at the same time, so that one does not expose oneself to those people who do not understand. One should be clever and not just childish.

362   When you begin to play with the inferior function, you touch uniqueness, which is at the bottom of all psychological tests! In the tree test, or the Rorschach test, you tell people to do whatever comes into their minds, and they give themselves away at once because play is genuine and therefore also unique. For this reason, children play. In two minutes, they reveal their whole problem, for by doing so, they are themselves. I often suggest to feeling types that they should take some striking motif in a dream, a numinous motif, and try to do some real thinking about it; they should not look up the indexes

in Jung's books, but really to try to find out what they think about the symbols themselves. And then very often they suddenly get quite passionate about it and have the most amazing thoughts — which sometimes seem to be very naïve thoughts to a thinking type.

363   I often notice that when feeling types begin to think, they do so exactly as the early Greek philosophers, the pre-Socratics, did. They have thoughts like those of Heraclitus or Democritus and are as fired by these ideas as were the early Greeks. If you read Empedocles or Heraclitus, there is an eternal youth in the way they think. That is why I love these philosophers so much. Nowadays, it seems like mythological thinking and not very scientific. For instance, the atomic theories of Democritus are awfully naïve if looked at according to modern theories, but there is a kind of wholeness and enthusiasm about them, together with the idea that they now see the whole picture. Naturally, the material is full of projections of the symbol of the Self, so one gets quite carried away when reading it. It is a kind of springtime of the spirit. Early Greek philosophy is like the blossoming of spring. If a feeling type gets down to his own thinking, he very often comes to this kind of experience, and if a thinking type witnesses this, he must retire to his own estate and not say that one knew that twenty thousand years ago! The same thing applies to the thinking type if you once get such a type to bring up naïve, real feeling. Usually, the thinking type is so much a thinker that he even organizes his feelings appropriately, and because he does not get along with his real feelings, because they are so unadapted, he generally has a pseudoadaptation to feeling. I would say that the main method of getting to the playfulness of the inferior function is to scratch away the pseudoadaptation with which we all cover the inferior function. The feeling type, for instance, is usually full of school and university theories and imagines that those are his thoughts. But they are not; they are pseudothinking adaptations to cover up the fact that his real thinking is awfully embryonic and naïve. The same holds true for the thinking type who has very naïve feelings; for instance, "I love you; I hate you." If he went around the world saying this to everyone, or saying "I can't stand you," you can

imagine what a stumbling block he would be! It would not work for two minutes! At school, too, you could not tell your teacher that you could not stand him! I am a thinking type myself and I loved certain teachers and hated others. I could never dissimulate my feelings sufficiently and always showed what I felt, though I knew it would have been much more diplomatic not to show too clearly how much I despised a certain teacher, but it was always obvious. When you become an adult, you hide these reactions and then acquire a pseudofeeling adaptation. Thinking types are often quite amiable and seem to have balanced feeling reactions, but never trust that! That is just a pseudoadaptation because the other is so painful and helpless and childish that one cannot show it. But if you want to get to it, you must again dig up the naiveté of your thinking or your feeling and get the crust off your pseudoadaptation.

364   Intuitive people very often have no relationship to their body and are likely to dress badly or be dirty, but since that does not work, they learn to wash and put on nice clothes, but although they may be quite correctly dressed, there is no personal style. If they were to dig up their real sensation, their taste would be artistic, but weird and very much out of the ordinary. Intuitive people who get down to their sensation cannot buy ready-made clothes; everything must be made for them. Neither can they eat restaurant food; they must either have a cook or cook for themselves, and it must be very special. It gives them a lot of trouble to discover this, and what is worse, it is a nuisance and expensive both in money and time. You can have a tailor and a cook, but that is not quite genuine. Or you can go down into your inferior function, which is the greatest time-thief of all because it is primitively slow.

365   In primitive countries it is impossible to hurry people. If you travel in Egypt, it is no good ordering the cars for 9 a.m. and expecting to be in the Kings' Tombs at 10. Everyone who travels in the Orient knows that one must put up with being two or three hours late and not arriving on time, as Europeans do. But once you have made the adaptation, life is much nicer because you have all kinds of experiences: One's car breaks down and causes a lot of fun,

and instead of arriving at the Kings' Tombs, you find yourself in the desert again with a lot of swearing going on, and so on. But that is life too! You cannot organize the inferior function. It is awfully expensive and needs a lot of time, and that is one reason why it is such a cross in our lives: It makes us so inefficient if we try to work our way through it. It must be given whole Sundays and whole afternoons, and nothing may come out of it, except that the inferior function comes to life. But that is the whole point. A feeling type will only bring up his thinking if he begins to think about something he cannot use in this world, neither for examinations nor for study purposes. But if he thinks about something that interests him, that is how to get going, for it is not possible to yoke inferior playfulness to utilitarian motives. The essence of play is that it has no visible purpose. I would tell a feeling type to learn by heart what he needs for exams, and not to try to think, because he will not be able to do so. He should make pseudoadaptations, and if a thinking type gets into a situation where he must behave — for example, he must attend a funeral — then on no account may he express his personal feelings; he must just behave and do the conventional thing with flowers and condolences, and that is the right pseudoadaptation. To get at his real feeling, the thinking type must find a situation where he can play, and then it will be quite different. Thus, the first thing to do is to take the inferior function out of the adaptation field and keep the pseudoadaptation for those cases where it is necessary. I think nobody can really develop the inferior function before having first created a temenos, namely a sacred grove, a hidden place where he can play. The first thing is to find a Robinson Crusoe playground, and then when you have gotten rid of all onlookers, you can begin! As a child, one needed a place and time and no interfering adult audience.

366   To return to our book; after this climax of happiness where they have found a well, the tragic end follows relatively quickly. The little prince asks Saint-Exupéry to draw him a muzzle for the sheep in order that it may not eat the rose on his asteroid, and by this, Saint-Exupéry guesses that the little prince intends to leave the earth.

Saint-Exupéry continues working on the repair of his engine. The next evening, he is almost finished when he hears the little prince arranging a nocturnal rendezvous with somebody. He rushes to see to whom the little prince is talking.

367   Beside the well, there was the ruin of an old stone wall. When I came back from my work on the following evening, I saw from some distance my little prince sitting on top of it, his legs dangling. And I heard him saying, 'Don't you remember? It was not quite here!'

368   No doubt another voice answered him since he replied, 'Yes! Yes! It is the right day, but not the right spot...'

369   I continued walking towards the wall but still could neither see nor hear anybody. Yet the little prince answered once again, '...Yes, of course. You will see where my track begins in the sand. Just wait for me there. I shall be there tonight.'

370   I was a mere twenty metres from the wall and yet I could see nothing. After a short silence the little prince spoke again 'Is your poison good? Are you sure it will not make me suffer for too long?'

371   I stopped in my tracks, my heart aching, but I still did not understand.

372   'Now, go away...' he said. 'I want to get down!'

373   Whereupon I dropped my eyes to the foot of the wall and what I saw made me leap into the air! It was there, raising its head towards the little prince, one of those yellow snakes which can kill you in a matter of seconds. Groping in my pocket for my revolver, I started running, but because of the noise, I was making the snake gently slipped back into the sand, like the dying spray of a fountain, and, in no apparent hurry, disappeared among the stones with a light metallic sound.

374 I reached the wall just in time to catch my little prince in my arms; his face was white as snow.

375 'What does this mean?' I asked him. 'Why are you talking with snakes?' I had untied the golden muffler which never left him. I had moistened his temples and given him a little water to drink. And now I didn't dare ask him any more questions. He looked at me gravely and put his arms around my neck. I could feel his heart beating like the heart of a dying bird shot with someone's rifle.

376 He said to me, 'I'm so glad you discovered what was the matter with your engine. Now you can go home...'

377 'How did you know?'

378 In fact, I was coming to tell him that, contrary to all expectations, my endeavours had been successful!

379 He didn't reply to my question but whispered, 'I too am going home today...'

380 Then he added a little sadly, 'It is much farther away...It is far more difficult...'

381 I could sense that something quite extraordinary was about to happen. I was holding him tightly in my arms like a child and yet it seemed to me that he was slipping straight down into an abyss, and I could do nothing to prevent it...

382 His gaze was grave and lost in the distance.

383 'I have your sheep. And I have the box for the sheep. And I also have the muzzle...'

384 And he smiled sadly.

385 I waited for a long time. I could feel that little by little, he was getting warmer.

386 'My dear little man, you were afraid...'

387 Of course he had been frightened! But he laughed gently.

388 'I shall be far more frightened this evening...'

389 Once again I was frozen by a sense of something irreparable.

390 The little prince trembles when Saint-Exupéry rushes toward him and takes him in his arms and scolds him, but Saint-Exupéry feels that he cannot hold him back, that it is too late and nothing will help him. The experience of helplessness, of not being able to save someone from death, has been impressed on him through the death of his little brother. When he describes somebody's death in his novels, he always describes this terrific feeling of helplessness. One stands there with the feeling that the person is slowly slipping away, floating away from you, and that you are utterly helpless. You cannot hold them back. Here is the same experience, for he realizes that the little prince has arranged a meeting with the snake to be killed by it. Saint-Exupéry feels that he can do nothing to hold him back from it.

391 The little prince then tries to comfort him, instead of being comforted or helped by Saint-Exupéry. He says:

392 'The stars mean different things to different people. For some they are nothing more than twinkling lights in the sky. For travellers they are guides. For scholars they are food for thought. For my businessman they are wealth. But for everyone the stars are silent. Except from now on just for you....'

393 'What do you mean?'

394 'When you look up at the sky at night, since I shall be living on one of them and laughing on one of them, for you it will be as if all the stars were laughing. You and only you will have stars that can laugh!'

395 And as he said it he laughed.

396 'And when you are comforted (time soothes all sorrows) you will be happy to have known me. You will always be my friend. You will want to laugh with me. And from time to time you will open your window, just for the pleasure of it ... And your friends will be astonished to see you laughing

whilst gazing at the sky. And so you will say to them, "Yes, stars always make me laugh". And they will think you are crazy. I shall have played a very naughty trick on you . . ?

397 And once again he laughed.

398 'It will be as if I had given you, instead of stars, a lot of little bells that can laugh. . ?

399 And again he laughed. Then he became serious again. 'Tonight . . . you know . . . do not come.'

400 'I shall not leave you.'

401 'I shall seem to be in pain. I shall look as if I were dying. It is like that. Do not come to see that. There's just no point. . ?

402 'I shall not leave you.'

403 But he was worried.

404 'I am telling you this . . . partly because of the snake. It must not bite you . . . Snakes are vicious creatures. They can bite just for the fun of it . . ?

405 'I shall not leave you.'

406 But a thought reassured him.

407 'It is true that they have no poison left for a second bite.'

408 Though Saint-Exupéry promises not to leave the little prince, he misses going with him.

409 That night I did not see him set out. He had left without a sound. When I managed to catch up with him, he was walking along with a quick and resolute step.

410 He merely said to me, 'Oh! You are here . . ?

411 And he took me by the hand. But he was still worrying.

412 'You should not have come. You will be unhappy. I shall look as if I were dead and it will not be true . . ?

413   I said nothing.

414   'You must understand. It is too far. I cannot carry this body with me. It is too heavy.'

415   I said nothing.

416   'It will look like an old abandoned shell . . . Not anything to be sad about . . .'

417   I said nothing.

418   He was a little discouraged. But he made one last effort.

419   'It will be nice, you know. I too shall look at the stars. All the stars will be wells with rusty pulleys. All the stars will pour me some water to drink . . .'

420   I said nothing.

421   'It will be such fun! You will have five hundred million little bells, I shall have five hundred million springs of fresh water. . .'

422   And he too said nothing more because he was crying.

423   'Here it is. Let me go on by myself.'

424   And he sat down because he was afraid.

425   Then he said, 'You know. . . my flower . . . I am responsible for her. And she is so weak, so trusting. She has four tiny thorns to protect herself against the world. . .'

426   I sat down because I could not remain standing any longer.

427   He said, 'There now . . . That is all . . .'

428   He hesitated a little more: then he stood up. He took one step forward. I couldn't move.

429   Saint-Exupéry sat down, and then suddenly the little prince got up and took one step — and now comes the decisive sentence:

430   'I couldn't move.'

431 Saint-Exupéry cannot do a thing. He remains sitting.

432 There was nothing more than a flash of yellow close to his ankle. He stood motionless for a moment. He did not cry out. He fell as gently as a tree falls. There was not even the slightest sound, because of the sand.

433 After a while, Saint-Exupéry remembers with horror that he had forgotten to draw the strap for the sheep's muzzle, so that the little prince will never be able to fasten it on. From then on, every time he looks up at the stars he is tormented as to whether the sheep has eaten the rose or not. Then follows the last picture. He says:

434 This is to me the most beautiful and saddest landscape in the world. It is the same landscape as in the last picture but I have drawn it once again to impress it upon your memory. It is here that the little prince appeared on Earth and then disappeared.

435 Look very carefully at the landscape so as to be sure to recognise it if ever one day you travel to Africa, through the desert. And if you should happen to come upon this spot, please do not hurry on. Wait a little, exactly under the star. Then, if a child comes towards you, if he laughs, if he has golden locks and if he refuses to answer questions, you will surely guess who he is. So be kind! Do not leave me grieving. Write to me quickly to tell me that he has come back. . .

436 We need to discuss this part at some length because it is full of symbolism. Firstly, it must be said that the little prince must be killed like a mortal human being to return to his star. He says that his body would be too heavy for that. This is a very strange motif because if you think of the little prince as an inner psychological inner figure — a symbol of the Self within Saint-Exupéry — then he certainly would not need to be deprived of his body. He would already be in the psychological realm and could return whenever he wanted —

could come to earth and go back to the star again. He came down holding onto a flock of birds, and at that time he had already a certain amount of body. He could not fly through the air or fall down through it to the earth but needed the help of the birds. It is strange that this idea does not occur to him again, but the only point I want to stress is that he consists of psyche *and* body. He is not a content of the unconscious which has remained in the Beyond, in the unconscious, but rather he has to some extent incarnated into the human realm. He has become physically real, and this shows that this symbol is a mixture of a childish shadow and an aspect of the Self. In a manner of speaking, the little prince is an impure symbol; that means, it is partly the childish shadow, which is already incarnated, and partly a symbol of the Self, which is not incarnated. As a symbol of the Self, it is in the Beyond and is eternal, and there is no such thing as death; there is only an appearing and a disappearing into and out of this realm — just as an experience of the Self comes to us, and then we lose it again. If we look at the little prince as the Self, it means that it sometimes touches the realm of our human consciousness and then disappears again. But in so far as it has a body, it has incarnated in us, in our realm. It has become visible and audible through our own actions; it has become a part of ourselves, and then the problem becomes difficult. The snake kills the shadow, for the snake can only poison this body and thereby free the symbol of the Self again from the body it had been in. The other possibility would have been that the incarnation would have gone on, and then the symbol of the little prince would have evolved, on a more adult and different level. But in this in-between situation, the development is suddenly interrupted by the snake poisoning the little prince.

437 Saint-Exupéry describes the encounter very poetically: At the very moment he can repair his engine and return to the human world and his fellow beings, the little prince makes up his mind to leave the earth. Saint-Exupéry departs toward a human world and the other departs to the Beyond. Because this story is such a mixture of right and fatal symbolism from the outset, one does not know at

this moment if this departure of the two is really a positive development. You could say that now, after this experience of the Self and the Beyond, Saint-Exupéry can return to his normal adaptation in this world, and the symbol of the Self, which was only meant to meet him at this crucial moment, can return to the place it had come from. That would be a positive aspect of this tragic moment. But, at the same time, one somehow feels that this is negative because Saint-Exupéry, in his own life, did not return to his adaptation to this world but soon after followed the little prince into the Beyond. Thus, we can say that the departure did not really take place or was not quite carried through. They did not really separate. The human part, namely Saint-Exupéry, followed the other part, and thus the departure of the little prince becomes an anticipation of Saint-Exupéry's death. Along with this goes the fact that Saint-Exupéry did not accept the departure, as you see from the last few words:

438   Then, if a child comes towards you, if he laughs, if he has golden locks and if he refuses to answer questions, you will surely guess who he is. So be kind! Do not leave me grieving. Write to me quickly to tell me that he has come back. . .

439 Saint-Exupéry had not given up. He cannot accept the departure as such, though it is quite unlikely that the little prince will ever return. He has not sacrificed the relationship. That is another fatal hint because if one does not sacrifice such an experience after having had it, then there remains a constant pull toward death and unconsciousness in the hope of finding it again.

440   That is a very dangerous and typical experience. It belongs to the neurosis of the *puer aeternus* who, because he is so close to the unconscious, generally has overwhelming experiences of it which convey to him a positive feeling of life. But then he cannot let them go. He just sits there, waiting and hoping for the experience to come back. The more one sits and waits, the less the inner experience can approach consciousness again because it is the essence of these experiences that they always come in a *new* form. The experience of

the Self does not repeat itself, but generally turns up again in those desperate moments when one is no longer looking for it. It has turned completely in another direction and suddenly again stands before you in a different form. As it is life itself, and the renewal and flow of life, it cannot repeat itself. That would be a contradiction of its very essence. Therefore, if ever one has an experience of the Self, the only way to not get poisoned by it afterward and to not get onto the wrong track is to leave it alone, to turn away — to turn to the next duty and even to try and forget about it. The more one's ego clings to it and wants it back, the more one chases it away with one's own ego desire. The same applies to positive love or feeling experiences: people who make childish demands on other people every time they have a positive love experience, or feeling experience, with another human being, always want to perpetuate it, to force it to happen in the same way again. They say, "Let's take the same boat trip because of the magical Sunday when it was so beautiful." You can be quite sure that it will be the most awful failure. You may try it, just to experience how it does not work. It always shows that the ego has not been able to take the experience of the Self in an adult way; instead, something that resembles childish greed has woken up. The positive experience has called up this childish attitude — that this is the treasure that should be kept! If you have this reaction, you will chase it away forever and it will never come back. The more you long for and the more you seek the experience, the more you get into a cramped state of conscious desire and the more hopeless the situation becomes.

441   The same thing applies to an artist's work when, through an inspiration from the unconscious, he produces something outstandingly beautiful, and then wants to go on in the same style. It has been a success, and the work has been admired, and he feels that now he has got it and that something of value has been produced. He wants to repeat it, to repaint or rewrite in the same manner, but it's gone! The second, third, and fourth draft are just nothing — the divine essence has disappeared; the spirit is out of the bottle, and it cannot be put back in again. It often happens that young people

produce something that is a big "hit" and then they become sterile for a long time, for they cannot go back; ego greed has got into it. This is the downfall of the "Wunderkinder" — outstandingly gifted children; afterward they are sterile because they cannot get out of this difficulty. The only way is to turn away and not look back for a second. But Saint-Exupéry looks back: "Write to me quickly to tell me that he has come back. . .," as though he were constantly hoping to recapture the experience. That is fatal.

442 The snake bites the little prince on the heel, which is obviously where a snake would bite. But this is also a mythological motif. You know of the Achilles heel, the only place where Achilles could be wounded. Many other savior gods were often wounded in the feet. For instance, Philoctetes, written about by Kerényi in his paper *Heros Iatros*[2] — the healing hero. There he has collected all the Greek material on the healing gods and demons: Asclepius, Chiron, and so on, all of whom are wounded and therefore can heal others. One must be wounded to become a healer. This is the local image of a universal mythological motif, which is described in Eliade's book about the initiation of medicine men and shamans[3]. Nobody becomes either one or the other without first having been wounded: One is either cut open by the initiator and certain magical stones are inserted into his body, or a spear is thrown at his neck, or some such thing. Generally, the experiences are ecstatic — stars, or ghostlike demons, hit them or cut them open. But they have always to be pierced or cut apart before they become healers, for that is how they acquire the capacity for healing others.

443 If this were only about knowing the whole process of suffering and of being wounded and healed, then everyone could become a healer or a shaman, for we have all suffered. The psychological difference between an ordinary person who suffers and the healer is that the healer finds a way to overcome his suffering. The indigenous peoples of the Polar regions see the difference between an ordinary person who suffers and a healer by how the healer finds a way of

---

[2] Kerényi, *Heros Iatro*.
[3] Eliade, *Shamanism*.

overcoming his suffering and without external help. He can overcome his own suffering; he finds the creative way out, and this means that he finds his own cure, one that is unique. Eliade tells of a very successful reindeer hunter, a provider of food and therefore a big man in his tribe, who has no thought of becoming a shaman. However, he develops a neurosis which keeps him from going hunting, and then he discovers that as soon as he learns to drum like a shaman, his disease disappears. As soon as he begins to "shamanize" by drumming, calling ghosts and making cures, he is all right. But once he is cured, he has had enough of being a shaman and goes back to hunting. Then the illness gets him again. In the end, he sulkily puts up with it and becomes a healer since it is the only way he can keep himself fit. Against his wish and his will, reindeer hunting is finished forever. This is a striking illustration of a man finding his own cure after having been wounded by a neurotic disease and of him being forced into a healing activity. Naturally, at first, when he was confined by his illness, he got a shaman to try to cure him, but no shaman could. He had to cure himself; he had to shamanize, and then he was cured. The healing hero, therefore, is the one who finds some creative way out, a way not already known, and does not follow a pattern. Ordinary sick people follow ordinary patterns, but the shaman cannot be cured by the usual methods of healing: He must find the unique way — the only way that applies to him. The creative personality who can do that then becomes a healer and is recognized as such by his colleagues.

444   That, I think, is the most convincing explanation of this motif and the simplest. But you can also see it differently and that comes into our story.

445   When the Self and the ego get in touch with each other, who is wounded? As soon as they come together, both are wounded because to get in touch with the ego is a partial damage to the Self, just as it is a partial damage to the ego to be in touch with the Self. The two cannot meet without damaging each other. One way in which the Self is damaged is that instead of being a potential wholeness it becomes a partial reality. It becomes partially real

within the individuated person — in the actions and words of the person that reflect this partial realization of the Self. This is a restriction of the Self and its possibilities. The ego, however, is wounded because something greater breaks into its life. This is why Jung says that it means tremendous suffering to enter the process of individuation. It causes a great wound because, to put it quite simply, we are robbed of the capacity of arranging our own lives according to our own wishes.

446   If we take the unconscious and the process of individuation seriously, we can no longer arrange our own lives. For instance, we think we would like to go somewhere, and the dream says no to it, then we must give up the idea. Sometimes it is all right, but sometimes such decisions are very annoying. To be deprived of an evening out, or a trip, is not so bad, but there are more serious matters where we greatly want something which is suddenly vetoed by the unconscious. We feel broken, caught in a trap, or imprisoned, nailed on the cross. With our whole heart and mind we want something, and the unconscious vetoes it.

447   In such moments there is naturally an experience of intense suffering through our encounter with the Self. But the Self suffers equally because it is suddenly caught in the actuality of an ordinary human life. In this connection, Jung refers to the saying of Christ in the Acts of John, in the Apocrypha: Christ stands in the middle of the dancing apostles and says, "It is your human suffering that I want to suffer." That is the simplest way of putting it. If it is not in touch with a human being, the divine figure has no suffering. It longs to experience human suffering; it does not only long for human suffering but also causes it. Man would not suffer if he were not connected with something greater, or he would suffer as an animal does: He would just accept fate and die from it. If you submit to everything that happens to you, as an animal does, you do not suffer intensely but in a kind of dumb way. Animals accept things as they happen: A leg is lost in an accident, and they hobble along on three legs. Or they are blinded and try to carry on without eyes and will probably die. This happens all the time in nature, but man *feels* what

happens to him. He has a greater capacity for suffering because he is more conscious. If his legs are cut off or he is blinded, the feeling is deeper and more intense because there is more ego and therefore the ability to rebel against fate. If you have ever worked together with people who have met a horrible fate, you will have seen what a terrific revolt can mean. Such people say, "I cannot accept it! I cannot! Why has this happened to me? It is irreversible, but I cannot accept it!" An animal does not show such intensity of suffering. It tries to carry on until it dies; even if its hind legs are paralyzed, it tries to move, and usually ends by being eaten — a quick and merciful end. For us it is worse, because with modern medicine a human being is not killed quickly. We are cared for in hospitals, and then comes the problem: What does this mean? Why do I have to go on living? In such cases, the suffering becomes more intense and terrible, to the point of being a real religious problem. One can say therefore that we are more open to real and intense suffering, and this has to do with the fact that there is something within us that thinks this should not be so. But if it is a part of my life and inescapable, then I must know what it means. If I know its meaning, I can accept the suffering, but if I do not, then I cannot. I have seen people who could take what had happened to them with a certain acceptance and composure when they saw a meaning in it. Although the suffering continued, they had a kind of quiet island within because they had the relief of feeling that they knew why they suffered. But to discover the reason for such suffering, we must follow the way of our own individuation process because the reason is something unique and different in each individual. One has therefore to find that unique meaning. In seeking the meaning of your suffering, you are seeking the meaning of your life. You are searching for the greater pattern of your own life; this is why the wounded healer is the archetype of the Self — one of its most widespread features — and is at the bottom of all genuine healing procedures.

448   I have been asked if suffering, when it is accepted, could become a medium of communication with the Self. This depends on whether

it is accepted in the right way. If it is accepted with resignation, it does not work. Many people accept their suffering, but with a tinge of resignation. They put up with it, and then it does not help. It must be a positive acceptance; you can only get to the meaning of it if you accept it. It generally plays out as an endless struggle and then, in a moment of grace, one can suddenly accept it and then the meaning dawns upon one. One could not even say which comes first. Sometimes it is the meaning and then the acceptance, or one makes up one's mind to accept it and then at that moment the meaning becomes clear. But it is strangely interwoven.

449 Even though there is a long and rich tradition in Christianity of the idea that suffering is of value, one still comes across a lot of resignation among Christians. At bottom, it is a question of faith: If they have a living faith, they accept suffering without resignation because they already have understanding, and then it is all right. But if a person tries to accept their suffering — as they have been instructed to do by the preacher — "because Christ suffered on the cross," then it does not help at all; then nothing is understood because then the person is merely preaching to his own consciousness, and there is no inner experience to back it up.

450 Now let us turn our attention to the last image in our book, the most tragic one of all that is without any color and shows only a single star above two lines that indicate a landscape. It is lifeless, without any feeling experience. The emotional participation has receded. But from what? At the beginning, there were highly colored pictures. There was the one that Saint-Exupéry himself called the "urgent picture" — of the baobab trees which he says he drew much better and with more color. And now we have this image that is without color. It is an image of the loneliness left after his departure. The picture shows the crossing point of two sand dunes and there is the star, the idea being that the prince returned to that star. It is a picture of the loneliness which is left. It would be natural to feel lonely and lifeless after the little prince had departed. This is not a bad symptom, but rather quite normal; indeed, a desert without any life in it — that is how it would feel if the divinity left. I would say

that this drawing expresses his disappointment, and therefore its sadness and emptiness are right. But what is objectionable about it is that it lacks intensity. It is a poor and inadequate drawing of disappointment and loneliness. You must think about it because its feeling tone is not immediately grasped. Try to draw or paint a picture of how you feel when you are deserted by the god and you will see — or I hope so for your sakes — that your imagination will run in a more vivid way than this. It would take some artistic effort — but after all Saint-Exupéry was an artist — to depict the loneliness of the desert. But draw a wide, wide plain, and get the feeling of the atmosphere into it, its nothingness, and try to express the sad coldness of a sky which has only one star looking down on the earth, with its cold light. You have all seen paintings of being lost, of despair, which wring your heart, in which you feel all the lostness and despair and emptiness, but here you do not. Here you must put all your imaginative powers to work to work out what it is he is trying to express. You think it must be the loneliness, but it does not hit you or wring your heart because there is no color. Why did he not make it all gray? If it had been a sad gray, you might have got the feeling of it. Why not make the sky so that it appears as a vast cold orb overhead, so that it chills you to look at the picture? Here you feel neither sad nor chilled. You must replace this reaction with your thinking. There is something lacking. It is just dead — it is not even a disappointment, nor does it even express sadness! The description in the book is full of nostalgia, but not the drawing, and although the description is nostalgic, it is very childish. There is just the hope of getting back what he has lost. "Write to me quickly…". It suggests a postcard, the cheapest means, some form of public assistance — just like a radio announcement for some missing person — a request that the next police station be informed. But, except for the wish of a greedy child who wants to have his toy back, and the poor expression of this feeling, it is a very weak goodbye. Perhaps he did not realize that it was a god. Otherwise, he would never have asked to be sent word like that. Imagine putting out a call to the world, "If you find my god…." Again, we are confronted with the extinct volcano. The emotional intensity is not great enough, and that is the dangerous thing. It is typical of the person who in such tragic situations simply reacts by saying, "Oh, yes, yes!" Sometimes it is pretense, an understatement. They pretend to have no emotion, but then you can tell by their cold hands and other symptoms that emotion is there; and then it does not matter, for it is just pretense. But if they really have no emotion — when the volcano is burned out — then it is dangerous.

451   Someone might object by saying that Saint-Exupéry himself was quite intuitive and he thought that it was an episode which had to come to an end, similar to when he crashed in the desert. Do you not have the feeling throughout the book that the experience is only meant to last for a short time and will then be over? Could not the flatness in his picture, together with the experience and feeling of being left alone, express that there is no disappointment because he knew that it would have to come to an end, and he could do nothing about it? But that would place too much weight on the intellect, and it would be a morbid reaction on the part of Saint-Exupéry. Suppose there is someone you love, and that person dies from an incurable disease. Your intellect knows this! It knows that the experience must come to an end. The relationship must end, the doctor has warned you, saying that the patient will last another three weeks, but that does not mean that you have no other reaction. Even if you know that the relationship has inexorably to come to an end, that does not stop your feeling. That is exactly it! Such an experience as Saint-Exupéry had in the desert with the little prince had to come to an end. Experience teaches us that it must do so. But that is exactly the weakness of a personality such as Saint-Exupéry's. People who cut themselves off from their feelings and the emotional layer to avoid suffering, or because they are incapable of feeling and suffering, replace all that by reflection. They simply say, "All right, that had to come to an end." That is an intellectual argument, and precisely therein is a lack of feeling intensity. Constant awareness of the transitory nature of life, and a sense of always preparing for an end before it arrives, is typical of the *puer aeternus*. For instance, when

he makes friends with a girl, he knows that the end will be a disappointment. He therefore does not give himself wholeheartedly to the experience. Instead, he is always getting ready to say goodbye. As far as reason is concerned, he is right, but then he does not live. Reason has too much say in his life, and he does not allow for the unreasonable human side that does not always prepare for the retreat because there will be a disappointment. Why can one not say, "Of course there will be disappointment because all experiences in life are transient and may end in disappointment, but let's not anticipate it. Let us give ourselves with full love to the situation as along as it lasts." The one does not exclude the other. One need not be the fool who believes in nothing but happiness and then falls from the clouds, but if one always retreats at the beginning in anticipation of the suffering, that is a morbid reaction. Many neurotic people do this. They try to train themselves not to suffer by always anticipating suffering. They say, "I always think ahead of the suffering to come and by doing this, I am trained against it. I anticipate it in my fantasy." But this completely prevents you from living. A double attitude is required: that of knowing how things are likely to turn out, and that of giving oneself completely to the experience all the same. Otherwise, there is no life. Reason organizes it ahead of time so that one may be protected against suffering — so that it does not catch one unprepared. In this case, reason and consciousness have taken too much away from life. This is exactly what the *puer aeternus* tries to do all the time. He does not want to give himself to life and tries to block it off by organizing it ahead of time with his reason.

452   Sometimes, one thinks about how much more alive such people would be if they suffered! If they cannot be happy, let them at least be unhappy, really unhappy for once, and then they would become human. But many *puer aeterni* cannot even be quite unhappy! They even lack the generosity and courage to expose themselves to a situation which could make them unhappy. Like cowards, they build bridges by which to escape — they anticipate the disappointment in order not to suffer the blow, and that is a refusal to live.

453   How could the locked-up, rejected feeling express itself? Even if it is refused, it must still be there. I do not see it here, except in the temperamental spontaneity of the rose and in her emotional outbursts that she fully gives in to. When she boasts, she boasts thoroughly; when she is angry, she is thoroughly angry; and when she is haughty, she is thoroughly so. She has a certain totality of expression. She is fully in her momentary mood, one could say, and that, at least, is something. Apparently, that was the case with Saint-Exupéry's wife. She was amazingly spontaneous, even to a shocking extent. This shows itself in a more negative form throughout the book, in its slight sentimentality, that always indicates a lack of feeling — it does not replace real feeling. This is another aspect of this image.

454   We now need to ask ourselves what it means that the little prince wants a muzzle for the sheep so that it should not eat the rose? You see how the thing must work: He wants a sheep to eat the baobab shoots, and, naturally, if he just lets the sheep loose on the asteroid it will not be able to distinguish between rose and shoots and will eat everything. So, the little prince probably plans to put the glass shade over his rose and then let the sheep eat up all the baobab shoots; then put a muzzle on the sheep and take the glass globe off the rose. This is how he plans to keep sheep and rose naively apart. As drawing is a form of creation in his world, he wants Saint-Exupéry to draw the muzzle which he can put in the box with the drawing of the sheep and thereby prevent the rose from being eaten. But the strap for the muzzle gets forgotten in the upset of the departure, and when Saint-Exupéry suddenly thinks of it afterward, he says, "I keep wondering what has happened on his planet. Perhaps the sheep has eaten the flower...." And then he thinks that he will be tortured to the end of his life by wondering whether the sheep has now eaten the rose or not? To that question he gets no answer, but it is a thought which will torture him from now on.

455   When I began to interpret the sheep earlier, I spoke of it as being possibly the little mistake which causes a deadly accident, as for instance, when there are sheep on the airfield and the plane lands

on one of them and crashes. We also spoke of it as representing the mass-man, the crowd soul. The sheep's negative aspect is the collective nature of its instinctual make-up. In earlier times, there were always a few goats among the sheep because if wolves attacked, the goats did not lose their heads and the sheep might get away. If a ram were the leader, it would panic and the whole flock after him. To compensate for the stupidity of the sheep, goats were kept, but the wolves learned to kill the goats first to make the sheep panic. If the sheep is the collective thing that destroys the process of individuation by its collectiveness, it would not be surprising if it ate the rose. As a mandala, the rose is also the nucleus of the process of individuation, and the terrible thing in the book is that it is destroyed on the other side — in the Beyond. On this earth, the sheep is not wholly negative; the *puer aeternus* needs collective adaptation. He is usually a wrong kind of individualist who does not adapt sufficiently to the collective. Most *pueri*, for instance, flunk their military service because they do not want to be sheep. In such cases, it sometimes does them a lot of good to be sheep and to have to adapt to the collective. But in Saint-Exupéry's case, the collective extends to the star, where there should not be any sheep. This is a tragic mechanism: If one is too extreme in one's refusal to adapt, then one gets collectivized from behind and within. If you pretend to be more individual than you are, and avoid adaptation by thinking you are someone special — with all the neurotic vanity of being unique and misunderstood by everybody because you have such a delicate soul — if you have these false pretensions and because of them do not adapt to humanity, then you will be the very person who is actually not at all individual.

456   I have already mentioned that when I talk of the *puer aeternus*, people always have the same reaction: They know many such men, and can think of a whole crowd of examples, which goes to show that the *puer aeternus* is not at all original. He is really a very collective type — the collective type of the *puer aeternus*, and nothing else. The more he plays the part of the prince, with the idea that he is something special, the more he is really an ordinary type

of neurotic — a type you could describe clinically and cover almost the entire personality with clinical concepts. Precisely because the *puer* entertains false pretensions, he becomes collectivized from within, with the result that none of his reactions are very personal or very special. He becomes, as it were, an archetype, and if you become that, you are not at all original, not at all yourself and therefore, not at all special. This is why, when you are confronted with a *puer aeternus*, you are sometimes able to say to him, "Isn't that, and that, and that, your philosophy? And do you not have trouble there, and there, and there? And isn't this the case with girls? Do you not have this and this experience with girls?" And then he replies, "But heavens! How do you know? How can you know me so well?" If you are identical with an archetype, I can describe all your reactions because an archetype is a definite set of reactions. One can for the most part foretell what a *puer aeterunus* will look like and how he will feel. He is merely the archetype of the eternal youth god, and therefore he has all the features of the god; he has a nostalgic longing for death; he thinks of himself as being special; he is the one sensitive being among all the other tough sheep. He will have a problem with an aggressive, destructive shadow which he will not want to live and generally projects, and so on. There is nothing special about him whatsoever. The greater the identification with the youthful god, the less individual the person will be, even though he himself feels so special. If people are schizophrenic and think they are Jesus Christ, they all say the same thing. Jung once had two Jesus Christs in the asylum. He put them together and introduced them saying, "Here is Mr. Miller. He thinks he is Jesus Christ, and this is Mr. Meyer, and he thinks he is Jesus Christ." Then he went out of the room and left them alone. After a while he found one sitting in a corner drumming with his finger on the table and the other was standing drumming on the window. He asked them if they had made out who was the real Jesus Christ, and both turned to him and said, "He is a complete megalomaniac!" Each saw it clearly in the other. The diagnosis was correct as far as the other was concerned.

Part 2

A Practical Study

◊

Chapter Four

Life

457   To illustrate what we have seen in the book *The Little Prince*, I would like to draw on some practical material. I cannot call it case material because, as you will see, my contact with this *puer aeterunus* was rather strange; one could not call it therapy.

458   It concerns a young man who was thirty-one years old when I first met him. He came from a central European country. His father, who had been a decorator, had had a small florist's shop; when the boy was six years old, his father committed suicide by shooting himself. I could not find out why the father had killed himself, and the boy did not know. The marriage apparently was very unsatisfactory, and the boy remembered that there had been constant quarrels. His mother had brought him up and continued to run the florist's shop after his father's death; the boy himself wanted to become a painter. I think he was quite gifted in this way. From the age of about eighteen, he had suffered from a prison phobia to such an extent that he could hardly go into any town, for as soon as he saw a policeman, he became so frightened that he ran away, thinking he would be arrested and put into prison. This made life very difficult for him as he was always running away and sneaking around corners, as if he were a persecuted criminal. He was also very much afraid of the night, and every dusk was agony to him. He was frightened at the approach of evening, and at night, he could not sleep, and lay awake all night long, and naturally he masturbated. Another phobia, that came out much later, was that he was unable to cross any frontier or border, and it is disagreeable to live in Europe if you cannot cross a frontier. It was in connection with this difficulty that I first heard of him.

459   I had gone abroad somewhere and had lectured on some Jungian theme. Afterward, I received a postcard from him saying that there were a few things about my lecture which he would like to discuss with me, and that he also had a personal problem; he said he would arrive at such and such a time and date. I reserved some time for him, but nobody came. Later I received another postcard, with no apology, simply saying, "This is me again, and I am coming at such and such a time." Again, nobody appeared. I found out later that he always got to the Swiss frontier and then could not cross it, and so returned home. As he did not want to explain this in writing, he simply did not turn up. Then I received a third postcard, again without apology, and again saying he would be coming, but this time I decided not to reserve any time for him. Then, suddenly, a young man stood at my door and explained, quite politely, that he had written twice and not come because he had been afraid. The only explanation he could give of his phobia was that once he had been painting very near the frontier somewhere without knowing that he was practically on the border. He had been arrested by a frontier guard who had asked him for a passport, and since he did not have one, he had been locked up for two or three hours while the guards telephoned his hometown to make inquiries, after which he was let out with many apologies. He said that this experience had not really frightened and upset him, for he had had this fear of crossing the frontier beforehand. Thus, this incident just reinforced the existing phobia. He also told me vaguely that he had once had some shock treatments and had been in an asylum, but I was never able to find out any details, as he did not want to talk about that. In a way, you could probably call it a postpsychotic case. He had practically no money and he wanted to camp out nearby and consult me. Very tall with golden locks and blue eyes, he looked just like a beautiful young sun-god, and he wore a Jean Cocteau cloak with a hood in a heavenly blue, which suited him very well. I talked to him for a few hours that afternoon and found out what I have told you above. Then he took his tent to sleep in a field nearby, but in the night — it was summer-time — a thunderstorm came up, and he got so frightened of the night and the

storm that he had to rush into a hotel, and so spent the little money he had. He left the next day, and I never saw him in person again. In that one short discussion, I told him a few things about the *puer aeternus* and outlined a few of his problems, which he did not like at all. I did not expect ever to hear of him again, thinking he would be just like a meteor in my life, coming and disappearing forever. But after a fortnight, I received a letter in which he said that he had very much disliked what I had told him, and that he had been angry with me and disappointed that the heroic expenditure to meet me had ended so badly. Then, afterward, he had thought it over and had reached the conclusion that I was not quite so wrong about the things I had told him after all, and, moreover, something had happened which proved that I was putting my finger on the right spot. Then he told me the story which I will tell later. He asked if he might write from time to time and if I would answer his letters. That went on for about a year, during which time we exchanged only about three letters, and then the correspondence lapsed. That was at the end of the 1940s, and I knew no more until about five years ago, when I met someone who knew him who told me that he was all right and working at his painting. Since then, I heard that he married and that later he died from cancer at the age of forty-five.

460   At the end of his first letter, he wrote, in a very challenging kind of way, that he had had a dream shortly after he had left me. He said he could not make anything of it, and he wondered what I would say. The dream was as follows:

461   I was on the crest of a mountain and was walking with a girl along the ridge. I did not know the girl. Two men jumped up from below and attacked me. During a wild wrestling match with them, they took me and threw me down into the gorge below. I had the feeling that I was lost, but there was a lonely fir tree in which I got caught thereby preventing me from falling to the bottom of the gorge.

462   This shows the problem of the *puer aeternus* in a nutshell. He is too high up, and that was his attitude. He always wanted the cream of every experience. Furthermore, he was the Don Juan type and had been with any number of girls with whom he usually lived for about a fortnight or three weeks before walking out on them. As soon as things became a bit too personal and too binding or too committed, he just walked off. He did not know, or had not realized, that this was an unsatisfactory way of behaving; he thought everybody behaved like that, that that was the right way for a man to live. He was, in a way, completely innocent about this. The valleys in which people live, jammed together, but also rooted, held problems about which he knew nothing. For example, he had never dealt with the money problem. He got some money from his mother and lived on that somehow, very modestly, saving money and, for example, living in a tent. But he never thought of earning any himself, even though he was thirty-one. When I suggested that a sexual relationship with a woman might also be a human relationship with some feeling and some commitment in it, he stared at me in amazement, for such a thing had honestly never occurred to him. He did not like the idea, but he was quite innocent about it. This somewhat removed attitude would be the crest of the mountain; if you walk along the ridge, whichever way you go, you must go down — you cannot go higher for all sides lead down. This shows his situation very clearly, for he could either get stuck or in some way come down from his height, which is what I wrote to him. It is, however, very dangerous to have a dream analysis by correspondence with someone whom you do not know at all. I kept to vague generalities such as, "You are too high up. To go on like that will simply mean that somewhere, or somehow, you will have to go down," and I left it to him to make the practical application, for I did not know what possibilities he had.

463   We know that he was afraid of the night because, when he was lying awake in the dark, he often had the hallucination of a big, very strong, primitive type of man who stood near his bed and stared at him. He said he was like a boxer, and he would stand and stare steadily at him. This terrified him. It is obvious that the man

represented a split-off part of his masculinity. He did not look very feminine, but he was quite nervous and anxious and did not go in for any kind of sport. It was clear that this other man represented a part of instinctive masculinity which was lacking. This type of shadow is very common among *pueri aeterni*. Because of the mother complex, they are usually split off from the physical spontaneity of masculinity. In the case at hand, the shadow is relatively harmless, and I thought that the prospect was not too bad because such a type is not very dangerous, whereas a cruel gangster-type is a highly dangerous shadow.

464   It is this physical spontaneity that the animus of the mother likes to split off, for the mother who intends to keep, or destroy, her son, instinctively fights his masculine spontaneity. I once experienced an amazing illustration of this. A woman in my neighbourhood had a little boy of four to whom the parents gave a watering-can as a Christmas present. Because it was winter, he naturally could not use it, and when he was given the can, he was told not to use it in the sitting-room. The boy probably would not have thought of this, but now, of course, as soon as his mother was out, he took the can and sprinkled the carpet. His mother blew up, ranted and raved, beat the child terribly, making a fuss out of all proportion. I heard the noise and decided to interfere. The boy was screaming at the top of his lungs, and when I asked the mother what the matter was, she told me the story, and I could not help laughing. I told her that she had put the idea into his head, and that of course he could not wait until spring. She said, "Perhaps not, but this behavior must be stopped because otherwise, when he is sixteen, he will go out and kiss girls." That was literally her answer. The child had shown a little bit of spontaneity, of independence and disobedience — the wish to enjoy life and to do something on his own — and the mother realized that this was the little man in the boy, who must be crushed at once. Naturally, there is also the symbolism of the watering-can — the obvious one — which would later lead him into kissing girls in the dark at the age of sixteen. The mother's fantasy had already

anticipated that. She felt the little man standing up and being spontaneous — and she could not tolerate that.

465   There you see how the mother's animus pounces on these manifestations, such as coming in with dirty shoes, spitting, using bad language, or the phase that young boys go through of speaking of women in a belittling way, as though women were God-knows-what — despised because one is attracted to them. Such things are primitive — one could even say ape-like — manifestations of masculinity. A certain wildness is natural in a boy, a certain lack of adaptation, and while one must oppose such behavior to a certain extent, some of it should be allowed to live. Every mother who has a healthy instinct just shrugs her shoulders and says, "Oh well, boys are impossible," or something like that. But she leaves them alone and tries to ignore what they do, although she sometimes must swear a little bit. This mother, however, revealed exactly what the fantasy was about; she felt the germ of future independence in her little boy's action. That is why, when the mother has "eaten" the son, she has largely destroyed such physical manifestations of masculinity as being dirty, wild, aggressive. But such things strengthen the boy's feeling of being alive.

466   Probably in your youth, you have been to Bacchanalian, Dionysian festivals of wildness where you felt on top of the world and completely alive, when you felt you could conquer the whole world. This feeling of vitality is typical in a healthy young person. It makes one feel alive and enterprising, and that is what the devouring mother hates most. She hates it in the son because that is the impulse of life which will lead him away from her. He will forget her. This is why, in such a son, one usually finds this split-off shadow of a gorilla, or a big strong boxer, or a criminal, who represents the split-off masculinity, and compensates for the weakness of the ego.

467   In the dream, the shadow figure which turns up is double. Two men spring at the dreamer and wrestle with him. As I have pointed out before, when a figure appears in a dream in a double form, it generally means that it is approaching the threshold of consciousness. In this instance, it means something else, namely,

that the shadow has a double aspect: a dangerous and a positive one, a regressive and a progressive aspect, which, in this case, is only too obvious. The shadow figure could, for example, come into the life of the dreamer in the form of homosexual seduction; he could easily be seduced by a homosexual man of this type. Actually, as we shall find out later, he had a friend of that type, although nothing homosexual ever happened between them, but the fascination was quite tinged in this way. One could say, therefore, that this boxer-shadow is now doubly constellated in his unconscious: It is either something that can blend with him and, in that case, will add to his consciousness and strengthen his lacking masculinity, or it can remain outside and be projected, in which case he will probably become homosexual and run after this shadow in an outer projected form. Thus, this split-off content can either hurt him, or can get him into a wrong way of realizing it, or it can help him. From its behavior, one can also see how ambiguous this double shadow figure is: The two men throw him down the side of the mountain. If there had been no fir tree, he would have fallen to his death. If this kind of shadow suddenly attacks ego-consciousness, that is what is responsible for the sudden death, or the accidents, of the *puer aeternus* type. This shadow can save him or possibly destroy him. I have seen cases where the latter happened.

468   I remember the case of a young man who was completely eaten up by his mother and was half a girl. He was a kind of artist, and terribly unrealistic. When his parents died and he was left in a difficult financial situation, a very cynical, realistic type of cousin turned up and gave him the opportunity of joining in a scheme to cheat the insurance company. The young man had never worked before, had never faced reality, and was suddenly stranded. Then this criminal appeared and said that everybody behaved in this criminal way and that he should just sign the paper and he would get the insurance. He did so, without realizing the consequences of what he was doing, and he soon landed in prison. The cynical, realistic cousin had carefully arranged that *he* should not go to prison!

469   Another case where the shadow produced a sudden crash was also of a mother-bound boy who up until then, had been kept completely away from life under a plastic cover, got away from his home for the first time in his life and went to a big town. Having never had any kind of freedom, sexual or otherwise, and having always had to be so overcivilized at home, he ran completely wild for a time. He went to a group of young people with anarchistic inclinations who lived a very free life, and there he drank too much and had a different girl every night. He switched right over to the shadow side. There would have been nothing wrong in it if he had not done it in an exaggerated, nervous, hectic kind of way. I only met him once in my life and I saw that he was absolutely worn out, and that his health was completely run down. He looked at me mockingly, as if I were a kind of clucky aunt, and that was all the response I got. Three weeks later, he rang me up. He had caught polio and was lame for the rest of his life. I am sure that the fact that he was in such a poor state of health had added to the bad outcome of his illness. That is how the shadow hits the *puer aeternus* in practical life: He either crashes to his death in an airplane, or dies in a mountain accident, or in a car crash, or he lands in prison — in many instances, half innocently. Those are all examples of what falling down the mountain means or what it means to be thrown into the abyss. Thus, we see this shadow has a double aspect: It contains the necessary vitality and masculinity but, in addition to that, a possible destruction — something that might really destroy the conscious part.

470   The two shadow figures (he had no associations to them) fling him down. Thus, he has to go deeper, and that might be the right or the wrong thing for him. If he goes too far, it is wrong, and if, as here, some saving force comes along, it turns out well. In this dream, it becomes clear for the second time what I pointed out in my interpretation of *The Little Prince* material: In the *puer aeternus*, the material is very often double in some strange way; the healing and the destructive factors are close together, and it is possible to interpret almost everything on two levels. An optimist might say

that the *puer aeternus* is too high up and thank God the shadow seizes him and brings him lower. There is the tree, a symbol of growth, so what happens must be right. It appears to be unfortunate, but this ambiguous shadow forces the *puer* to come down from the heights. But the tree that breaks his fall embodies not only growth and life, but it can also mean death. In the state he was in when I saw him and when he had this dream, this man was in great mortal danger. He could have died at any moment, and therefore, I found the dream to be highly ambiguous, especially as the shadow figure was also of a double nature. Even if we cannot say how the crisis will end, we know that there is a lysis, a solution, in the dream: He does not fall down the whole slope of the mountain, which would probably have killed him, but that something stops him halfway — an isolated fir tree which stands just where he falls and in which he is caught.

471   There were several mother-cults in Asia Minor and Syria whose center was the mother-goddess Cybele. She was also later identified with the goddess Aphrodite. Her son, and in some versions her priest-lover, Attis, embodies the archetype of the eternal youth. When he became attracted to a nymph and was no longer interested in the mother-goddess, she drove him into madness out of jealousy, so that he castrated himself under a fir tree. According to other versions, he was also persecuted by the god of war, Ares, the lover of the mother-goddess Cybele/Aphrodite. We could say that it was the aggressive animus of the mother-goddess that killed or castrated the young god. In Rome, and in several towns in Asia Minor, there was a spring festival in which fir trees were carried through the streets. In the crown of the trees was an image of Attis, generally only his upper torso. There are also mythological versions according to which, after his death, he himself was changed into a fir tree. All this naturally belongs to the mythological cycle of the young dying son-god, and the mourning and the spring ceremonies connected with the cult of this god. The great problem here is the tree. Attis is suspended in the maternal tree. Christ, suspended in the tree of life, or of death, portrays the same idea. One could say that Attis

regressed into a prehuman form; he became a tree numen, the vegetative spirit in a tree. He has grown out of the tree; that is, his life comes only from his mother complex, or from his connectedness with the collective unconscious, and he has no living system in himself, but lives like a parasite from the tree. This is a very serious thing. There are cases of mother-bound young men where it is not advisable to try to detach them too much from their mother complex because they would die. You could say that they can only survive in that parasitic connection with the maternal tree. If you put them on the earth as an independent living system, a fruit of the tree, they cannot survive for they do not have the vitality to become an independent individual — which shows that one should approach such problems without prejudice. If such a man goes about with an elderly woman, many people say that he is just going about with his mother and should be thrown into life, and so on, but one should never be guided by such common-sense general opinions, because they are destructive. Instead, one should follow the dream and the unconscious material, for only that can show if the detachment from the maternal tree is possible. If it is not, one is just working for the death of that individual.

472   The suspended youth in the tree is an ambiguous figure. You can interpret the dream positively and say that the tree is a symbol of life, that it is something rooted, which grows, and has a place on the earth. Seen in this way, we can say that through the clash with the shadow, the young man is forced into being rooted, into having a place in life, and into beginning to grow or mature. But if you interpret it negatively, seeing the tree (the mother) as a coffin and therefore death, you can say that through the clash with the shadow, the young man is thrown back into the symbol of the death-mother and returns to the source of life, namely, into the mother — in this case, into death. The *puer aeternus*, is, in a way, the opposite of a tree, because he is a creature who inhabits lofty heights, and roams about. He always refuses to be in the present and to fight for his life in the here-and-now, which is why he avoids finding a relationship to a woman. A woman represents being tied to the earth, particularly if

she wants to have children. A family would permanently tie him to the earth. For the bird that flies about, the *puer*, a woman is the tree principle. In accepting this side of life, he accepts the just-so situation of life, which he is constantly trying to avoid. The tree shows clearly that being tied inevitably means losing one's freedom and the opportunity to roam about. The *puer aeternus* and the tree symbol belong together. The tree fixates the *puer*, fastens him to earth, either in a coffin or in life.

473   On the afternoon when I met the dreamer, he told me principally of his outer life, mostly in a superficial way, without any relationship to the unconscious. Then, in the middle of the conversation, he pointed out that when he was in a certain town of his home country, he had suddenly lost all his symptoms — his night-time fears, his border and police phobias and his fear of being imprisoned, and he had no longer masturbated. Then he looked at me very sadly and said that three weeks later, it had all started again — even worse than before. I said that we should look at those three weeks more closely, that it was always very interesting when someone temporarily lost their symptoms because it means that, for a short time, the person must have been in a situation where things were right, which was very important. I therefore asked him what he had been doing during that time. At first, he seemed to ascribe the beneficial influence to the town and its atmosphere. But then it came out that he had lived with a girl there, whom he had left after three weeks and had gone somewhere else. I asked him if that were not strange and if he had never made any connection between the fact that while he was with the girl all his symptoms had disappeared. Such a thought had never occurred to him. I asked him why he had left, but he said he had just gone. After further questioning, I got from him the following story, to which I referred previously.

474   He had known the girl since his boyhood. She was the daughter of a rich neighbor, and he had always admired her from afar. She was introverted and very unapproachable and respectable, and he had always looked upon her as the beautiful girl whom one admires and can never get. From his early twenties onward, he had been

friends with a very masculine type of man, a sculptor, who in a way resembled the man in his nightmare. The two were always in contact, and one evening in the sculptor's atelier, they began talking about this girl and whether it would be possible to seduce her. The sculptor, who was a Don Juan type, was quite sure that he could do it — one could get any woman if one only knew how to set about it! But the dreamer said in this case it would be impossible, and while they were a bit drunk, they had a bet on it. The dreamer then arranged a meeting at which he introduced her to the sculptor and helped the situation along a little bit. Somehow the poor girl got caught in the plot, and the sculptor succeeded in getting her for one night. The girl must somehow have felt unconsciously that she had stepped into an intrigue and that this episode had nothing to do with love, but was rather a cold, devilish plot. After that night she ran away terrified and completely avoided both men.

475   The young man got a terrific shock from the fact that the sculptor had succeeded with the girl, not only because he had lost his bet. He did not understand why he was so shocked and did not trouble to think much about it. He had no further contact with the girl until he met her again by chance in the town and spent three weeks with her. And that was the time when he lost his symptoms, which only returned after he had left the girl.

476   In our conversation, it became clear that it was he who wanted the girl, but that he did not have the courage or the virility to approach her himself, and so made his shadow friend do what he should have done. It was so much a projection that he had not realized that if his shadow friend succeeded in getting the girl, he himself got nothing out of it! He was so identified with the sculptor that, at the time of the bet, under the influence of drink, it had seemed as though he were to get the girl himself. Then, when the sculptor triumphantly showed the scalp, it dawned on him that he was "out of the picture," that the other fellow had won out and he had made the other live his split-off shadow. To me, that was the simple explanation of the shock. Then — again swimming along in his unconsciousness — he started once more with the girl and lost

his symptoms, but again did not wonder what that meant. The girl seemed to me to be a very important factor in his life, for with her he had once been happy in the normal way. But when I suggested this, he saw me as a matchmaker and a witch. I had, therefore, to retreat and to say that I did not want to push a relationship with her, but that I did think it would not be bad if he perhaps carried on the contact, or at least that he should try to think about the possibility of a relationship. But even this very careful kind of advice made him so mad that he left. He wrote telling me that it was the one part of our afternoon's conversation which finished me for him — apart from the fact that he had no money. He then sadly went back to his studio and thought that it had not been worthwhile seeing me and that he had wasted his money. But after a fortnight, he decided that perhaps there might be something in it after all, that he might write to the girl suggesting a meeting — nothing more. At that time, she lived in another town. He wrote in the evening but did not mail the letter, for he wanted to sleep on it. The next morning when he opened his own letters, there was a letter from the girl. She had never taken the initiative in any way. Thus, it struck him tremendously that he, the evening before, had made up his mind to write to her but had not mailed the letter, and then, that very morning, he had received a letter from her! Both made the same proposition in their letters — that they should meet once more, and as there was a national festival day during the next week, they should spend it together. The girl put it in practically the same words as those he had written. It was a typical synchronistic event. Of course, he knew nothing about synchronicity, but it had a very convincing effect on him. He thought then that perhaps I had not been quite so wrong. He forgave me and wrote to me, telling me all about it. If this synchronistic event had not taken place, he would never have resumed contact with me because what I had said had upset him so much.

477   They met up again on the day of the national holiday. They went on an excursion together during which the young man had a dream which, because of its significance, I would like to discuss at length in its own chapter.

Chapter Five
The Big Dream

478 These two young ones went on a summer's day bicycle trip. They stopped at the edge of a wood and lay down in the grass. He put his head in her lap and while lying in her arms, he had a little nap during which he had the following big, archetypal dream:

479 He was standing at the edge of a cliff. [He made a drawing in the letter, showing himself standing at the edge of the cliff looking down into the valley below — it is much the same as in the Grand Canyon with the plain on either side.] He looked down: There were white cliffs on both sides of the valley, but at the bottom of the valley were the heavens with the sky and the stars! He crawled down very slowly toward the valley, making movements with his legs as though he were bicycling in order to slow up the slow descent even further [he had bicycled quite a while before, so in part it is the continuation of a physical stimulus when he bicycles in his dream, but there is a deeper meaning] and to keep his balance. There is a certain amount of anguish, and he is a little afraid of what is happening, but he is still in control of the situation. He has the feeling that there is something near him but it is very blurred; it might be a dog. Suddenly, below, there is a sort of explosion, the welling up of an enormous outburst of light. The light spot expands and he has the feeling that he is absorbed in it, but he continues to fall down through the air. Then the scene changes; the whole thing disappears and below him he no longer sees the sky but rather a quadrangular pattern, similar to how a landscape looks from

480 an airplane, with the fields in rectangular patterns. There are no trees. Then there comes another shift and once again he finds himself in the same landscape as before. At the bottom of the valley is stagnant water. It is gray and dirty, and does not reflect. He wakes up and says to himself, "I am not afraid, but this water is a symbol of the mother and I don't want to fall into that. [He had had some Freudian analysis so he knew that he had an Oedipus complex, but his conception of it was only in a narrow Freudian sense of the word.] It is like ice at the bottom of the valley and it does not mirror." [He repeats that twice.] He is a bit afraid. Suddenly, this spark of light appears once again at the bottom of the valley. It is quite round, but the borders are a bit blurred. It explodes like a soap bubble, and in the spark, he sees a skull and thinks to himself, "How funny! What does death have to do with all of this? What does death mean here?" He is not terribly afraid but is still falling slowly at the same spot [which means that he is falling and not falling; it is a dream paradox]. Then the valley with the light disappears and is replaced by a floor covered with linoleum at the bottom of the valley. The linoleum is yellow with brown spots. [At first it was the sky with light stars, and now there is a yellow linoleum with brown spots on it.] The landscape has completely lost its gigantic proportions, and he asks himself what a piece of linoleum is doing at the bottom of the valley. [This is surrealistic.] He can see it all very clearly. He laughs a little about the idea of the linoleum.

481 In his letter, he then added that he did not like linoleum; he thought it cold and not aesthetic. It was very difficult to get his associations. Those he did not write voluntarily, I could not get, so I had to make do with what he gave in his rather superficial letters.

482 This dream contains in a nutshell the problem of the drama of the *puer aeternus* who must come down into life. A landscape in dreams, especially if it is worked out with so much detail and love

as in this case, can usually be said to be a soul-landscape, as can be seen in the paintings of the Romantic period in which the landscape takes on the atmospheric qualities of the painter's soul — a storm coming up or the peace of evening or a dark, threatening forest. These typical landscapes are attractive and mirror certain moods or convey a certain psychological situation. Therefore, where there is a worked-out description of a landscape in a dream, it can always be taken as a description of the psychic situation. Here again, the dreamer has come to the edge, to an end, as in the dream of the crest of the mountain. He can go no further along the way he is now going, which is why he alighted so briefly in my neighborhood — like a bird lighting on a tree and flying off again. He felt he had come to an end and could not go on as before. There is a very deep split in his psyche, but from a clinical viewpoint it is important to note that his is not a typical schizophrenic landscape. In the landscapes of schizophrenics, there are several splits: There will be canyons here and there, indicating that the earth of conscious reality is falling apart. These types that have only *one* split, I have often seen in compulsion neuroses, which are frequently diagnosed as being borderline between neurosis and psychosis. There you often find this kind of very deep split, but only one, and naturally that is more hopeful because there is only one problem to solve. In this case, you can say that there is one big problem behind his border-frontier phobia but that the whole structure is not dissolving.

483   I have not commented on the symbolism of this man's phobia because I thought it obvious: the policeman putting him in prison, and the frontier. When he must go over the border into another country, then he projects the idea that now he is going to fall into the hole in his psyche. The prison phobia is also obvious. He is like a bird — he never gets pinned down to earth; he never stays anywhere, neither with a girl, nor in his profession nor anywhere else. He does not even stay in the same town all the time but wanders around with his tent. Thus, the prison is the negative symbol of the mother complex (in which he sits all the time anyhow), or, seen prospectively, it would be exactly what he needs, for he needs to be

put into prison — into the prison of reality. Wherever he turns, prison threatens, and he is constantly on the run. At bottom, the only choice he has is which prison he will inhabit — that of his neurosis, or that of his reality. Thus, he is caught between the devil and the deep blue sea. That is his fate, and that is the fate of the *puer aeternus* altogether. It is up to him which prison he prefers: that of his mother complex and his neurosis, or the prison of being caught in the just-so story of earthly reality.

484   He comes into a situation where he is confronted with his inner split and he is slowly falling, and while doing so he makes bicycling movements with his legs to stop the rate at which he is falling. There might be some sexual implication in this, but there may also be a physical stimulus because he was cycling beforehand for several hours. It is positive that he does not stop moving. He does not just passively sink into the situation, rather he maintains a certain amount of movement, and, in that way, his fall is slowed down. This is very important, for when someone falls into an inner split — a depression or an inner accident, so to speak — if the ego complex can keep a certain amount of activity, can keep moving, the danger is less. This is often done instinctively by people when they are going off into a psychotic episode. One of the last attempts to save themselves — I have seen it in several cases — is that they feverishly try to write down all their fantasies. They write day and night and keep on and on until they snap. It seems rather crazy, but it is really a last attempt to keep a certain amount of initiative, to keep going with the ego complex and to do something about the flood of unconscious material by separating it and putting it down on paper. The ego complex is drowning, but still has an instinctive need to struggle and keep moving. If one can encourage that, it is sometimes possible to bridge the dangerous moment. If the ego keeps a certain amount of initiative, it does not just sink completely and inertly into the unconscious. If we liken this with the actual situation, the very fact that this man went on a bicycle trip with the girl was such a movement. Instead of waiting till his bad fate caught up with him, for once he met the relationship half-way and showed some

enterprise by establishing contact with the girl on a feeling level, which was exactly the movement that kept him from falling completely into his split. We have noticed that throughout the entire dream, he keeps on repeating that he is not afraid, or that he is only a little bit afraid. Such insistence always means that people are afraid. The very fact that he must keep asserting that he is not afraid shows his tremendous fear of falling into the split, but, with a kind of autosuggestion, he tries to keep his head.

485   This is a great improvement on the other dream in which he was thrown down into the gorge by the shadow and was saved by sheer chance. This time, he keeps a certain amount of movement himself, and that slows the fall. We see here how important it is not to push a man caught in this kind of constellation too abruptly into reality, because that might constellate being thrown down by the shadow. It is as if an airplane, too high up, were running out of fuel, and had to land slowly to avoid a crash. That is the great difficulty in dealing with such cases: on the one hand, helping them to approach reality and, on the other, not pushing them too much because there is the danger of crashing. The dream shows it very delicately, how one can fall slowly, like a parachutist, but also shows that this man has such a severe split that he needs very careful handling.

486   We have already seen examples of what a "crash-landing" looks like in reality with the above-mentioned examples of the young man who fell ill with polio, or of the other young man who landed in prison after being persuaded to cheat an insurance company. It can also happen completely inwardly, not visibly and physically outside. Then, instead of being a brilliant *puer*, such a man suddenly becomes a cynical, disappointed old man. The brilliance has turned into a cynical disappointment and the man appears to be too old for his age; he has neither belief nor interest in anything any longer. He is absolutely and thoroughly disillusioned and thereby loses all creativeness and *élan vital*, all contact with the spirit. Then money, ambition, and the struggle with colleagues become paramount, and everything else disappears with the romanticism of youth. There is

very often an embittered expression on the face of such a man. The following case is a clear illustration of this problem.

487   A very romantic young man of the Don Juan type, with a positive mother complex, married and built up a profession. Unfortunately, taking his wife and children with him, he decided to go back to the town where his parents lived. Naturally, there were the usual quarrels between his wife and parents-in-law. The man had a good sexual relationship with his wife but not much human contact with her, and he did not really know her. He also had tremendous illusions about his own mother, whom he had idealized, because of his positive mother complex, just as he idealized his wife. When the two women started fighting, he could not help but be very disappointed by the way in which the quarreling women behaved. It involved lies and slander and outbursts of affect, with both taking him aside and telling him poisonous things about the other — the usual weapons which women use in such situations. He fell literally out of the clouds and resigned himself to the situation. He drowned himself in work and just tried to ignore the fighting cats who made his life a hell. Instead of shouting at one or the other from time to time, he did not take a stand. When I met him again, I was absolutely shocked at the change in him. He was a disappointed, pale-faced old man with a bitter expression. I asked him how his work was, and he said it was going well and that he had a lot to do, and then the whole story came to light. He had not admitted his disappointment to himself; instead, he thought that that was just life and that he had dealt with the situation quite well, but he had not realized the shock to his feelings. Then he told me the following archetypal dream:

488   He came into a strange town where there was a prince who had loved a beautiful woman, but she had become a film-star and left him, and he was now engaged to a second woman. It was doubtful, however, whether he loved her as much; it looked as if he still loved the film-star, to whom he had given, as a kind of farewell present, a jewel he had had made for her — a huge diamond in the form of a tear. Then suddenly the

dreamer was standing in the street of this strange town, and he saw the prince walking away with the second woman. He had his arm around her. A lot of cars were racing by, and the dreamer thought the couple would be run over, but they succeeded in crossing the street, and then they went into a rather slummy part of the town, into a dark backyard. Dark men jumped out of a nearby building, intending to attack the prince. But there came a shift in the story, and the dreamer himself was lying sprawled on the pavement, knocked out but not dead, wondering if the attackers were still around or whether help would come.

489 In this dream we see that the prince is the archetype of the *puer aeternus* with whom the dreamer is no longer identified. This man has fallen out of identification with the prince and is no longer a *puer aeternus*; the prince is now an autonomous figure within him. Ten years earlier, he had been a prince himself, a typical *puer aeternus*, but now he has come into reality. He has dis-identified with that archetype which nevertheless is still alive in his psyche, independent from his ego. When the ego has dis-identified, then the figure which before was a mixture of the infantile shadow and the Self becomes a symbol purely of the Self. The association he gave me was that the prince had loved a beautiful woman who had now become an American film-star and gone completely into cheap extraversion. This is a normal development where one part of the anima seduces the man into life — that was the part which had seduced him into marriage, into a career, and into getting involved with life, founding a family, finding a big flat, and so on. A part of his will to live had been fascinated into life. That was all right, but it left out the romantic prince within him, who could not follow into this part of life. The prince, then, chose another woman as his fiancée, which would mean that now another part of the anima — probably not the exogamous but the endogamous aspect — is linking itself with the Self.

490   Often, in the development of the anima, youths have a girlfriend they admire but cannot marry because they are not yet of an age to do so, and later they marry another type. Then, perhaps between forty and fifty, this admired anima-imago frequently turns up again and generally plays the symbolic inner role of being the one who leads to the Self. This aspect of the anima takes on the role of Dante's Beatrice, namely, that of the leader into the inner person, while the other part of the anima which gets projected onto a real woman is what seduces the man into marriage and into life. Thus, we can say that there is an aspect of the exogamous anima that leads into involvement with outer life, while the endogamous aspect of the same image remains within and later becomes the guide toward the realization of the inner life. The new fiancée of this disappointed man would be this endogamous aspect of the anima, but she is nondescript, not yet defined, and he has not yet grasped what she means.

491   The prince gives a diamond in the form of a tear to the film-star, who is leaving which clearly expresses his sorrow at her departure and alludes to the fact that he still values her highly and is tragically upset by her departure. Probably he would still cling to her if she had not left. Although this man had an expression of deep sadness and bitter disappointment, he had not realized how profoundly he was hit by the disappointment in his past life, how much he felt betrayed by the fact that he was now involved in the human, all too human, ordinary life on this planet. The prince in him was, in a way, still longing for that lost *élan vital* that had seduced him into life and had now faded. When he connects with this new form of the anima, who is devoted to inner development, he is nearly run over by a lot of cars when he crosses the street.

492   When a man turns to the inner life, the pace of outer life works against him. It demands that having started a family, he should go on building up a career, earn more money and a better position, and strive to become the boss and super-boss. Here, however, the dreamer in the middle of life ought to give that up and turn to another sphere of life. He is not supported in this but is threatened

by the speed and demands of outer life. The dreamer was in a situation where he was completely overworked. He was very successful, and it was hard for him to see that despite his great success in outer life, he had the face of an embittered old man.

493   The prince is not destroyed by the mechanical speed (that is, the dreamer's occupation, indicated by the traffic in the dream), but rather he has the courage to go into the darkness of a city backyard, which means into his inferiority and human misery, to the inferior function — to poverty and dirt, where dogs eat out of dustbins, cats mate, women gossip, and so on. The backyard represents the hidden life of the big city — a beautiful image of the neglected unconscious, and for the neglected inferior part of the soul. As in a fairytale, the prince must now enter the darkness of this aspect of life, and in this moment the gangster-shadow attacks the archetypal prince. The gangster personifies a danger in the dreamer's psyche, namely, to throw away his secret longing for a meaningful life. He had already begun to do so. His cynicism is now attacking his inner prince and he is in danger of giving up the search for an inner ideal or truth, or for what he once had felt was the aim and meaning of his life. And then, suddenly, he is in the situation of the prince himself and lies helplessly on the ground. I told him then that he was completely flattened, awfully "down," depressed. He could not answer for five minutes, he was so surprised by the idea that he was depressed. I said, "Well, you are lying on the ground, just knocked down by the situation and don't know what to do. You feel helpless and you had better realize it because then you might do something about it. You might get up and call for help or find people who would pick you up, or something like that." This clicked with him at once. The dream really wanted him to realize that nothing could happen until he saw how deeply disappointed and depressed he was by the way his life had developed.

494   That is a typical situation and *the* crisis in the middle of a *puer aeternus's* life who has successfully moved out of his *puer* neurosis but is now confronted by a second difficulty. It is always like that, for once you have solved a problem, and feel the problem is, indeed,

solved, just wait. The next one is just around the corner! This man had managed to pull himself out of the mud of a *puer's* life for only two years when the wheel was turned again by the unconscious. Once again, he had to reevaluate the whole thing and do just the opposite. He was very angry when he heard this interpretation, but it clicked. Here we see the danger of crashing, of falling down: If you have succeeded in falling down, you are not at the end of the story; you must just get up again. Falling down is only one rhythm in life. The glorious spark of genius is like a star falling from heaven into the mud. But then it must once again rise out of the mud.

495   Now we come to the abnormal theme of the other dream, to the theme of the stars below. It is concerned with an old image of the earth being flat instead of a sphere. At one time, it was supposed that the earth was like a pancake, or something shaped like that, and when there was a split in it, you could see the stars below. From the dream we can draw one conclusion, namely that the dreamer had a flat world, that his reality was not round but flat, which was true. There were no dimensions and no polarities in his psyche, as can be seen by the way in which he walked into and out of situations and into and away from relationships with women, never wanting to waste a thought on them. Naturally his life lacked any kind of conflict or polarity and was just flat.

496   The dreamer looked down into the valley below and saw that much had been transformed there, but what he first noticed was the stars. His field of consciousness is like thin ice over the abyss of the collective unconscious. He has not yet built up any solid reality of his own. You could also call it the picture of his ego-weakness. In the middle of this flat world there is this huge split, and he sees the stars below, as if you could see through the firmament to what was below.

497   There is a famous alchemical dictum which says,

> Heaven above,
> *Heaven below,*
> Stars above,

Stars below.
All that is above
Is also below.
Grasp this
And rejoice.[1]

498   I was at once reminded of this saying, whose origin we do not know, and about which we only know that it comes from an ancient Hermetic manuscript. In general, the stars can be interpreted as the archetypes of the collective unconscious, as nuclei in the dark sky of the psyche. We see them as luminosities, as single lights, and usually they are interpreted as gods or archetypal contents. For instance, the Lord of Sabaoth is the Lord of the Heavenly Army because it was thought that the stars were his army, the soldiers of God, and that God led this heavenly army. Then there is the theory of the stars as the individual gods. The order in which they are constellated would then represent the secret order of the contents of the collective unconscious. In mythology, there are also the motifs of the many eyes or the many stars. The dragon Argos, for example, is covered with eyes, and it is also sometimes projected onto the sky.

499   The Zodiac was thought of as a huge snake, a kind of Uroboros biting its own tail, and it, too, was represented as being covered with stars. In a Gnostic treatise, the oldest representation of the Uroboros is that of a snake eating its own tail, with its head speckled with stars while the rest is black. This illustrates the double nature of the unconscious totality with its dark, nefarious aspect and its light aspect characterized by the stars. The same representation is to be found in the alchemical treatise of the so-called *Codex Marcianus*[2], in which there are drawings that characterize the "whole in one." The tail of the Uroboros is the material and dangerous end and is very often the seat of the poison (quite in contrast to a real snake). The head part is the light, spiritual aspect. This image was projected onto the sky because the Uroboros always appeared at the borders

---

[1] Ruska, *Tabula Smaragdina*, 217; cf. also Jung, *Practice of Psychotherapy*, vol. 16, *CW*, § 384.
[2] Berthelot, "Codex Marcianus."

of human knowledge. In antiquity, for instance, it was believed that the ball of the sky was this huge Uroboros snake upon which the signs of the Zodiac constellated. In the flat form of the world, the ocean circled the earth in the form of a round snake biting its own tail. In the old maps, the Uroboros stood for the outermost circle. Whenever man reached the end of his field of consciousness, he projected this type of snake. Whenever man came to the point where he could say that he did not know what was beyond, there would be the picture of the snake with the stars on it. Thus, we see how much the star motif has to do with unconsciousness, especially with the collective unconscious.

500   If we look at this above cited saying naively, we see that it must have to do with a double aspect of the collective unconscious which is above and below us, as though it surrounds us in two forms. When interpreting dreams and mythological material, people again and again make the mistake of identifying what is above with consciousness and what is below with the unconscious, the *Unterbewusstsein* — that which is below consciousness — implying that consciousness is what is above. If one goes downstairs in a dream, that is taken as going into the unconscious, and going upstairs is going into consciousness. But that is a superficial and wrong way of seeing things. If you look at the mythological maps of the world, you see that above there is a realm that is made up of the mysterious, of what is unattainable for human beings, where the gods live. In Sumer and Babylon, there is a myth about a man who tries to fly up to heaven with the eagles, but he is incapable of transcending a certain barrier above and is turned back by the gods and falls down. He encounters the same difficulties and obstacles in going to the gods below. If we are objective, we must admit that there is a field of the unconscious both above and below us. This same duality applies to the symbolism of the house: The cellar often represents the unconscious in some form, the area of the drives and instincts. There are innumerable dreams in which coal and fire are in the cellar, or awful animals or burglars. But the same things can happen in the attic. A crazy person, overwhelmed by the unconscious, has, for example, "bats in

the belfry" or "mice in the attic." Ghosts usually rattle their chains in the attic and walk about over our heads. Up in the attic, then, where it is dark and full of cobwebs and we are a bit crazy, there is just as much a realm of unconsciousness as in the cellar. People frequently dream of thieves getting in from the roof, or of demons sitting up there and taking tiles off the roof.

501   We must therefore look at the above and the below from a different standpoint and see if there is any kind of qualitative difference between representations of the unconscious powers above and the unconscious powers below. There are exceptions, but it can be said that in general the above is associated with what is masculine — ordered, light and sometimes spiritual — and the below with the feminine — fertile, dark (not evil; there are no moral designations in the original mythological counter-positions), chaotic, and the realm of the animals. The sphere above relates to birds and angels — with winged beings of the spiritual world. If in a dream something comes from below, we might expect something to come up in the form of, for instance, an emotion or a physical symptom, such as sleeplessness, or some affective disturbance of the sympathetic nervous system. It often also comes in the form of synchronistic occurrences, but then it materializes in the outer world. If an invasion from the unconscious comes from above, it can take the form of an enthusiasm: for Communism or Nazism. Such an "above" unconsciousness erupts into the system in the form of an archetypal idea. If it is characterized as positive, then it can be said to be the Holy Ghost; if it is considered negative, then there are the winged demons, bats in the belfry, and other pernicious winged creatures — that is, destructive ideas. Whether constructive or destructive, such ideas have a strong collective energy of their own. Dynamic representations belong to the "above" aspect of the unconscious, while emotional, instinctive representations belong to its "below" aspect.

502   Egyptian mythology is an exception to this formulation because certain aspects are inverted in it. Thus, as far as sexual symbolism is concerned, the heavens above are feminine and the earth below is

masculine. This probably has to do with the Egyptian concept of life being inverted: The main value was placed on life after death, while little value was placed on life in this world. The amazing pyramids were, for example, built in connection with life after death, but until the very end of the Syncretistic Period, except for the king's palace, there were no decent houses for the living. To the Egyptians, ideas were concrete and real, while actual life forms were abstract, and therefore masculine. Studying Egyptian religion, one is struck by what could be called the concretism of ideas. The idea of immortality, for example, had to be realized by the chemical treatment of the corpse. We consider immortality to be symbolic, but to the Egyptians it was not (as in very primitive magic), and the preparation of the mummy was meant to establish immortality. This shows the concreteness of the idea. To the ancient Egyptian, the earth was masculine; spirit and ideas were concrete. While these conceptions were specific to Egypt, there are traces of this reversed constellation in other civilizations. Therefore, whenever above and below appear, we must think in a qualitative way and study the context carefully, and not simply identify what is above with consciousness and what is below with the unconscious.

503   In his paper "On the Nature of the Psyche,"[3] Jung compares the psyche to a color spectrum, with the infrared at one end and the ultraviolet at the other. He uses this simile to explain the connection between body and psyche — the instincts and the archetypes. Our consciousness is like a ray of light with a nucleus in it to represent the ego, a kind of field of light that can shift along the spectrum. The infrared end would be where things become psychosomatic and finally end in physical reactions. At this end of the spectrum the psyche is somewhat connected (we do not yet know exactly how) with physical processes, so that its activity loses itself in physical processes of some kind: initially psychosomatically and then somatically. This would be the end representing the body. At the other end, the ultraviolet end, would be the archetypes. From within, but also from without, we only know what the body is to a certain

---

[3] Jung, "On the Nature of the Psyche," vol. 8, *CW*, § 414.

extent. Here there is a big question: the mystery of the living organism. At the ultraviolet end is the mystery of that same thing expressed in the representations, realized as ideas, emotions, fantasies, and so on, of which this end is the source. The origin of dynamic fantasies and ideas that come up in our psyche is unknown, but we ascribe such fantasies to the activity of the archetypes. Probably these two poles are in some way connected. Although we do not know how, these may be two aspects of the same reality. At one end is the body, while at the other end are the ideas and representations that suddenly seize upon the human mind. Our consciousness generally shifts between the two poles. We know that somatic processes and physical behavior are directed by the instincts, namely, the sexual instinct, with its play of hormones in the body and its physical aspects; the instinct of self-defense with its automatic fighting gestures; the instinct to flee, a part of the instinct of self-preservation, which takes over automatically in certain life situations without any thought on the part of the subject, as when we run away from danger or the reflex action of withdrawal on contacting a burning object — an automatism of the body that we could call instinct. The difference between instinct and archetype is the following: Instinct is represented by physical behavior, similar in all human beings, while archetypes are represented by a mental form of realization, similar in all human beings, i.e., *homo sapiens* mate in the same way throughout the world; they die more or less the same way; they stand erect and flee. But there are certain patterns of behavior that characterize us as different from other animals. *Homo sapiens* also tend to have emotions of the same kind, ideas of the same kind, religious reactions of the same kind, seen best in the mythological motifs which are similar all over the world. So, at the one end are the instincts and at the other the corresponding inner experiences.

504   Jung does not assert it with certainty, but he says he has not yet met an archetypal constellation that does not have a corresponding instinct. Thus, one can say that every archetype has a corresponding instinctual counterpart. Take the archetype of the *coniunctio*, for

example, which appears in all the myths of the origin of the world, and in some form in most religions of the world. It is concerned with the mating of a male god and a female goddess and the creation of the world, or being together in an eternal embrace, such as Shiva and Shakti. The *coniunctio* appears in the mystical experience of the union of the soul with God in a feminine or masculine form. The corresponding physical instinct would be the sexual instinct. Self-preservation in the form of fighting relates to the archetypal idea of the shadow or the enemy, the dangerous counterpart, the figure which appears in dreams as the attacker or the person from whom one runs. On the physical side, that would be represented by the instinct to fight, or to flee, which is physically inborn in us.

505   As we have not yet met with any exceptions, it would seem that every archetypal content has a counterpart in some form of instinct. According to this way of looking at things, instincts are what we see from the outside, while representations — ideas and dream fantasies and images — are what we observe from within. If we observe the human being from the outside (we can photograph him in all his actions) then we get the infrared aspect. This is what is commonly done nowadays in anthropology, and in anthropological papers, for the focus is upon what the human being does in contrast to other animals; how it mates, builds its abode, fights and survives, and so on. These authors try to describe humans objectively, as though we were just one species of animal, as compared with elephants, tigers and other creatures. In this way, one obtains a scientific photograph of physical, instinctual human behavior which is correct. But if one follows up the same thing from within, which is what we do as psychologists, we observe what wells up in the human being: ideas and representations. Thus, we have an anatomy of the human being photographed from within, an introspective picture of man, by which we discover the realm of the archetypes. In an unknown way, the two are probably one — the same reality observed from outside and from within. If we now adopt the idea presented in mythology of human consciousness and the unconscious as being between two poles — the heavenly pole above and the underworld pole below —

we might compare this to the scientific model of the psyche and call the infrared end of the spectrum the "heavens below" and the ultraviolet end the "heavens above."

506　　Our dreamer is in the middle field of consciousness. Through the break, he can see the heavens below, and the movement of the dream is to make him sink down into that. One should also remember how the little prince had to come down onto the earth, investigating, or rather rejecting, certain qualities on his way down. Usually, the *puer aeternus* is too caught up in the realm of archetypal representation. Through his mother complex he is generally possessed by it. This means that he underestimates the "lower" experiences, the infrared realm. It is quite a different thing if I think about a steak or if I eat it: The thought of the steak and *sauce béarnaise* can be delightful, but if I eat it, I will have still other experiences. The same is true for the archetype of the *coniunctio*. It is certainly one thing to fantasize about a love affair and try to imagine every detail of the experience, but the actual living experience is different.

507　　The *puer* generally tends to avoid the immediate friction of reality. He does not go into the heavens below, which he under-estimates, and neither does he go into the instinctual realization of life. That is why the little prince meets the fox on earth and needs the sheep, but, as we know, in that case the realization of the heavens below did not work out. This is a generalization, however, and the *puer* does sometimes live a certain amount of instinctual life, but he blocks off, as it were, the psychological realization. He makes a cut and lives his experience automatically — as a split-off shadow affair. In that form, his archetypal fascination with the idea of the great love and the *coniunctio* remains a wishful fantasy: One day he will meet the woman who will bring perfect love, perfect warmth, perfect harmony, a lasting relationship, and so on — clearly a mother-image illusion. In the meantime, he does not abstain from sexual contacts for that would frustrate him too much, so he has twenty or thirty affairs with women, as in this case, but he does not let himself be affected by them. He does not completely undergo the experience.

We could say of such people that they are innocent, in the wrong kind of way, as though they had not lived at all, because they live it without being in it. They make a mental reservation, saying to themselves that this isn't *it*, but that in the meantime they need a woman. Then they have the physical union, but it does not count mentally or in the inner aspect of fantasy, in the feeling of the man himself. If it is not taken seriously, if one does not let the impact of the experience touch the psyche, then it is as though it had not been lived.

508   I once analyzed a prostitute who looked exactly like an old maid. Her dreams always showed untouched little girls or women who had never had any sexual experience, and this was completely true. She shut herself off from what she lived. She just wanted the money: she did not identify with her job: she neither admitted to herself the pleasure of certain contacts not her disgust over others. She made a rational decision that she needed the dollars and said to hell with the rest of it. Thus, in a way, she was untouched by life. Although she had rather severe psychic symptoms, she was not miserable. One of the results of the analysis was that she suddenly realized her own miserable condition, which had not been the case previously. It had all been carried on by intellectual decision. She had never admitted that certain men disgusted her while others attracted her, for that would have disturbed business. Therefore, although she was really a very emotional woman, she did not allow herself to have the emotional experience of what was happening, for if she had done so, she would have earned less money by refusing certain men.

509   The same thing happens sometimes with the *puer aeternus* who, although he lives the instinctual side, he does so in a cut-off way: He makes an artificial emotional barrier by separating what he is living from his real self. In such a case, the stars below are not seen. This is why the alchemical saying says: "Grasp this [stars above, stars below] and rejoice." Life is incomplete if you live it in its fantasy aspect; it must be lived through on the instinctual level. But that means really accepting it, letting yourself be moved by the experience and not limiting it by living it in a conditional way. To

have a mental reservation about life means that it is not lived at all, and that is why the *puer aeternus* is sometimes cut off from the stars below. And this is why the solution for the dreamer is that he should sink into that world.

510   Often people who are regarded as *pueri aeterni* by their associates are very much envied for being able to throw themselves into life with great vigor so that they appear to be living successful lives. We could say that was the shadow and that we know that they are really cut off. But how do they achieve this appearance of so vigorous a life? They can act! Many people are actors, and to act something simply means to play a part. As far as I have come to know them, these people play a part, even to themselves, to convince themselves that they are living, until they land in analysis and must confess that this is not the case and that they are not happy. Others may consider them successful, but they themselves do not feel so. The criterion is simple: Do you feel that you are living? Those who do not feel alive describe it as being as though they were acting, even for themselves. People fall for that unless they know some psychology and look at the eyes to see the real expression. Then one can tell that something is wrong, even though such people seem to be so successful.

511   If one were fixed at the ultraviolet end, then I suppose one would find this archetypal pole too beautiful to seriously allow oneself to experience the infrared opposite pole, and even if one were to have nineteen experiences, they would all be sordid and miserable because one would always be looking for the ultraviolet. We could say that if you live one end in a split-off way, then one end cannot communicate with the other. Put quite simply, you have the experience, but it is not meaningful, and an experience which one does not feel to be meaningful is nothing. It only becomes real when it relates to an emotional perception of meaning. Without that, one is just bored. I knew one man who had a lot of affairs, but he was so much not in it that in the middle of the sex act, he would look at his watch to see how much time he had left. It clearly meant nothing to him, or else it was purely narcissistic, for all he experienced was his role as a man.

512   Any woman who would go into a relationship with such a man generally makes the same cut with her animus. The prostitute, for example, had the idea that if she tried to earn her living as an office-worker, she would have to be at the office from 9 a.m. till 6 p.m. for weeks and weeks on end and would never be able to do anything else. As she was a very undisciplined and childish person, that was unacceptable to her. Her animus said that that would go on forever, which is the most common thing the animus tells a woman. She could just as well have started an office job and found a boyfriend all the same, but her animus logic was that if she worked in an office, she would have to submit to discipline — which she hated — and never have a love affair. Why one excluded the other one does not know, but her animus thought so. And then, at fifty, she would be an ugly old woman still typing in an office! She wanted to live and did not want an office life, but because she needed money for food and could not afford to live freely with a lot of men whom she may have chosen, her animus said that she should combine the two things and to hell with her moral prejudices. One could say that she just resigned herself to it because she had no faith in the irrational. She had landed in New York as an immigrant, and when she saw that immense city, she felt she would be lost in it. She had no faith either in herself or in life, not in her own personality and not in God. Thus, she mapped it all out and thought that being a prostitute was the thing to do. In the case of a woman, it is the animus who engineers things, and he is always a professional pessimist who excludes the *tertium quod non datur* — the third party.[4] The animus says to the woman that he knows there are only so many possibilities. He says the thing can only go in such and such a way, thereby blocking off any possibility of life itself producing something new.

513   A woman who had a good relation to her instincts would not fall for such a man. Or she might start a relationship on this unreal level, but then she would try to pull the man into a definite or meaningful relationship. I have an illustration of this, though it does not quite fit because in this case the man took the initiative. It is the case of a

---

[4] Jung, *Archetypes and the Collective Unconscious*, vol. 9/I, *CW*, §§ 285 ff.

woman who had many affairs which she ran in accordance with her animus decisions. But then she met a man who really loved her and whose instincts were sounder than had been the case with the other men she had been involved with. He was very sensitive and felt that very often she went to bed with him without being inwardly present herself, or in tune with him on a feeling level. He felt the autonomy of her sexuality and revolted against it. He got nasty with her because it hurt him. He said that was how she was with all her other lovers — of whom he was jealous, feeling himself to be just one of them. He knew nothing about psychology, so he was rather clumsy. He became nasty, calling her a "cheap" woman, and such things, which was not just, for she was not that at all, but her feeling had been cut off. But through his strong, emotional, and instinctual reactions, and the fact that he was a mature man who had had much experience and had great physical self-control, he was able to help her to get her feeling back — naturally a very difficult task. Usually, the man is sexually so impulsive that he cannot hold himself back, but this man said that he would not go on unless they were on the same feeling level. She had a dream that there was a dirty, poisonous, muddy hole in the ground into which he dived and brought up a golden key to her. I think we can say that he really rescued her feeling because he loved her as an individual and did not just make use of her. He wanted her as a whole person with her feeling and he resented it when that did not function. Through his resentment and after a lot of quarreling and trouble, he brought up her feeling personality.

514   One can naturally go on discussing and expanding this problem endlessly because it is really the key to the whole dream. A Russian fairy tale, "The Maiden Tsar,"[5] illustrates this:

515   At a dinner party, the Tsar says that none of his sons had yet picked his flowers. His sons ask for his blessing and set out on the search. Each takes a horse from the stable and sets forth. All three come to a signpost which says, 'He who goes to the right will have enough to eat, but his horse will be

[5] Löwis of Menar, *Russische Volksmärchen.*

hungry; he who goes to the left will have enough for his horse but will himself remain hungry; and the one who goes straight ahead will die.' The first brother would be robbed of the instinctual experience and therefore his horse would be hungry. The son who goes that way finds a copper snake on a mountain. When he brings it home, his father is furious and says he has brought back something dangerous and demonic and puts him in prison; that is, he only finds a kind of petrified life and falls back into the prison of the traditional spirit, that is, the father. The next son goes to the left and finds a whore who has a mechanical bed to which she invites him. Jumping out of it herself, she presses a button and the bed turns over and he falls into the cellar where there are a lot of other men – all waiting in the dark. That's the fate of the one who goes to the left! Then comes the Great Ivan, the hero of Russian fairy tales. When he gets to the signpost, he begins to cry and says that a poor fellow who has to go to his death will find neither honour nor glory, but he gives his horse the whip and goes ahead. Then his horse dies and comes to life again, and he finds the witch and conquers her. He then finds the princess and returns home and becomes the Tsar.

516   He has a normal, successful, fairytale career: The hero chooses to remain in the conflict, which seems death to the ego, for ego-consciousness wants to know what is ahead. If this woman who arrived in New York had had the strength and the psychological courage to accept the fact that she faced nothing but misery whatever she did, and that she could not see a glimmer of light or life ahead, if she could have faced moral death and still have remained herself, then the path of individuation would have begun. But she could not, and in her case, she chose the path to the left. Others choose the path to the right.

517   It can therefore be said that human consciousness must always be crucified between the pull of the two poles: If you fall into either one, you die. Life, in its essence, means crucifixion. To the rational

ego, it seems to be death, and that is what this Russian motif expresses in a most beautiful and clear form. The third son chose what seemed to his ego to be the road to death, but, in fact, as the story says, he chose the road of life. The others, who wanted to be clever and chose the relatively lesser evil — one, the way on the right, and the other, the way on the left — had not the nervous strength or the guts to face the unknown. The most difficult thing for a human being to do is, apparently, to face the unknown — to not know in advance what is coming and yet be able to keep steady in the dark. Man's most ancient fear and cause of panic seems always to have been the unknown.

518   The first time a primitive sees an airplane or a car, he runs away, for everything unknown is inevitably terrible! That is the old pattern. It is the same thing in analysis. When people are confronted with a situation where they cannot, by their own inner reason, see what is coming, they panic. That is painful, but it would not matter so much, if then they did not rashly come to some decision — to turn to the left or the right — and thereby fall into the unconscious because they have not been able to stand the tension of not knowing what is ahead.

519   If the *puer* were to go too much to the right or left, it would not be so bad because sometimes one must first find the copper snake or land in the cellar to find out only afterward that it would be better to go on the road that leads to death. But the *puer* does something much worse: He risks neither way completely but ventures a little both ways to be on the safe side. He bets on the one horse but puts a little on the other too, and that is self-destructive. That is worse than going too much one way, for any excessive action will be punished and one must wake up and pull out of it. The natural interplay of psychological opposites corrects any one-sidedness. Life forces one onto the middle path. But in order to avoid suffering, the *puer* plays a dirty trick which boomerangs back onto him: He splits himself by throwing a sop to the dragon but remains on the other side inwardly and has illusions about himself. Thus, he arrests the process of life and gets stuck, for he thwarts the interplay of the

opposites. His weak personality that wants to escape suffering tricks him into it.

520   As the match-making witch that the young man considered me to be, I had tried to push him into taking up a relationship with a woman whom he had already had his Don Juan affair with and cast aside. But when, after he had planned and written his letter saying that he wanted to see her again, this synchronistic event took place: She wrote a letter similar to his own, which he had not mailed, and then, for the first time he got a whiff of meaningfulness with this woman. After this strange synchronistic event, he could not avoid naively thinking that this woman must stand for something beyond what had already passed between them, and that the relationship must have some meaning. Thus, for the first time, he accepted something unknown. The doubt which I cast into his mind would not have helped without the synchronistic event. But now his attitude toward life was touched by an experience which seemed marvelous and mysterious. He therefore went on the bicycle ride with a different attitude, without knowing everything ahead of time. For the first time, he was puzzled about a relationship — we saw what the unconscious produced when he slept in her arms. It was as though the heavens below — the meaningfulness of such sexual experience — dawned on him, which explains why, while making the motions of riding a bicycle, he fell slowly into the heavens below.

521   The next theme in the dream is the explosion of light in the heavens below, which would mean a sudden realization and an illumination from below. It is a very interesting motif if we compare it with the experience of medieval mystics, who most often spoke of a light that came from above. Here it is the light experienced from below, which comes from accepting the unknown side of life and the unknown unconscious. We might say with the alchemists, "Heaven above, Heaven below." It is the same light, but it comes from the midnight sun and not the sun above. When Apuleius was initiated into the Isis mysteries, he described how he was illumined not by the heavenly sun, but by the midnight sun which he met face to face when he descended into the underworld, to the gods below.

This would mean an experience which cannot be reached by intellectual effort, or exercises in concentration, or yoga, or the *exercitia spiritualia*; rather, it is an experience of the self that one can only have by accepting the unconscious and the unknown in life, and by living with the difficulty of one's own inner conflict. When the dreamer gets further down, suddenly the heavens below solidify and look like the earth as seen from an airplane, with a quadrangular pattern of fields. It is a very positive image, for now the split is beginning to close. There is still a difference of levels, however, for between the earth above and the earth below there is a very sudden change of level, such as often appears in the psychological geography of a dream where there are the two levels and no connecting steps. Such a dreamer might switch in his way of living between intellect and instinct without there being any bridge between. But this is not a very dangerous situation since it is one that occurs frequently in the case of young people who have not yet harmonized the relationship between the two levels. The wound in this dreamer's psyche is healing. The earth level is rising — thanks to the fact that by accepting, for once, an unknown situation and venturing into it, he is, for the first time, touching human reality, the earth upon which we live. He could have seen woods below, or just the ground, but he sees cultivated fields.

522   It is cultivated earth on which labour has been expended and which has been distributed among different individuals, with the disadvantage, also, of the many walls, fences, and roads, and all the different regulations and controls concerning admittance and respect of property. It is the civilized earth and suggests work, so that one is reminded of Jung's words that work is part of the cure of the split and difficulties of the *puer*; just ploughing some plot of earth, no matter which, would be helpful. I remember him saying once to a *puer aeternus* type, "It doesn't matter what job you take. The point is that for once you do something thoroughly and conscientiously, whatever it is." This man insisted that if only he could find the "right thing," then he would work, but that he could not find it. Jung's answer was, "Never mind, just take the next bit of

earth you can find. Plow it and plant something in it. No matter whether it is business, or teaching, or anything else, give yourself for once to that field which is ahead of you." Everybody has a field of reality to work in if he wants to. The childish trick of saying, "I would work if it were the right thing," is one of the many self-delusions of the *puer aeternus* by which he stays within the mother realm and his megalomaniacal identification with the gods — for the gods do not work. Except for Hephaestus, who was despised by all the others, there are no gods who work in Greek mythology. Fields would also imply limitation. That is the drawback of getting in touch with reality: There are restrictions. One comes into the miserable human situation of having one's hands tied as it is not possible to do as one would like, something particularly disagreeable to the *puer aeternus*. What one produces is always miserable compared with the fantasies one had lying in bed about what one would do if one could!

523   Next in the dream comes an autonomous change of scenery, for the valley is suddenly replaced by stagnant, icy water. The dreamer thinks that this is the mother complex into which he does not want to fall. It is treacherous, and what previously had looked like an explosion of light now resembles a soap bubble with a skull in it. The same world into which he is sinking now shows its completely destructive aspect, without anything happening in the dream to justify such a change. If in a dream the dreamer does or thinks something, after which the whole landscape turns negative, we can say that there was a wrong thought which caused things to go wrong. If, while sinking, the dreamer had had the thought that he did not like this narrow reality and then the change had come about, the dream would have been easy to interpret. If one refuses the earth, it becomes eternal stagnation and being haunted by the mother complex and, at the end, death. That would be a cheap and easy way of interpreting the dream, but here the thing is very mysterious, for he goes on — one would think rightly — toward the bottom of the valley and the earth. Quite of itself, what had looked so positive turns into something uncanny — stagnant ice water and a soap

bubble with a skull in it. I do not pretend to have understood this in all its aspects; rather, I simply intend to state what I think about it.

524   Let us begin with the stagnant ice water. It suggests stagnation, where the water of life does not flow. Ice suggests being frozen in the cold. Obviously, this man was very cold. If he were not, he could not have behaved as he did with his girlfriend. His feeling was either nonexistent, or it had been destroyed by the family situation, or he was so tied to the mother that he had no feeling for other people. I had met him only once, so I could not say where his feeling was — whether it was tied up with the mother, or whether he was just an unfeeling cold fish; but in his behavior he was certainly cold. He associated the world below with the mother complex, into which he did not want to fall. Here, I think, we are on track to finding the trouble. A soap bubble, in general, is a simile for an illusion, which can be pricked. It has great volume and a marvelous, beautiful surface if the sun shines on it, but it is an empty sphere which, when it encounters some real body, dissolves into nothingness. With little children it is connected to happy fantasies: they love to make bubbles with their spittle which is accompanied by joyful fantasy. Building castles in the air, or fantasizing, is like an inner cinema where we get to be the powerful stag or the beautiful woman. All those wonderful daydreams are bubbles that can be pricked. Here something appears below which means stagnation, coldness, illusion, and death, apparently without any fault on the part of the dreamer except that when he sees the stagnant, icy water, he says that it is the mother complex, which he is not going to fall into. I think this gives us the key. We must not forget that this man had had a Freudian analysis, and the effect that that has on a human being. It produces an intellectual attitude toward life that robs it of its mystery; one knows all about it, and if one does not, then the doctor in the white coat who sits behind your couch does. Freudian analysis explains everything to you as the Oedipus complex, and so on, and dreams are no mystery; they are quite clear! All long objects are phallic, and the others are feminine, and the rest have some sexual connotation. If you know just a little anatomy, you know all about it; you need

only make the connection. In this way, dream interpretation becomes very monotonous and easy. Freud even once complained to Jung that he no longer worked much on dreams because it was too monotonous! Of course! He knew what would come out, so he played the magician's trick and first dropped a rabbit into the hat and then pulled it out! That is Freudian dream interpretation: One knows what it is driving at, namely, the Oedipus situation. Your mind is no longer open to the fact that something might exist which you do not yet know. Our ego is therefore fed with conscious illusions, namely, that it is just a question of knowing all about it, and this brings with it a complete stagnation of life.

525   There is a certain type of man with a mother complex who is much attracted by Freudian psychology because its effect on the individual is similar to that of the mother complex itself: It is another prison, and this time you are imprisoned in a situation which is known to your intellect. The Freudian system has its gaps, but these were not approved by its founder. Freud created the system as something entirely known, except for the physical aspect where there are openings left for biological chemistry. On the religious or philosophical side, there are no openings: There everything is precisely defined. For this reason, Freudian analysis seems attractive to the victim of a severe mother complex, with his anxious and ungenerous attitude, because it offers him another cage of protection. One learns the language easily, and one who has had a Freudian analysis for six months or so knows all about it. A patient like this will bring his dream to you with a cheap, ready-made interpretation. You feel puzzled by the dream and wonder what it means, but he will interrupt you and ask if it is not again the Oedipus situation. Such people have it all down pat, and therefore life cannot flow.

526   Freudian analysis is often completely without feeling. This is also expressed factually in as much as the doctor is not allowed to have any personal feeling for his patients and avoids them by sitting behind the client. Any personal feeling or feeling-reaction is suspect. (I am referring here to the strict Freudian school of thought; today, there are modified versions, but I am referring here to the original

approach.) If the patient's feeling function is already damaged, the situation can become a catastrophe and the split will be worsened. Our dreamer, like a clever monkey, had assimilated the Freudian standpoint as a justification for his Don Juanism. I am not accusing his Freudian analyst of this. I rather think that this, at least, was his own trick. Every time he felt rather too close to a girl, he thought that it was the mother complex again, so he got out. In this way, the Freudian way of thinking helped him to carry on his Don Juanism. What is so damnable about it is that there is even truth in it. Naturally, in Don Juanism, the partner who is looked for in different women is the mother complex, so that to have an affair and then walk out of it because it is again the mother complex is quite justifiable. It is a wonderful excuse for escape! And it is quite true that these first fascinations — that is, these first games of the anima — do have their origins there, and that they do, in fact, prove to be an illusion. I have not seen a man who was somehow connected with a woman for a longer period who has not suffered from certain disillusionments and disappointments, and who, in the end, has not realized the transience and corruptibility of all earthly life.

527   I would therefore propose to take this dream more philosophically: If you venture into life, into reality, instead of keeping outside of it to avoid suffering, you will find that the earth and women are like a fertile field on which you can work, and that life is also death. If you give yourself to reality, you will be disillusioned and the end of it will be that you will meet death. If you accept your life, you really, in the deepest sense of the word, accept death, and that is what the *puer* does not want. (I heard that the dreamer died when he was only 45 years old. This part could, therefore, also be seen as a premonition.) He does not want to accept his own mortality, and that is why he does not want to go into reality: At some point he would be forced to recognize his own weakness and mortality. He identifies with the immortal and does not accept its mortal twin, but if he were to go into life, he would assimilate the mortal brother. Therefore, we could say that this dream contains a kind of philosophy of life that would not surprise an Easterner. No

Indian would be surprised by it. He would say, "Certainly, if you go into life, if you love a woman, then you embrace an illusion, and every illusion will show itself as Maya, as the great illusion of the world, the end of which is death." All those who have read some Eastern mythology and philosophy will not be surprised by this, but it is surprising that in a modern European young man's dream such deep philosophy is brought up. The thought is put plainly before him: life and meeting a woman mean coming together with reality; to work means to meet the earth — disillusion, stagnation, and death. That is an honest answer to one who has doubts about whether he should live or not. We should not forget that as a child, this young man had met death in a very shocking way. His father shot himself when the boy was six. As he lived in a small town, the child doubtless heard gossip. It seems probable that he also peeped into the coffin and saw the remains of his father. As a sensitive boy, he had met death in a terrifying and shocking form, so death already belonged to his experience, and probably this partly accounts for his hesitation about going out into life. The unconscious does not pour any balm over the facts at this moment, nor does it comfort him about them, but presents him with the plain truth: Life is death, and if you accept life and move into it, you are moving toward your own death. Death is the goal of life.

528   From a therapeutic standpoint, this fascinated me because the tendency of analysts is to look at one part of the analysand's life and endeavor to infect the other with a certain amount of optimism; namely, that one ought to go into life, one should believe in its meaningfulness, and so on. But see what the unconscious does here! It shocks the dreamer with the absolute dual aspect of reality. If he wants to say yes, he should have no illusions about that, for this is how it is. Now he can say yes or no on an honest basis. And if he prefers to kill himself, that can be his honest solution, too.

529   Then, later on, the dreamer left the girl again, in spite of all that had happened. In a big town, he fell into the hands of a Russian prostitute whose chief customers were black. These black men hated the young man because he was her only white lover, and they made

several attempts to kill him. The Russian prostitute was the Mother Earth aspect of his mother complex — which the girl in whose arms he had dreamt was not, for she was a sensitive, introverted girl and not a very earthy person. With the Russian, he did indeed fall into the stagnant water of his mother complex and nearly meet death.

530   When our dreamer sees a skull where a round spot of light had burst like a soap bubble on the floor of the valley, he asks himself what death has got to do with all of this, and he repeats that he is not terribly afraid and continues to fall slowly in the same place. Then the whole thing disappears and is replaced by a yellow linoleum floor with brown spots. The landscape has completely lost its gigantic proportions, and the dreamer wonders why there is linoleum at the bottom of the valley and says that it is surrealistic. It is all very clear. He laughs a little about the linoleum, and he added in the letter he sent with the dream, "I don't like linoleum. It is always cold and not aesthetic. I don't like it." He obviously has a strong feeling against it.

531   We have discussed the problem of the skull and said that, in a way, the dreamer is right in saying that falling into this water would be falling into the valley, where the skull is; he would be falling into his own mortality and the stagnating aspect of matter. I have already mentioned that he left the girl in whose company he had had this dream. With the Russian prostitute, he really did fall into a dirty pool and risked death and complete stagnation. The Russian prostitute was a large, earthy woman, obviously a mother figure. Thus, despite his not wanting to fall into this condition, he did afterward go through this phase and completely lost, as it were, his wings. He was already afraid that a woman would land him there when he made his contact with the girl, which was why he was afraid of continuing the relationship. It was also the reason why he always left women so quickly, feeling that behind every woman there was this whirlpool of matter that sucked one down. Falling into death does not always take such a concrete form, and many *pueri* die between thirty and forty-five for this very reason.

532   After the *puer* loses the ecstatic, romantic *élan* of youth, there is danger of an enantiodromia into a completely cynical attitude toward women, life, work in general, and money. Many men suddenly fall into an attitude of disappointed cynicism. They lose all their ideals and romantic impulses and, naturally, their creativeness, writing it all off as the fantasies of youth. They then become petty, earth-bound, small-minded people who just want to have a family, money, and a career. Everything else is regarded as romantic nonsense — what one wanted and did when one was young, which now must be written off. It is as though Icarus had fallen into the mud and life had stopped. This is due to a weak consciousness, which cannot conceive of the possibility of enduring the difficulties of reality and not sacrificing one's ideals but instead testing them on the touchstone of reality. Such men take the easy way out and say that ideals merely complicate life and must therefore be written off. This is a great danger.

533   As has already been said, this dreamer was very weak on the feeling side, and the cold ice at the bottom of the valley mirrors his own basically cold attitude and lack of feeling. It is the feeling function that gives life its color and value. Certainly, this boy suffered a great shock when his father committed suicide, and life then became icy, stagnant, and boring. If you talk to such people, they say that there is always the same human dirt and that from now on, they will just get up in the morning and have breakfast … and just continue to exist.

534   I would like to return to the example discussed above of the man who had fallen into this state and then dreamed of a prince whom he had to follow. There the *puer aeternus* reappeared and wanted to be followed, but as a figure separate from the ego. After having been identical with the prince, the man fell into the mud of the road, after which they became two. Then the prince reappeared, still in love with his bride to whom he gave a jewel in the form of a tear. The man had to follow him and the bride but got knocked down by shadow figures. One could say that to avoid this stagnation, it is necessary to face the shadow again and again. When you are

identical with the *puer aeternus* archetype, the shadow must be seen clearly to come down to earth. But when you are identified with the shadow, the archetype of the *puer* must be faced again to connect with it, for facing the other side is what leads to the next step. I have seen several cases where this disappointment was not so much concerned with the mind and the spiritual side but rather with the man's attitude to marriage.

535   When Icarus loses his wings and falls into the stagnating aspect of the mother and matter, some very independent men cannot make up their minds to marry. They feel that marriage would be a prison, a thought that is typical of the mother complex and the *puer aeternus* mentality. Jung once said of a man like this who did, finally, decide to get married, "He curled up in his little basket like a nice little dog and never moved again." They never move again; they do not dare look at other women, and they generally marry (even though she may be beautifully disguised in youth) a devouring-mother type of woman. If she is not already that, they force her into the role by being submissive and boylike and sonlike. Then the marriage situation is changed into a kind of warm, lazy prison of habits which, with a sigh, they put up with. Such men continue quite efficiently professionally and generally become very ambitious, for everything at home is boring — there is the basket for the dog, the sexual problem is parked, as is the food problem, so all ambition and power go over into the career where they are quite efficient. On the eros side, however, they completely stagnate. Nothing goes on there anymore, for marriage is the final trap in which they got caught. That is another way in which the *puer aeternus* can fall into stagnating water — either on the mental side, when he gives up his creativeness, or on the eros side, when he gives up any kind of differentiated feeling relationship and curls up in the habitual conventional situation.

536   We also said of the skull that, naturally, it could be taken as representing the problem of death. One of the problems for a *puer* is that, if he enters life, he must then face the fact of his own mortality and of the corruptible world. He must accept the fact of

his own death. That is a variation of the old mythological motif where, after leaving Paradise, which is a kind of archetypal maternal womb, man falls into the realization of his incompleteness and mortality. From this skull, this realization of death, the dream then says, light explodes again, showing that in such a realization there is still more light to come, i.e., the dreamer would be illuminated if he could think about and accept these facts of life.

537   Afterward, the landscape changes completely and loses its gigantic dimensions. Now there is the linoleum on the floor of the valley. First the dreamer looked down into the split and saw the stars below, then came the dark sky with the light stars, and then comes the yellow linoleum, upon which what were light stars have now become brown spots. He is looking at the same picture, but an enantiodromia has occurred in the color: What was light is now dark, and vice versa. This, he says, is surrealistic. I have no amplifications for the linoleum other than his dislike of its coldness and its unaesthetic effect. We must add our own material, even if it may be arbitrary to do so.

538   One could say that linoleum is the typical floor covering in little bourgeois dwellings and poor people's homes. It is cheap stuff and brings to mind the rather disgusting atmosphere of cheap little flats that smell of cabbage. Now, for the first time, nature no longer covers the ground. Instead, there is an artificial man-made substance in all its smallness, and this ties in with the fact that the landscape loses its gigantic proportions and that everything is flattened. The stars have become dark spots, and what before was the brown earth has now become a yellowish linoleum. This shows the danger of falling into banality. I discussed this part of the dream with Jung. In response, he wrote the following:

539   'Linoleum is the essence of the unaesthetic, banal and petty bourgeois reality: marriage, taxes, formal greetings, the milkman, the cleaning lady, rent....it is the squareness of the earth with its harsh angles in which no symbols are to be found. (It is) what crushes, smothers and imprisons the just-

so nature of life. This is the very daemonic power of a true symbol that the *puer aeternus* would like to flee from, but which pins him down, like a magnet, and to which he needs to submit – he who approaches the place of terror overcomes fear. The secret of being hidden in the banal; whoever turns his back on this is gripped by an imaginary fear. Being in the just-so-ness is 'satori', being close to the self. One has to become small and ugly to shed the egg-shell of the Bardo. Only in extreme smallness can one see and reach greatness. He should sit down on the linoleum and meditate: Tat twam asi (thou art that). A mother's boy can find himself only in matter."[6]

540   In the dream, the gigantic dimensions disappear; they are leveled up, which means that, when he fell into banality, the great polarities and the — at least for his weak personality — too great a tension in his psyche have been flattened out and the opposites are nearer each other. The stars, however, which are the illuminating aspect of archetypal complexes in the collective psyche, have now turned into dark spots.

541   How does the archetypal kernel of the complexes of normal people appear? They would say that life was quite clear except for a few disagreeable spots, the dark spots — the complexes! When Jung discovered the complexes of the unconscious, he did discover them as dark spots, namely, as holes in our field of consciousness. By making the association experiment, he found out that the field of consciousness was tightly put together, that we can associate clearly and correctly except when a complex is touched, and then there is a hole. If a complex is touched in the association experiment, there are no associations, or there is a delay in their coming. The normal view of the unconscious is, therefore, that everything is clear except for those disagreeable dark spots of the complexes, behind which are the archetypes. This is, for example, what one always realizes if

---

[6] From an unpublished letter of C. G. Jung's, dated 28th August 1952, with kind permission of the Jung family.

there is a strong enantiodromia. After a psychotic episode, if people go through what one calls the regressive restoration of the persona, they then call what previously had meant illumination to them (the source of the too bright insight which one has when one has fallen into the collective unconscious), the dark spots which must be avoided. This is a very unhealthy situation. If you get people out of their psychotic episode by pharmacological means, they then tend simply to push away the whole experience of the collective unconscious, with its excitement and illumination, and call it a dark spot about which they want to hear nothing more. This is the typical compensation in a case where the ego is too weak to stand the opposites and to see both sides of the thing, namely, that the archetypes are the source of illumination on the one side, but that one must also keep one's feet firmly on the ground at the same time. In this dream, it looks as if the dreamer were in danger of falling into the opposite, into complete banality. When I wrote him about the dream, I said this was a phase he had to go through, and that after he had fallen into it, he must trust the unconscious to take him to the next step; that for the time being this is where he has to land and it is a process which cannot be stopped. He will fall into utter banality and write off all his former ideals — and become an angel who has lost its wings.

542   There are, in fact, two changes in this dream: There is the fruitful earth, then death, and then something he can stand upon. I think it is a pity that the dream did not stop when the fields appeared, for that would have been a complete solution of the problem. But he was not capable of looking at reality as something that one could form and work with; his nature was too passive. He needed something on which to stand, but he could not turn to the masculine attitude toward reality and say that if things were not as he liked, he would change them, form them, and impress his own mind upon them. The creative masculine gesture of taking clay and molding it according to his own ideas was what he could not do. He remained passive and accepted reality, but then it had to support him and be something upon which he could stand. This is, however, better than

before when he would have fallen into a bottomless abyss. He has not yet found his masculinity but is still dependent upon the mother-base. The degree to which this is still a problem of not having found his masculinity is shown in the next dream.

543 But before we turn to it, a few words about the color of the floor. Yellow has to do with intuition, and for an intuitive person, reality always causes difficulties, and it is what they come up against in life. Nevertheless, I cannot quite fit this floor as intuition — except that the dreamer was clearly a very intuitive kind of person, and it might mean that at least he had now found the basis of his main function. He was so completely "unborn" that he had not even developed a superior and an inferior function. The ego-complex was weak, and there was no developed consciousness, so at least his function of intuition could become something he could rely upon. Its opposite would be reality (which is related to through the sensation function), and intuition is always at odds with reality. To the intuitive type, earthly reality is the great cross.

544 Thus, at first glance, it might seem that he initially needs the linoleum upon which he is able to stand to be able to find the stars. But the first step in the birth of consciousness is to develop a main function and this normally occurs between the ages of twenty to thirty. In this case, practically speaking, it would mean that one is dealing with a human being in such an unborn state that one would have to concentrate on developing their main function. He can move on to the inferior function only after many years, to discover the problem of what is behind the irritating factors of reality.

545 In the next dream which he wrote to me he says that he is in a sort of *razzia* (a rounding up by the police). He does not try to run away because he thinks that his innocence will be revealed. He is put in a room, and after a while he opens the door and sees that his guard is a woman. He asks her if she will let him go since he is innocent, and she answers, "Yes, certainly I shall let you go because you are innocent, but first there are some questions to be put to you." Then, behind the

wall, he hears moaning and realizes that the questioning is accompanied by torture. Actually, people are being beaten on the sinus. He is very much afraid of the physical pain and wakes up.

546 He did not give me any other associations, but this clearly refers to his prison and police phobia complex. We recall that he could not cross the Swiss border because he thought he would be put in prison, and he always ran when he saw a policeman. In connection with the woman guard, he wrote to me that he had once painted the portrait of an unknown, imaginary woman. For four years, he worked on this painting, which became so vivid and significant for him that he had to keep it covered with a cloth, especially at night, because he was always afraid it might come to life and threaten him. He could not sleep in the same room with it for that reason, so he painted and then quickly covered it up, and sometimes he did not look at it for weeks because, to him, it was a living thing. This is an amazing example of what the anima is. The painting itself did not remind him of any concrete woman. It was the representation of the anima, of the imago of *the* woman within him, and it had become so alive to him that he was terrified of it. The old Pygmalion motif!

547 Now we should focus upon this strange police-prison complex that was a kind of phobia he had.

548 The dream is very important because it begins to link up with what I wish to arrive at by the end of my lecture, namely, that we are dealing with a problem that is not only personal but belongs to our time: The police state, the totalitarian system, that tortures thousands of people, is becoming more and more the great problem of our day. The strange thing is that it is mainly the *pueri aeterni* who are the torturers and establish tyrannical and murderous police systems. Thus, the *puer* and the police-state have a secret connection with each other; the one constellates the other. Fascist and communistic regimes have been created by men of this type. The real tyrant and the real organizer of torture and of suppression of the individual are therefore revealed as originating in the not-

worked-out mother complex of such men. That is what possesses them, and it is out of this state of possession into which such a complex plunges people that they act in this immoral and outrageous manner.

549 Since the dreamer is in the street, it can be said that he is in the collective. At present, he has no relationship to the collective: He is an isolated, lonely human with an entirely asocial attitude. He is nowhere linked up with his feelings. He has no real friends — only the man to whom he gave away his girl, but that had not been a strong feeling connection. Therefore, he is lost in the collective. He is the anonymous man in the street, and that is where he is caught by the police system. Anyone who has a weak personality and has not worked on his individuality is threatened from both sides: Not only is he threatened with being swept away by collective consciousness, but also by the outer collective. A person with a weak ego-complex swims between Scylla and Charybdis — between the devil and the deep blue sea. He is then caught either by the collective unconscious or conventionality in some form — very likely by collective movements. Identifying with the persona or identifying with a collective movement is therefore as much a symptom of a weak personality as to go mad and fall into the collective unconscious. They are merely variations of the same thing, which is why the carriers of these collective, absolutist movements are generally very weak as far as the ego is concerned.

550 I remember a medical doctor telling me that at the beginning of the last war, when he was a stomach specialist and very well known, it happened that he had a patient with stomach ulcers who was a high Nazi official. He succeeded in curing this man, and as a result, he was spoken of in Nazi circles as being a good stomach doctor. Throughout the war, an enormous number of high-up Nazi officials then came to him for private treatment. Because of the *religio medici* (the medical code) he could not, of course, refuse to accept them as patients. He said it was amazing to see those concentration-camp torturers, those so-called heroes, take off their beautiful uniforms and shirts, disclosing bodies tanned by sun and sport — and then

to find nervous, hysterical stomach trouble underneath. These pseudoheroes were merely weaklings — spoiled mamma's boys. A large percentage he had to dismiss, telling them the trouble was purely psychological. It was an eye-opener to the doctor — not what he had expected, although to us it makes sense. If he told them of a cure or a regimen which was the least bit disagreeable, they would not try it. If he poked into their troubles, many of them would begin to cry. He said that, when the beautiful hero-persona had fallen off, he felt as if he were confronted with a hysterical woman.

551   Our dreamer thinks he can get away because he is innocent. He still has the old-fashioned idea of a regular juridical state, such as we have in Switzerland, where one can only be arrested if one has committed some crime. One need not fear the police, for if one has done nothing wrong, one can get away. It is quite clear from the end of the dream that the question of right or wrong plays no role here. He will get away, but he will be tortured by the police all the same. His endeavor to plead innocent is not going to help him. Concerning his belief in his own innocence, we should think about this beautiful, delicate, blond, young being with the heavenly blue coat, and ask ourselves what wrong he has done in his life. We could say that he has done practically no wrong, other than doing no wrong! He has sinned by not sinning. He has not lived. If you live, you are forced to sin: If you eat, then others cannot have that food. We shut our eyes to the fact that thousands of animals are butchered so that we may live. Life relates to guilt, and he, by not living, has not accumulated much active guilt, but he has accumulated a tremendous amount of passive guilt. We need only think of all the girls he has just walked out on. True, he has not shouted at them or given them illegitimate babies. He has not done all those things that a more virile man might perhaps have done. But he has let women down by disappearing, which is as cruel and immoral as to do something which is called wrong. He has committed the sin of not living, and he is typical of the kind of man who, on account of his mother complex, has a too aesthetic and high-up attitude toward life, who thinks that by staying above it all, he can keep up an illusion

of purity and innocence. He does not realize that he is secretly accumulating dirt. The dream tells him quite clearly that he will not get away with that illusion. Life will catch up with him. He cannot continue as Mamma's innocent little boy who has never done anything wrong, for it will catch up with him all the same. Therefore, he is caught by collective forces in a negative form. You could say that the police represent his masculinity. Because he does not live it himself, it is lived against him. Whatever one has within oneself but does not live grows against one, and so the dreamer is now pursued by these torturers and the police and discovers that the real devil is the anima figure whom he had painted for so long; she is the real torturer behind the scenes. This anima figure is obviously a variation of his mother imago. It is strictly speaking the anima, but the anima that is identical with the image of the mother who is the devil acting out behind the scenes. We know of the sphinx as an image of the Great Mother, who asks torturing questions of those who want to remain innocent. Oedipus, too, wanted to remain innocent. He ran away from home to avoid fulfilling the prophecy that he would kill his father and marry his mother, and by running away from it, by trying to avoid the guilt, he ran straight into it. In the dream we have a modern version of the Oedipus motif; this man, too, thinks he can run away from fate, and he, too, falls into the grip of the Sphinx, who asks him an unanswerable question.

552   The motif of the Sphinx who propounds the riddle — or here, the sphinxlike woman who asks him questions while he is being beaten on the sinus — leads to an essential problem which is widespread and archetypal, and which has not yet been sufficiently addressed. It has to do with what I call pseudophilosophy, the wrong kind of intellectualism induced by the mother complex. The best example of this is to be found in the Russian fairy tale "The Virgin Tsar," which I spoke about earlier (see p. 181). The story is about the Tsar's three sons who go out at his behest, whereby the oldest brother takes the path to the right, and, upon his return, gets caught by his own father, i.e., he regresses into tradition, whereas the second brother, who took the path on the left, is caught by a prostitute, i.e.,

is imprisoned within his sexual drive. The third brother, on the other hand, the hero, goes straight ahead despite having been warned that he would be going to his death. His horse goes through a death and resurrection process, but the hero stays alive. Then he comes to the great witch, the Baba Yaga, who is spinning silk and who watches the geese in the field with her eyes, scratches the ashes in the stove with her nose, and lives in a little rotating hut on chicken's feet with a cock's comb on top. Firstly, he says a magic verse to stop the hut from rotating. He then enters and finds the old witch scratching the ashes in the stove. She turns around and says, "My child, are you going voluntarily, or involuntarily?" What she really means is whether he is on this quest of his own free will. Since the boys had been challenged by their father at the dinner party, when the father said that none of his boys had yet done as much as he had, in a way they did start involuntarily: The impulse came from the traditional past, from the father. On the other hand, it is voluntary, particularly in the case of the youngest, who has been laughed at as someone who must not go because he will never get anywhere and should stay at home by the stove. Thus, although one can say that he really did go voluntarily, there is something wrong with the question. Firstly, however, I would like to give you the answer because it shows how the problem should be dealt with. Ivan answers, "You should not ask a hero such questions, old witch. I am hungry and want my dinner, so hurry up!" And he ends up with some threats — very vulgar and very delightful! He knows quite well that the witch does not want an answer and that the question is a trick designed to lame him. If he were to answer the question, it would be like slipping on a banana-skin. It is just a diversion — not something that should be discussed.

553   The question of free will is one of the philosophical problems which man has never solved. Free will is a subjective feeling. Intellectually and philosophically, there is a pro and a con, and you can never prove either side. If you ask yourself whether you are doing something because you have to or because you want to, you will never find out. You can always say that you feel as though you

wanted it, but perhaps it is only an unconscious complex which makes you feel like that. It is a subjective feeling, but it is tremendously important for the ego to feel free to a certain extent. It is a feeling problem about the mood in which one finds oneself. If you cannot believe in a certain amount of free will and therefore free initiative of the ego, you are completely lamed because then you must go into all your motives. You can go into the past and investigate the unconscious more and more deeply, but you will never get out of it. And that is the spider's trick of the mother complex. That is how she tries to catch the hero: She wants him to sit and ask himself whether he really wanted it or not, whether it is really a question of opposing his father or not? If he does this, is he just falling for his father's suggestion, or is he simply showing off because he was ridiculed at home? And, finally, does he even want to do it at all? You can be sure that he will sit there forever, and the witch will have him in her pocket. That is the great mother-complex trick.

554   Some *pueri aeterni* escape from the mother by means of actual airplanes; they fly away from mother-earth and from reality. Many others do the same thing in "thought airplanes" — going off into the air with some kind of philosophical theory or intellectual system. I have not given much thought to it, but it has struck me that especially among the Latins, the mother complex is combined with a strange kind of strong but sterile intellectualism, a tendency to discuss heaven and earth and God-knows-what in a kind of sharp intellectual way and with complete uncreativeness. It is probably a last attempt on the part of these men to save their masculinity. This simply means that certain young men who are overpowered by their mothers escape into the realm of the intellect. There, mother cannot follow. Especially if she is the earth type who has a stupid, unconscious animus, she will not be up to it. Since it is an initial attempt to escape the mother's power and the animus pressure by getting into the realm of books and philosophical discussion, which they can think mother does not understand, it is not altogether destructive. Such a man has then a little world of his own — he

discusses things with other men and can have the agreeable feeling that it is something which women do not understand. In this way, he gets away from the feminine, but he loses his earthly masculinity. He saves his mental masculinity but sacrifices his phallus. He leaves behind his earthly masculinity, that masculinity which molds clay, which seizes and molds reality, for that is too difficult, and so he escapes into the realm of philosophy. Such people prefer philosophy, pedagogy, metaphysics, and theology, but it is a completely unvital, bloodless business. There are no real questions behind such philosophy for these people have no genuine questions. For them, it is a kind of play with words and concepts, and it therefore lacks entirely any convincing quality. One could not convince a butterfly with such "philosophical" stuff. Nobody would listen to it.

555   The pseudophilosophical intellectualism is ambiguous because, as I said before, it is a way by which to make a partial escape from the dominant grip of the mother figure, but is done only with the intellect, and only the intellect is therefore saved. That is what one sees in the tragedy of the Oedipus myth, where Oedipus commits the mistake of entering into the question instead of saying to the Sphinx that she has no right to put such questions and that he will knock her down if she asks such a thing again. Instead, he gives a very good intellectual answer. The Sphinx drives the play forward very cleverly by apparently committing suicide. Oedipus pats himself on the back and steps right into the middle of his mother complex, into destruction and tragedy, just because he complimented himself on having got out of that difficulty by answering the question.

556   To my mind, the way Freudian psychology has taken this myth and generalized it is quite wrong, for the Oedipus myth cannot be understood without the background of Greek civilization and what happened to it. If you think of Socrates and the Platonists, you see that they discovered the realm of philosophy and pure mind in its masculine mental operations. But when you know what happened to Plato when he tried to put his ideas into reality, then you see that they had escaped reality and had not found a philosophy with which

they could form it. It was a complete failure. They discovered pure philosophy but not a philosophy that could be tested with reality. In the same way, they were the founders of basic physical and chemical concepts, but the Egyptians and the Romans had to change these concepts later into experimental science, for the Greeks could not put their ideas to the test in chemical experiments. Their science remained purely speculative, even in its most beautiful forms, and with it came the endless split of the little Greek towns and the tragic decay of Greek civilization. As soon as they were up against a nation with masculine and military self-discipline — the Romans — the Greeks were at a loss. Therefore, although they were the great philosophical fertilizers of the Mediterranean world, they themselves could not follow up their own attempts in a creative way because they never understood the riddle of the Sphinx. They thought that the intellectual answer was the solution — an illusion for which the Greeks paid. The Oedipus myth is, indeed, the myth of this level of cultural development. It is also the myth of all those young men who have this same problem. That is why it is also a general myth.

557   The question of this Russian witch — her philosophical question at the wrong moment — shows that this is an animus trick of the devouring mother. Later, when the man is on his own, it is a trick of the mother complex to put a philosophical question at just the moment when action is needed. This trick is often played out in actual life, for instance, when a young man wants to go skiing or go off somewhere with his friends. He is filled with the élan of youth, which carries one out of the nest, eager to be with others of the same age. He and his friends are enthusiastic about taking a boat down the Rhine to Holland. The boy tells his mother what he plans to do. It is just youthful exuberance, but the mother begins to worry about his being away. The boy is living and learning about life in a natural way, if only the mother does not hang onto him. But if she does, then she starts, "Ought you to do this? I don't think it's the right thing. I don't want to prevent you. I think it is quite right for you to go in for sport, for instance, but I don't think you should go just now!" It is never right "just now." Everything must first be thought over. That

is the favorite trick of the devouring mother's animus. Everything must be discussed first. On principle, says she, there is nothing against it, but in this case, it seems a bit dangerous. Do you *really* want to do it? And then if her son is somewhat cowardly, he begins to wonder, and then the wind has gone out of his sails. He stays at home on Sunday while the others go off without him and once again his masculinity has been defeated. He really does not care if it is right or not; he just wants to go! The moment for action is not the time for discussion.

558   I feel somewhat skeptical in this regard for those children whose parents have had Freudian or Jungian analysis because I see that the mother's animus even uses psychology to lame the son: "I don't know if it is psychologically right for you to go skiing," or whatever. In the second generation, even psychology is dangerous. The children of parents who are not psychological are often more fortunate. They can start something new, but not those whose parents' minds are already spoiled by psychology. The same thing applies to analysts who want to keep the patient, for the moment the analysand wants to go into action, the analyst may say that one must look first at the dreams to see if it is right psychologically. The *puer aeternus* shadow often does the same thing if no mother or analyst plays that role. Every time he wants to go into action, he will argue that he should not act until he has thought it over very carefully. One could call it neurotic philosophizing, philosophy at the wrong moment just when action is needed. That is the trick behind the myth of the riddle of the Sphinx and the devilish question of the Baba Yaga in the fairytale. It is the mother-animus who says, "Oh, yes, you may go, but I must just ask a few questions!" And whether he answers the questions or not, he is tortured.

559   But there is also a positive, prospective aspect in the dream, for when the men are tortured, they are beaten on the sinus. In this young man's country, the language has Latin roots, and he knows what *sinus* means in Latin: the curve, the bay at the seaside (or any kind of curve), but specifically a female curve, namely, the bosom. Therefore, when he is beaten on the sinus, he is hit on his hidden

femininity. The sinus is also a cavity that can get infected easily. It is therefore a hollow empty place, and "sinus" refers to something which, in a hidden way, is feminine and within the head. It refers to the fact that this kind of head activity, this pseudophilosophy and pseudointellectualism, has hidden feminine qualities. Being this kind of a philosopher implies having hidden femininity, and though it is the mother-devil who induces the man into this, that is where she hits him. One sees in real life how mothers do everything they can to castrate their sons. They keep them at home and make women out of them, afterward going about complaining that they are homosexual, or that at forty-three, the son is not yet married and how happy she would be if he would only get married; that it is so irritating to have him sitting about at home so depressed, and how much she has to suffer because of him; how anything would be better than to have him at home in that awful state. But if a girl comes on the scene, then she goes off on another tack, for it is never the right girl. The girl in question will never make him happy, she can guarantee that. Thus, the mother plays it both ways: She castrates her son and then perpetually hits that weakness, criticizing and complaining about it continually. That is how it looks on the personal level. The same thing applies as far as the archetypal complex is concerned, for the cure can only be found where the destructive complex lies.

560   In this case, you could look at such torture as a meaningless "neurosis-causing" activity of the unconscious psyche. He was terribly tortured by his symptoms at the time of the dream, for he could not go anywhere because of his prison phobia. The symptom by which the mother complex tortured him was also a question, and if he could have understood it as such, he could have asked what it wanted of him: What was the trouble behind it? And then he would have found the answer. The torture has a completely double aspect: If he understands it as a question put to him by fate, then he can solve his problem; if, however, he only runs away from it, then it is eternal torture imposed on him by his mother complex. The decision is up to him. Unfortunately, the dream ends: "I am very much afraid

of physical pain, and I wake up." This shows that this is his basic problem. It is the quite simple but widespread problem of a man who has fallen too much into the mother: He cannot endure physical pain. Generally, that is where the mother who intends to devour her son begins, when he is quite young, with her perpetual fussing care — putting cream on the sore place – telling him not to go with the other boys who are so brutal, and so on. When he comes home after having been beaten up, she says she will speak to the other boy's parents about the awful things their son does, instead of telling her own boy not to be such a coward but to hit back. Thus, she turns him into a physical coward, and that forms a base for all the rest, for a coward has no foothold in life. I knew a man of fifty who would not go out with a woman because, he said, if he went with her to a bar and a drunken man challenged him, then he would be forced to fight, and that he would never be able to do. To be sensitive is a different thing. There are people who feel pain more keenly, but the question is whether you give in to it. There is the story of a Frenchman and an Englishman who, during the First World War, were in a trench together. The Frenchman nervously smoked one cigarette after the other and walked up and down. The Englishman sat quietly and then said mockingly to the Frenchman, "Are you afraid? Are you nervous?" And the Frenchman said, "If you were as afraid as I am, you would have run away long ago." It is not a question of being afraid. There are thick-skinned people who do not feel things, who have some lack of sensitivity and are not so badly hurt, while others feel pain much more. The question is whether one has sufficient stamina to stand it. As the Frenchman intimated to the Englishman, it is not heroic not to be afraid. The Englishman was just unimaginative and therefore quiet. Many people are tremendously courageous, simply because they are not sensitive and cannot imagine what might happen. They cannot imagine what might take place and that is why they do not get nervous. Highly strung, imaginative people naturally suffer much more, but the real problem of courage is whether one can stand it, or at least not lose one's fighting attitude, one's feeling of self-defense and self-respect.

This is a very deep-rooted instinct which exists not only in man but also in the animal realm, for the male of many species cannot lose self-esteem and honor without paying for it. It is essential to basic masculinity, and to lose it means castration in a hidden way.

561 Among the cichlidae — a certain breed of fish — a male cannot mate with a bigger female. The reason is that these fish do not see very well, and there is no great difference between the two sexes. They swim toward each other, and the first thing the male notices is that the other is bigger, which alarms him slightly in case there may be a fight, and he goes pale; then when he approaches and sees that it is a female, he cannot mate. A female meeting a bigger male may also be frightened, but she can still mate. The result, as the zoologists put it, is that, in the male, sex with aggression can be combined, but not sex and fear. In the female, sex and fear can be combined, but not aggression and sex. And there you have the animus-anima problem in a nutshell. In other areas of nature, it has been discovered that if certain male animals lose their self-esteem, they die. There is a beautiful story by Ernest Thompson Seton of a particularly good leader and cattle-thieving wolf in a pack of wolves.[7] This lead wolf was caught with much difficulty and, being such a famous animal, was not killed but tied up and brought home. At first it got wild, with manic eyes, but then, suddenly, to his astonishment, Seton, who had the wolf on his horse and was watching him, saw that the animal's eyes became quite quiet and had a faraway look, and the animal relaxed. He was left tied up in the courtyard, as no decision had been made as to what was to be done with him, and the Government had offered a tremendous price, but the next morning the wolf was dead for no apparent reason. It had died of humiliation, and that is not uncommon among male animals.

562 The same thing happens in primitive masculine societies. Statistics were compiled (by the Red Cross) during the last war to discover whether primitive or more highly educated people stand imprisonment best. It was found that the more primitive the person, the greater was the rate of suicide. Bushmen, for instance, cannot be

---

[7] Seton, *Wild Animals I Have Known.*

imprisoned, for no matter how well they are treated, they just fade away. They lose hope and die for psychological reasons. Thus, it can be said that it is essential for the human male to have feelings of freedom, self-esteem, and honor, and, with that, a certain amount of aggressiveness and the ability to defend himself. That belongs to the vitality of the male, and if that is destroyed by the mother, then he falls an easy prey to the mother's animus.

563 Another very wicked way by which it can be done is through mockery. I know of a mother who completely lamed her son by her witty tongue. Every time he wanted to assert his masculinity and be enterprising, she would make a little mocking remark which killed all his élan and made him look ridiculous. A young man who goes off to perform his heroic deed should not be ridiculed by the adult, but should be respected, for it means the growth of masculinity. If boys play at cowboys and Indians, they are funny, but one should recognize the necessity for the assertion of self-esteem and feeling of freedom and independence. That is essential, and stress should not be laid on what is ridiculous about it. For that reason, in many primitive male societies where they endeavour to keep their independence and masculinity, when the males walk around wearing animal masks and tails attached to their behinds, and so on, the women may not look. In most male initiations in primitive tribes the women are kept out, for they could so easily just make a little mocking remark about the heroes, or something like that, and immediately the thing would fall flat. The men know very well that they look completely ridiculous in those demonstrative displays of masculinity and for that reason exclude the women. Women also have their women's mysteries, with the girl's first attempt at make-up and hair styles, and the mockery of their brothers is terrible. They laugh at the way she has made her first shy attempt at being a little feminine, so that usually girls prefer to get into groups at school and make their first attempts there.

564 Finally, let us turn our attention once more to the dreamer who is beaten on his sinus by a woman while being held by the police. I have never found out what its medical function is. Like the appendix,

it seems to be a remnant from the past, a rather meaningless thing. I think that makes it more meaningful and supports a prospective interpretation. The woman in the dream hits him on something that is unnecessary, and this is what gives the dream a meaning which is not only negative. In other words, if he had not got such a cavity, this unnecessary feminine weakness in him, she could not torture him. One can say that if he were masculine and strong and not already infected, and therefore weak, she would not be able to do anything. His lack of masculinity shows in the babyish cry that he is innocent. As if that matters! Instead of saying he is innocent, he should be furious and try to free himself. But he has this passive reaction, his hope that his innocence will save him — as if that would help in our world! According to Christian teaching, evil does not exist, and if one is innocent, everything will be all right. But by being misinterpreted in this way, Christianity has made us all infantile, and it has robbed us of our sound instinctual attitude toward life, because we are all trying to be innocent sheep, and then, of course, we are helpless. There we link up with the sheep problem of Saint-Exupéry and the idea of sheep-mentality and infantilism. It is a certain kind of wrong Christian attitude where one is innocent so nothing can happen, for the protecting angels will take care for you. But reality contradicts this kind of teaching because in this world, and in nature, innocence does not help. It invites the wolves.

Part 3

'The Kingdom Without Space' (Bruno Goetz)

◆

Chapter Six
The Boys

565 Next, we shall go into the puer aeternus problem as mirrored in Germany, taking for this the book Kingdom Without Space by Bruno Goetz that was published in 1919. It is interesting that this book was written and published years before the Nazi movement came into being. Bruno Goetz certainly had a prophetic gift about what was coming and, as we will see, his book anticipates the whole Nazi problem, throwing light upon it from the angle of the puer aeternus. Goetz predicted the whole movement in his book, even what is now happening in Germany, and I believe that through the book, we shall get to the point at which I am aiming, namely, the religious and the spirit-of-the-time aspect of the puer aeternus problem.

566 Goetz was born in 1885 in Riga. His novel begins with two poems which I would like to summarize:

567 Encircled in death's mighty folds of darkness,
Our burning spirits strove
After the dream which led us on.

568 Far from our home and our maternal land,
On undetermined waves our ship drives on.
Laughing boldly we had ventured forth
As Vikings, searching undiscovered shores.

569 And if by night and horror overtaken, thou sing'st
Us songs of other homes,
Then phantoms vanish into gentle mist,

570   The world dissolves in dance and rhythm,
The stars disperse a fortune long delayed,
And radiant shines the kingdom without space.

571   Then comes a second poem dedicated to "Fo," who, as we shall see, is the puer aeternus figure in the novel.

572   When the dark cloud
Withdrew not from the sky
And from all the world
The sun was hid,

573   Out of the depths
A new light neared,
And in our sleep we knew
That Thou wert there.

574   O the suns that come
From the depths of thine eyes,
And from thy lips
The flowing streams of love.

575   Across the waves of an ethereal sea
The splendour of thy limbs
Entices us
To flaming courage.

576   Eternal youth,
Encircled by the music of the stars,
Giver of comfort,
Sparking, free, and beautiful.

577   Men and women
Dance in thy glory,
Driving into death
For sight of thee.

578   Forever into light
Thy white form calls
Wave after wave,
And never do we age.

579   The book came out in 1919 while the author was away. Either because they were so shocked or for some other reason, the publisher removed some of the chapters, making the first edition incomplete which in turn led to it being mistakenly taken for a political pamphlet. When the author returned, he insisted on a reprint, and explained in a postscript to this new complete edition, which also came out in 1919, that the novel had never been intended as a political document. A second, unchanged edition of this complete version of 1919 was published in 1925.

580   It must be remembered that this book was written after the First World War, the time of the great debacle in Germany, of mass unemployment and all the postwar miseries. The ruins alluded to in the first poem probably refer to the catastrophes of that time. It was at this time that a certain pathological dreamer went about holding political speeches, and gathering a group of young people around him who were enthusiastic about his ecstatic and crazy political programs — fourteen years before the Nazis seized power. It was a time of the utmost collective despair, aimlessness, and disorientation, a time that in certain ways was similar to what we are experiencing now. In the first poem, the author mentions the dream so passionately pursued that takes them away across the sea to new lands and into some unknown horror, and then he talks about one who speaks of a new country and of the emergence of a "kingdom without space."

581   The second poem in the book begins with the same motif of a darkened sky, and yet there is a new light which comes from the depths and which the still sleeping people feel as an invisible presence. This invisible presence is described as "eternal youth encircled by the music of the stars." The author makes it clear that the eternal youth is the ruler of this kingdom, and that one has to

go into death in order to see his transcendental kingdom. It is apparent that he entices people out of this world into another and seduces them into death.

582 The first chapter, entitled "Schimmelberg" (White Horse Mountain), says that the inhabitants of a little university town of the same name well remembered the old sea captain, Wilhelm van Lindenhuis. There had been a lot of talk about his sudden death. First his gentle, rather woebegone, and sickly wife had died, after which people noticed that he no longer took his evening walk. But when they saw a light in the house and his lean, furrowed face at the windows, they thought he must just have been indisposed for a while and was all right again. One evening, however, two unknown youths appeared wearing weather collars and leather caps rang his doorbell and he himself opened the door. Passersby said that when he saw the boys, he at first recoiled as if in surprise, but then he let them in and within a quarter of an hour they had left the house again. The next morning, when the postman could get no answer when he rang the bell, nor could he at midday, nor in the evening, he informed the neighbors. The door was broken open, and they found the old man sitting dead in his armchair. It seemed he had died quite peacefully from a heart attack. Upon going through the house, a crown of thorns and an ivory cross were discovered on Melchior's desk. Since there was no dust on these objects, they must have been placed there quite recently, for everything else was thick with dust. Every effort was made to advise Melchior of his father's death; telegrams and letters were sent to him in Rome where he lived at the time, but all were returned, and he could not be found. People said he had always been a strange young man, and the following old story was dug up about him.

583 When he was about fifteen years old, Melchior had had two friends — Otto von Lobe and Heinrich Wunderlich. Otto

von Lobe was a very slender, gentle, blond, aristocratic boy, and Wunderlich was a strong, brown, bold young man. The three became friends and founded a mystical secret club. They read a lot of alchemical and Rosicrucian literature and started alchemical experiments with the idea of finding an elixir which, when drunk, would enable them to change shape. After many attempts they believed they had succeeded in producing it. Each of the three wanted to be the first to try it, and since they could not agree, they called the whole of their mystical club together. The others had been more fascinated by the romantic horror of the undertaking than by the details, which had been left to the three friends, and they knew nothing of the poisonous makeup of the drink. Lots were drawn and the lot fell to Otto von Lobe. It was then decided to have an all-night carouse in which their fantasy ran off into future possibilities and what they would do when, like magicians, they could change their shapes, and how a new era would begin, and mankind could be transformed. They became more and more ecstatic, and in the early morning they ran down to the sea and turned to the East. Now when the first rays of the sun appeared, Otto von Lobe sprang up, tore off his clothes and, standing in the early light, laughed happily and then slowly drank down the elixir. In a few minutes he was dead. A strict investigation followed. Melchior was expelled from the school, having refused to make any statement, and the others were severely punished.

584   Wunderlich, the third in the group, changed noticeably after this event, dropping all unusual interests and becoming very cynical and conventional in a rather exaggerated manner. He studied medicine and retired as a general practitioner to a little village where he lived a very down-to-earth life as an odd ball.

585   Here we have the description of a phenomenon we can recognize from previous chapters — the fallen Icarus who, after the elation of creative fantasy, now drops once and for all into banality.

586   Melchior retires to his room for some months. His father, who was very much interested in magic and Rosicrucian writings and alchemy, pardoned his son. They begin to have long discussions on science and the possibility of transformation, but his father has no faith in the chemical transformation of the human being. Even if it could be done, it would only be meaningful if it were possible "to burn the original shape of the individual to ashes and make the earth a mirror of the stars." Melchior was unable to follow the astrological subtlety of his father's argument. They began to quarrel, and soon they did not understand each other and spoke less and less to each other.

587   Melchior then began to visit Henriette Karlsen again, the fifteen-year-old daughter of the director of the local museum. She was very beautiful, fair, slenderly built, with pale, amber-colored eyes and limp, long-fingered hands. Because of the activities of the secret club, Melchior had not seen her for some time. After having seen her walk past his house, he went to see her. She took both his hands in hers and looked at him for a long time without saying a word. Suddenly, her eyes filled with tears. Then Melchior turned and hurried home. Thereafter, he went to meet her every day in the museum. During this time, Henriette became paler and sadder. One day, by chance, the old director overheard the two of them talking. Melchior tells Henriette how every night since his childhood a face had looked in through his window. "When I was feeling very sad and father was away at sea and mother was sitting silently, bent over her Bible, I would hear a knocking on the window. Then it would appear — a small, brown face with eyes that looked like mine. But if I went to the window, it disappeared. And I would sit there for hours,

crying. … And now, about a year ago, it came back. But not alone: a whole group were with him. While I was attempting to make the elixir, they often looked on with scoffing faces. Since Otto's death, they have stayed away..." "Thank God," said Henrietta.

588   Melchior was enraged with this response. Since the boys had disappeared, he was completely alone, and nobody helped him. Henriette replied that if he loved her, he must promise to forget all that, and if the boys called him, he must not follow them. "How can I promise that?" Melchior cried out desperately, "how can you ask that of me? I want nothing more than that I may go with them. Then I would solve all the secrets. And you could help me. For you must come, too." "Never!" Henriette cried with deadly fear in her voice, "do you want to kill me as you killed your friend, Otto?" Melchior then got very angry and, calling her a coward, stormed out of the room, past the dismayed director, and back home. On that same day he asked his father to send him to another town to school.

589   Melchior leaves Schimmelberg and comes home only occasionally for a few days. Once he is studying at the university, he remains away altogether. No one knows anything about him other than that he was studying chemistry, and that he eventually got a Ph.D. for it at Oxford. In that same year, Henriette died of tuberculosis. The rumors about Melchior, that he was traveling and that it was only shortly before his mother's death that he returned to Schimmelberg were fueled when it was written in the paper that the young doctor van Lindenhuis had made a remarkable chemical discovery. At the same time the famous Professor Cux of the University of Schimmelberg needed an assistant and based on Melchior's publications, he had found him suitable. Thus, Melchior returned to Schimmelberg.

590 Naturally, everybody was very curious to meet the man about whose youth there had been such strange rumors, but he seemed disappointingly normal. While it is true that he gave the impression of being cold and strange, he nevertheless behaved amiably and seemed to be an important personage. Above all, people were enthusiastic about his charming and somewhat exotic-looking wife. As Professor Cux soon told Melchior, his father had, in the mean-time, died. When he mentioned the two boys, Melchior looked visibly shocked, but then pulled himself together and had him show him the crown of thorns and the ivory cross. He shook his head and made it clear that he did not recognize either object. "My father sometimes had strange ideas," he said. "God knows what came over him to purchase such things!"

591 Melchior then took over his father's house where, on the promptings mostly of his wife, he began to lead a very social life. The whole town met there, but Melchior himself always withdrew early, and went to his study where he remained studying and experimenting far into the night. With time, however, he began to neglect his scientific activities and took more and more part in his wife's social life, which through him now acquired quite a different character. People were indignant over the mocking way in which he spoke of State and Church institutions, and they were upset by his ever-increasing influence over the students, in whom he tried to imbue with radical skepticism against the foundation and outcome of scientific knowledge. To avoid a scandal, Melchior stopped lecturing. People withdrew from him, but a few remained faithful, including Professor Cux, who supported the views of his assistant, saying he was quite right and what was there in chemistry and science? Nothing! It was an intellectual illusion, a pseudofaith. When it was discovered that Cux had secretly married a young dancing girl, it was said that it was the fatal influence of a certain circle.

592 The circle met once a week at Melchior's house and became increasingly drawn in by him. The eccentric behavior of certain members began to be noticed, and soon it was being said that shameless orgies were being held at Dr. van Lindenhuis's house. People were even more astonished when the liberal-minded Lutheran priest of St. Mary's Church, Mr. Silverharnisk (silver harness) became a regular guest, who justified his visits by saying that he was able to gather information there on the disorientation and uprootedness of the modern soul!

593 Melchior himself grew more and more peculiar, withdrawing entirely from the circle. When strange boys who wore remarkable clothes were seen around the house in November, the townspeople remembered the curious conditions surrounding Melchior's father's death and the stories told by the old director of the museum about Melchior's conversation with Henriette. People became increasingly excited and irritated.

594 In the second chapter entitled "The Meeting," Melchior, in a very bad temper, is sitting on a bench in the heavy rain. He could not make up his mind to go home, for he was sure that his wife would have purposely forgotten to have his study heated to force him to join the weekly tea-drinking party. "Steps on the gravel startled him out of his apathy, and with a shock, he saw a boy wearing a high collar and a leather cap loitering along the leafless alley of the city park. When the boy came nearer, Melchior saw a small brown face out of which the determined yet shy, rather staring, grey eyes looked straight ahead." As he walked past Melchior, he smiles at him. He hides behind a bush at the edge of the path to hide himself from a tall man who appeared at the end of the alley and who looked uncertainly around. Before the man could have seen him, the boy suddenly rushed toward Melchior, sat down next to him on the bench and whispered to him, "Take my left hand! And then quickly put on your glove! Do not be

surprised at anything and do not tell anybody about me! Quickly! Quickly!" The boy's voice expressed such panic and fear that Melchior involuntarily seized his hand. Instantly, the boy disappeared as though he had melted into thin air. On Melchior's finger was a broad silver ring. Still under the influence of the boy's frightened request, Melchior put on his glove. Only then did he become aware of how tremendous it all was, and he was filled with happiness. Something he had long hoped for had now happened. His depression disappeared completely, and full of self-confidence, he looked at the man who was approaching him. He was clean-shaven, with clear-cut but rather faded features, and his eyes were like bright transparent stones. When he raised his hat, Melchior noticed that he had a very large forehead and fair, wavy hair.

595   The stranger asks him if he had seen a boy. Dismissively, Melchior replies that he had not noticed anyone. The man sits down next to him on the bench and says that he had been looking for his pupil the whole day. In response to the stranger's persistent questions, Melchior insists that he has not noticed anyone. Looking more closely, Melchior notices how the expression on the stranger's face seems to change constantly. Sometimes it seemed saggy and frail, sometimes there was a childish smile, and sometimes his features appeared threateningly severe, and his eyes sparkled cold and penetrating. Finally, he stands up and asks Melchior to let him know immediately if he happens to see the boy. He introduces himself as Ulrich von Spät, and his address is the Grand Hotel where he is staying. Melchior should trust him for there is something in him that connects them both. Upon saying goodbye, Melchior suddenly feels a tremendous warm sympathy for the man, an inner-relatedness to him. He forgets everything and takes off his glove and the man sees the ring, but he hides his excitement and walks away calmly. Melchior then remembers the ring and feels he has betrayed the boy. He can barely forgive himself his carelessness. "What

can that mean," he thought. "I am losing control over myself. Things happen to me as if in a dream. Who was that stranger? What power had he over me that I suddenly loved him so that I forgot who he was? He is my enemy."

596   The third chapter is entitled "Fo"— the name of the mysterious boy.

On the way home, Melchior felt as if he had dematerialized, and the houses seemed to be made of air; they divided like curtains in front of him and closed behind him like clouds of mist. Everything was changed: Mysterious buildings which he knew had existed in former times were suddenly there again; it was no longer the same town through which he walked. "The people also seemed changed. He caught fleeting glances and felt as though he looked into his own eyes as into a mirror. A smile, a wave of the hand, seemed to him an indication, a greeting, a sign of secret understanding." Near the station, he bought some apples off an old woman, and, to her astonishment, he stroked her wrinkled cheek saying, "Yes, yes. We know each other. We are old friends. Do you see this ring on my finger? You never saw it before, did you? Nobody else may see it. That means that I am going away now, far away." The woman does not understand and looks at him nervously. She becomes increasingly nervous when he maintains that they have known each other since childhood, and she asks him if he is not ashamed of talking to an old woman like that. "You don't know me?" asked Melchior. "Why, suddenly, don't you want to know me? You always sat at some corner when I was on the road. I always saw you when I left a place or arrived somewhere." He says that they met in a hundred towns, and he always bought apples off her. The old woman mistrustfully denies this. Finally, in a low voice, Melchior says, "I understand. You are careful. You don't want to be overheard. The stranger is here —our enemy. It was careless of me to talk to you. We may have been watched."

597   At this moment, he sees a boy passing by who looks at him
sharply and puts his finger to his lips in warning and then
rapidly goes around the corner. His face was smaller and
bolder than the face of the boy who had disappeared; only
their still gray eyes were alike. Melchior walks on, deep in
thought. He is disconcerted about himself, about his fantasies
— there are women selling apples at every station, and yet…
"What circle have I run into? What is it that surrounds and
captivates me?" When he nears his home, Melchior sees in
the dusk several boys who break up upon seeing him and
hide behind the corner of the house and peep out curiously.
He can hear laughter, confused talking and music coming
from his home in which the lights are on. Among the
murmur of many voices, he thinks he recognizes the clear
voice of Mr. von Spät. In order not to be seen, he goes in
through the back door and straight to his study. There it is
cold and dark. He turns on the light and lies down in his
damp coat on the couch. The ring, which was loose on his
finger, falls to the ground. In a fright, Melchior looks up. The
boy who had disappeared is standing by the couch looking
at him, smiling. While he turns on the heater, the boy takes
off his coat and cap and says to Melchior, "I knew that I
would find you, Melchior. I saw in your eyes that you would
help me. You belong to us even if you know nothing about
us. I thank you. We all thank you." Melchior asks him how
he knows his name. The boy tells him he has known about
him for a long time, and he introduces himself as Fo. He may
not tell him his real name. Who they are Melchior shall only
find out when he lives with them. Melchior need only call
out, "I want to leave" and they will come and fetch him. But
he should be careful of the stranger, who is their enemy. He
has a secret which makes him very powerful. Fo himself was
once caught in his power and he was only able to get away by
tricking him. But now he must return to the others who are
waiting for him. Melchior hears a noise and sees many faces

pressing against the windowpanes. Melchior does not want to let Fo go until he has told him everything. How can he follow them if he does not know who they are? How shall he resist the stranger if he does not know his secret? "You can only know who we are by living, not talking. You will follow us if your heart drives you to do so. We are always there when called. We ourselves do not know the stranger's secret; if we did, he would not have any power over us. I have answered you. Now let me go." "You want to run away from me," said Melchior, "but I know how to stop you. I shall take your hand and transform you back into the ring!" "The ring won't help you, Melchior," the boy said laughing. "It turns your life into mystery and confusion. Everything around you will change. But you won't get away. You will unravel nothing; you will take friends for enemies and enemies for friends, for you will not understand the signs that would explain them. Come with us and then you will be free." Melchior hesitates, but then gets up silently and opens the window, out of which the boy jumps. The group of boys surround him. They hold hands and from the center of the ring a flame rises up, bursts into sparks, and everything disappears.

598 This story is very suggestive. It is something like Edgar Allen Poe's stories and might have been influenced by Kubin's The Other Side and by E.T.A. Hoffman. It is the kind of novel in which suddenly banal reality is dissolved in the mysterious events of the other side, where, in psychological terms, the unconscious penetrates and dissolves the world of consciousness so that from then on, anything and everything can happen.

599 The name of the town, "White Horse Mountain," is also meaningful, for the white horse was a very well-known attribute, and sometimes a personification, of the old god Wotan, who either appeared riding on his eight-legged white horse Sleipnir or was replaced by this magic horse. Those who have read Alfred Kubin's The Other Side know that a mad white horse who races through a

destroyed world plays a similar role. Wotan retired to the mountain but will reappear at the end of time and reestablish his eternal and happy empire. The family name of the hero of our story, van Lindenhuis (Lime Tree House) references an old Germanic symbol. In olden times, there was usually a lime tree in the center of most small German towns and villages. As a feminine symbol, it is dedicated to the nature goddesses like Perchta, Hulda, Mother Holle (along with all her other names). It was thought that the souls of unborn children lived under the leaves of the tree, and it was the mystical tree in the middle of the village around which the whole of life centered, very like the central pole which, for instance, you find in the rituals of the indigenous peoples of America.

600   In the opening poem there is an allusion to seafaring people, the still-living Viking spirit which, for the Teutonic peoples, was a personification of restlessness and transcendental eternal longing. We can only interpret the details later, for, so far, we have no key as to what the ivory cross and the crown of thorns allude to, something that comes only in the later chapters.

601   The rumors which spread about the hero of the story contain typical features. For instance, at the beginning, the three boys are described: Otto von Lobe, an aristocratic type, dedicated to death, who is described as very delicate; and Heinrich Wunderlich, who is described as very vital; and Melchior. The first two are obviously opposite shadow figures of Melchior's: von Lobe could be called a personification of the sensitive, artistic personality with a strong suicidal tendency, while Heinrich Wunderlich could be the vital side of Melchior's personality which pulls toward adaptation to life and who therefore cuts off all the juvenile romantic longings. Otto von Lobe dies from drinking the elixir, and through the shock, Wunderlich becomes quite cynical and realistic. We could say that one part of Melchior dies and another part of him reacts to that with a tendency to cynicism. The ego complex, which would be represented by Melchior himself, is between the two, and, as we hear, after the shock, he retires into his room and into a deeply depressed introversion, while Otto von Lobe, the real puer aeternus in him, dies. It

is well-known that between the ages of fifteen and twenty, suicides occur frequently, for it is a period when the pull toward death is strong, and it relates to the puer aeternus problem.

602   Melchior describes his double at the window who always appeared when his father was away at sea and his mother was lost in her Bible. He was unable to speak to anyone about it, and his father gave him no answer. Naturally, we can say that this was Melchior's early experience which foreshadowed all that was to come later, but I think we should amplify this with a very well-known fact, namely, that in early youth, lonely children tend to produce a double personality with whom they entertain themselves. This double is the coming-alive out of loneliness of the unconscious personality. The description is typical: Melchior is a lonely child and in moments when he sadly realizes his loneliness, this apparition appears. There are children who invent such a double, personify it, and play with it for hours. Very often this fantasy figure of early youth later reappears in dreams and becomes a personification of the whole unconscious. It is the shadow, the anima, and the self, all in one — the whole other side of the personality.

603   If we are inclined to think of the unconscious in terms of the different classifications of Jungian psychology, we could debate whether this first apparition is the self or the shadow. We may not forget, however, that these concepts are only valid in certain psychological situations. When a human being first meets the unconscious in an autonomous form, either in childhood or, for instance, in the beginning of an analysis, there is no question of shadow, animus or anima, and self. The first experience we usually have when we encounter the unconscious is with what we could best call the other side which, in those early stages, is personified in different forms. It is advisable in analysis not to start introducing those formal concepts but to let the person first simply experience that there is another side to the ego and its ordinary world. It is only after some time, when the fact of a completely different part of the personality has been realized — that there is another inhabitant in our inner house — that we can then slowly discern figures in the

half darkness of the unconscious, such as that of the inferior man, whom we might classify under the name of shadow, and the figure of the opposite sex, which we might classify under the name of anima or animus, just to bring some order into that other side. But as a reality, it is really the impact of the unknown part of the personality. We shall see that the first meeting with the unconscious is often with such a personification, or a double, in which — throughout the world — shadow, self and animus or anima are completely one.

604   There is the same idea in ancient Persian religion, which says that after death the noble man meets either a youth who looks exactly like himself (for in death he turns again into his beautiful and noble stature) or a girl of fifteen (the anima), and if he were to ask this figure who it is, it will say, "I am thine own self." If the man was virtuous, then this figure is shining and beautiful. By living virtuously, with the right kind of religious attitude, he develops a double in the Beyond, and the moment of death brings reunion with the other half. This Persian myth has survived in certain Gnostic and Manichaean traditions in late antiquity. There it is irrelevant whether the figure appears as a shining youth or as a girl, for its answer to the dying person is the same, namely, "I am thine own self, thine other half." This is an archetypal idea. In many primitive societies, it is thought that upon entering this world, every human being is only a half, the other half being the placenta, that is, that part of the personality which has not entered this world. The placenta is therefore ritually buried, or dried and worn in a capsule around the neck, and it is the magic substance in which the double is supposedly located. After death, the two become one again. There is even a myth which says that the first man was complete in heaven, but when he was incarnated in this world, he was only a half, and therefore the first man, who is mythologically the same as our figure of Adam, is called the "Half One." Thus, we could say that any human apparition is only a half; the other remains in the land of death in the Beyond, and one joins it after death. What this ultimately means, we do not know because it is an archetypal representation whose

meaning we can never exhaust intellectually. But we can say that among other things, it mirrors the basic realization that the growth of consciousness, which begins in early youth and increases, is a halving of the total personality: The more one becomes conscious, the more one loses one's other half, which is the unconscious. It mirrors, as it were, the split of the human being into a conscious and an unconscious personality, and there are early-youth experiences in which this is realized.

605   I once read in a newspaper about a Hungarian officer which illustrates this experience. He was the only child of an aristocratic Hungarian family before the First World War and he was so lonely, having nobody to play with, that he invented a brother whom he called Stepanek and whom he imagined to be a very tough, red-haired little boy. In his imagination, this little boy would do all the mischief he would have liked to do, but for which he had not the courage. When he went to school and found real comrades, the figure faded and was forgotten. In the First World War, he was wounded. He fainted and came around after a time, bleeding and shivering. He saw a human figure bending over him, a red-haired man of thirty, and thinking it was somebody who had come to rescue him, he murmured, "Who are you?" The other whispered, "Stepanek!" The next thing he remembered was that he was being taken care of in a hospital and slowly coming back to himself. He was very much puzzled about whether he had had an hallucination, or whether he had projected something onto the man who had brought him in, who perhaps had been a black-haired Red Cross man. He tried to follow up the problem by asking the doctors and personnel at the hospital how he had got there, but nobody knew who had brought him there. The nurses only recalled that he had been brought to the ward after he had been found lying on a stretcher in the hospital courtyard, but no one knew who had delivered him there and he could never find out. He did not want to theorize about it, but stated simply that those were the facts. I have a rational explanation: As we have seen from the childhood story, Stepanek was his more ordinary and vital part, his inferior

personality, the red-haired fellow who dared to do all the things he did not dare do. He himself was rather an introverted, sensitive kind of boy, and I think it quite likely that in the war situation, in a half-dazed way, he managed to drag himself to the hospital, and was therefore literally saved by his inner instinctive personality, Stepanek. Then he broke down in the courtyard where he was found. His wound was not too bad. That seems to me to be the only possible explanation. The other possibility is that a man from the lazaret had picked him up and that in his dazed condition he had projected Stepanek onto him.

606   This is only to illustrate that a lonely child very often finds a companion in the unconscious other half and thereby experiences the unconscious. Normally at this age, these shadow figures and the other side are projected onto other children who take over the role of "the other." It also shows the problem of a certain dissociation of the personality, which we see in this rather exaggerated, romantic enthusiasm with which the boys work on their elixir.

607   They are fascinated by the idea that the human individual, in his material shape, could be transformed and dematerialized and then become, as Melchior says later to his father, a "mirror of the stars." At bottom, then, it is the fascinating idea of an alchemical transformation that haunts all those boys, and the accident happens through their attempt to put it into reality. There we see clearly that this double — the puer aeternus — has to do with the self, and that the realization of the self, as it is presented in the alchemical process, is the real fascinosum. We also see how the two rhythms set in, namely, the pull to death, expressed in Otto von Lobe, and the cynical pull toward reality, personified in Heinrich Wunderlich.

608   During Melchior's retirement into his dark room, his first meeting with the feminine principle takes place. Shut up in his room, having been expelled from school and quite under the shock of Otto von Lobe's death, he discovers the girl, Henriette Karlsen, who later dies from tuberculosis. He quarrels with her because she does not want to follow him into death — all the same, she dies afterward. In anticipation of the story, it is to be noted here that the

hero never unites with a woman in a real way. The marriage is nothing, for there is no relationship but complete hatred and disappointment on both sides: It is a complete fiasco. There is the same problem as in The Little Prince for the contact with the anima does not work, but here is a different variation. We recall that the little prince also quarrels with the rose and leaves her on the planet. There the anima figure is not described as being aristocratic and lacking in vitality but rather as being childish and haughty and difficult to get on with. This girl, however, is more the aristocratic "broken lily," a very attractive anima type. But how would you interpret this psychologically? The first love of a man is always very meaningful, for the girl then is more the anima than she is real. Usually, these love affairs do not end in marriage. In this story, we are dealing with an anima fascination linked up with the mother image — in this story, she was a sad, suffering woman who sat reading the Bible — and obviously Henriette is a replica of this mother-image. Sometimes men have different anima-figures: One of them is like this one here, but there are others to compensate. If that is the dominant type, however, we may conclude that his feelings-side, his eros, is weak. He himself is not necessarily weak, for Heinrich Wunderlich is a vital type, the one who becomes the cynical realist, so it could mean that it would still be possible for the ego to be quite realistic. What would you guess if you met someone between eighteen and twenty who had such an anima figure? What would he look like if you met him again at fifty? I would say that he has every chance of becoming either homosexual or remaining a bachelor. Those would be the two possibilities because the whole relationship to the feminine side and to feeling — to eros, relationship — is weak and very likely to die, that is, to fade away.

609   I have seen more cases like this among determined bachelors than among homosexuals. I know of a man who got engaged three times to a dying girl and never understood that this must have something to do with him. After the third time, he thought he was just persecuted by fate and gave up. I knew him as a very old bachelor — a very nice man. He never saw that his anima-

constellation made him choose such women, and that he had a real instinct for picking out doomed women! He always got engaged correctly and meant to marry, but the women died: one from tuberculosis, one in an accident, and the third I do not remember how. What was so striking about this old man was his terrific sensitivity that he tried to cover up with his odd and quirky behavior. He went about dirty, covered with tobacco, and lived in a flat like a cave, decorated with beautiful things, but ash and cigars over everything. He was an unbelievable aesthete, and he had a beautiful collection; he knew more about art, with feeling and understanding, than most people, and he was a spiritual, highly cultivated, oddball bachelor! You could see clearly that his anima was so sensitive that he could never get near a woman or make a friend of a woman or even make male friends. The only way he could survive was by keeping away from any close contact with other human beings. He also had a tremendous sense of humor and, to keep his shell whole, he always laughed at his own sensitivity, covering it up with ironic remarks. This is the usual behavior of a man with this special predilection for dying girls. The other option is a relation to someone of the same sex because there a certain distance and delicacy of relationship can be imposed and the snarls of passion and the realization of the marriage relationship with its disagreeable and wounding realities can be escaped. The similarity to the little prince is that the puer aeternus problem is here again connected with the problem of the weak anima figure and weak eros side, and relationship to the other sex is therefore a problem.

610   Then there is a strange paradox: Henriette, the only anima figure he meets before his wife, wants to prevent him from following up the romantic pull from the beyond, and then she herself dies. In a way, she does the right thing by trying to get him over onto this side and into life. But when she protests, the anima projection falls away. If she had cooperated and gone along with his romantic plans, she would have mirrored the anima role. But by calling him away from those plans she refuses to take on that role. The reason for this is not explained in the story, but at that moment, the anima projection falls

off because she would have had to have cooperated with his pull toward death for him to be able to continue his projection. Moreover, Melchior had chosen her because she was a dying person, which apparently the girl herself did not know and was consciously not attracted by death.

611   This also shows a typical weakness of young people. Melchior is the type of person who, when a projection falls off, does not carry on with the relationship — a further sign of his eros weakness. But there are also men who, when they notice that the other person is not what they had assumed, are pulled by natural curiosity to find out more about the matter. They think it odd that they were so attracted by a woman who ceased to attract when she proved to be quite different, and they try to find out what happened and why the attraction faded. In this way there is a chance of realizing the projection; but those who, as soon as they are disappointed, just finish it, always remain in the projection. If one is disappointed, that is just the time to follow the relationship, at least for a while, to find out what happened. That is how Jung discovered, in himself, the anima. Being again disappointed in a woman, he asked himself why on earth he had expected anything else — what had made him expect something different? Through asking such questions and realizing an expectation which did not fit the other figure, he discovered the image within of the anima. It is therefore always helpful if a relationship — not only a heterosexual relationship — disappoints you, to ask yourself such questions. Why did I not see that before? What did I expect? Why did I have a different image of this person? Where did the error come from? For the error is something real, too. If one can do this, it indicates a desire to hold on to the human relationship and take back the illusion. When one does that and tries to establish the relationship on its own level, then the illusions must be investigated as something interesting. But people with weak feeling tend to break off the relationship as soon as the other person disappoints them. They just walk out because it is no longer interesting, and questions about why one had the wrong expectation and why one is hurt are not asked.

612   Every projection, however, has a "hook" in the other person. But one can only discover what this is if one goes on after the disappointment. At first you think you know the other person, for when you project, you have the strong feeling of knowing a lot about the other person. At the first meeting there is no need to talk: You know everything about each other — that is a complete projection — and you have the wonderful feeling of being one and of having known each other for centuries. Then suddenly, the other behaves in an unexpected way and there is disappointment. One falls out of the clouds and feels that "this is not it." If you then go on with the relationship, you must do two things, for now there is a double battle: You must find out why you had such an illusion and who the other person is if he or she is not what you expected. Who is he or she in reality? That is a long job, and when you have done that — have found the root of your own illusion and how the other person seems to be when looked at without projection — then you may ask why your illusion chose that person to fall upon? And that is very difficult, for sometimes the hook is big, and sometimes very small, because the other person may have only few characteristics that fit the projection, so it may be more — or less — of an illusion.

613   Melchior is obviously the type of person who leaves as soon as the projection falls off, as soon as the other person does not behave as expected. He even calls Henriette a coward; he insults her and leaves her. This shows the weakness of his dying feeling function — his eros. He does not even appear to be sorry afterward or to suffer from his unhappy love and disappointment. He just writes the whole thing off, just like the little prince, only in a rather different form, for the prince leaves the planet and the rose, even though she is sad and says out of pride he should go. If someone writes off his relationship so quickly, you may be sure that he will write himself off equally quickly. This type of man's weak anima is typical of a suicidal tendency in the unconscious.

614   That is how, to a certain extent, one can discover suicidal tendencies beforehand. I have met two types: One is not suicidal but could finish himself off in a rage — it would be a kind of accident.

There are irascible people (really something of the murderer type) who get sudden fits of rage which may also go against themselves, when they can kill themselves by mistake. They lose their heads, and they would be very sorry afterward. That is not a genuine suicidal tendency, but rather an inverted aggression. The aggressiveness is not integrated and may suddenly turn against the person himself — like the scorpion's sting. But Melchior is the true suicidal type, and such people secretly, intellectually, and coldly, write off those in their surroundings and themselves. They never really trust themselves or those around them — there are no real relationships — and this is something which runs through this whole book: There is no relatedness. That is the fatal thing right from the start.

615   After this, the quarrel between Melchior and his father is described, which is very important as Melchior is still pursuing the idea of the transformation of the personality. His father is an astrologer, a magician, and is also interested in occult sciences, not, however, for the sake of the transformation of the personality but rather out of curiosity, or as a pseudoscientific occult occupation. Father and son clash emotionally and then again write each other off. This reaction is so important because it indicates the main problem: the enmity between Fo, the boy, and Ulrich von Spät. At the beginning, Ulrich von Spät pretends to be Fo's tutor. He wanted to catch him in some way and to keep Melchior away from his influence. The boy, on the other hand, is afraid of Ulrich von Spät and tries to bring Melchior under his own influence, and the battle continues. There are times when Melchior loves Ulrich von Spät — for example, when he takes his leave and shakes hands with him — while at other times, he hates him and wants to avoid him. We must go into this further.

616   Von "Spät" (Late) is an allusion to the fact that he is the elder and plays the father role in relation to the boy. He pretends to be the spiritual mentor, or guardian — a father. This conflict is, then, a further development of the fight between Melchior and his father. If the son believes in the transformation of the personality — admittedly in a most unreal and fantastic way — and the father is

also interested in magic and occult things, although for different reasons, then two worlds clash here: The father rejects the transformation and wants to uphold the status quo, while the son wants renewal.

617   If we refer this to the idea of the transformation of the personality in alchemy, then we come to the problem of mind and matter in the father-son relationship. In a certain way, the father — the old wise man and magician — embodies the material and the spiritual. As the one who studies books, he is the spiritual side — he explores the world intellectually — with a hidden materialism. Conversely, we could say that the Fo archetype is a spiritual archetype, namely, the élan vital of the spiritual element. But there is something materialistic in this, too, for the boys wanted to transform the personality with real poison. That is materialism. Thus, in both figures, spirit and matter fall apart. When the one adopts a materialistic trend, the other turns toward the spiritual; but when the other takes on the materialistic trend, then Fo, the puer aspect, pulls for the spiritual attitude. What is lacking in their relationship to each other, but also in their outlook, is the soul, the anima. This is why in both opposite positions there is a separation of mind and matter. There is no vinculum amoris (bond of love) to unite them, for the anima is lacking. Thus, the father has spiritual interests with a secret materialistic background, and the son has chemical-materialistic interests with a spiritual background. They clash and cannot understand each other.

618   We have the same problem today. Think of such movements as anthroposophy. In Los Angeles, for instance, there is a new sect, founded by Manley Hall, whose members consider themselves to be something like new Rosicrucians. We see a brisk revival of interest in magic, in Freemasonry symbolism, in Rosicrucian symbolism, and in astrology and the occult sciences, and the followers of these movements all reject psychology. They want the Beyond to be called the ghost world, or they claim that an apparition of the animus is an angel from the Beyond, and they give these factors, which we try to name in a psychological way, old names which they take out of the

old traditional books. This is really Mr. von Spät (Mr. Late) because these explanations have a backward pull. They regress to medieval, and even to Sumerian and Babylonian, magical concepts. Or the speakers use concepts of the sixteenth century, for example, Paracelsus, and they are all nicely muddled up. Behind this pot pourri of concepts from the past, that are all pulled out of their context and used as a name for the phenomenon of what we call the unconscious, is a tremendous power gesture. Such an interpreter would say, for instance, "Well, Fo is the Hermes infans, Mercurius infans, the young Mercurius." And then one feels that something has been said! That is von Spät. In this way, the outer and inner realms — matter and spirit — fall apart. If, for instance, a man has an obligation to his anima, and to the woman with whom he made friends, or married, then he gets into a typical duality situation in life where he always has a real conflict, a double obligation, and where he is always torn between obligations to the outer and to the inner side of life. This is an experience of crucifixion, or of the basic truth of life. Life is double: It is a double obligation, a conflict, because it always means the collision, or conflict, of two tendencies. But that is what life is made up of! This realization completely escapes von Spät, or he escapes the realization. It does not even occur to him, and that is one more of the small, but fatal, turns in the story which point toward its tragic end.

Chapter Seven
The Great Feast

619 Before further amplifying the figures of Fo and von Spät, whose conflict is an extension on the personal level of Melchior and his father, I would like to present the next chapter in the book.

620 After Fo and his crowd have disappeared, Melchior's wife, Sophie, knocks on his door and enters the room. She asks him to join the company that is in the sitting-room. Melchior tells her he has no time for those people. "You have no time for me either, then," Sophie says, "for with those people I can talk in a human way, but that bores you." Melchior complains that they always talk about the same thing, and chew over the same matters. Sophie controls herself and says quietly, "I only feel at ease and safe with familiar things. But you can't stand it when I feel safe. […] You don't like it when somebody knows what they want. You always try to pull the rug from under their feet. Since they met you, they've become quite stupid. We can no longer have a serious conversation. It immediately gets wild and crazy…" Melchior adds that she does not want to understand him. Her sense of safety is a complete illusion, and that the others are deluding themselves if they believe they are safe. "Only someone who knows nothing else, who doesn't know up from down, who knows nothing at all about who he is may talk about safety. I do not trust solidity, or form, or permanence, or security." Sophie grows impatient and says he should come along with her for everything is chaotic today, that there is someone there who generates more fear than Melchior. He holds such

strange speeches, as if he were the commander of a large army of ghosts. He is an old acquaintance from her childhood who everyone had to obey and even at that time, they couldn't play the games they wished to play. Today, fifteen years later, he just happened to chance by. His name is Ulrich von Spät and he is passing through. Melchior suddenly pays attention, and he gets very excited. "He must be here because of me. He is using the fact that he already knows you. Now I understand." He then hurries into the sitting-room. Already at the door he hears von Spät's shrill voice, "Ladies and gentlemen, you are only laughing because you want to dismiss the things I have been telling you. But I can do the things I have told you about before your very eyes. It is no fairy tale like the hundreds of fairy tales and stories you know. I can lock each one of you up in this little bottle which I hold in my hand."

621 Melchior enters with his wife, and they are immediately surrounded and feverishly greeted. He is puzzled by the nervous excitement of his guests. He asks himself whether Mr. von Spät is responsible for it all. Professor Cux then introduces him to his wife, the dancer. He openly praises her beauty saying that one is allowed to say what one thinks at this place, and he pulls up her skirt to show everyone her marvellous calves. Upon seeing this, several of the other women raise their skirts to show their legs, women whom Melchior otherwise knows to be honest, bourgeois women and who are, to his astonishment, all heavily made up. "I, too, have lovely calves, I, too, have lovely calves," they all cry out. The fat art critic, Mr. Trümpelsteg, exclaims that calves alone are not the measure of things, but rather "what accompanies the calves" is. He suggests they hold a beauty pageant. They should all take off their clothes so that their full beauty can be admired. Everyone cheers, and there follows a confusion of arms and legs and clothing flying through the air. Within minutes all the women are naked. Melchior looks for Sophie.

She, too, has undressed, is swaying her hips and is looking at him mockingly. "What on earth is happening here?" Melchior thinks, "Is this what it looks like when what I say enters other people's minds?"

622   When Mrs. Cux dances naked through the room, embracing first this man, then another, this is the signal for a general dissolution. Screeching, the women fall to the floor, hitting, scratching, biting each other, laughing, scolding, and kissing each other, while the men, completely out of themselves, applaud loudly. Melchior approaches Mr. von Spät who is standing perfectly still. He tells him he does not believe that this meeting is by chance. Trümpelsteg overhears this and takes the opportunity to remind von Spät of his skills with magic. The parson, Silferharnisk, wants to finally see the miracle that has been promised and demands facts. "We enlightened, free people of today submit only to facts! Facts, Mr. von Spät! Facts!" The others excitedly shout their support. Mr Trümpelsteg can no longer contain himself and he jumps up onto the table to give a loud speech on the meaning and duty of art. Art has nothing to do with facts, but with ideals. It makes possible what real life cannot: true love, all-powerful passion. "How we love, ladies and gentlemen, is a disgrace! [...] In art, it becomes a temple feast inspired by the spirits of the earth. There, we experience depth, eternity, revelation on heat, world views! And, gentlemen, if now our honoured wizard, Mr. von Spät raises us up, as it were, beyond the facts and reality with his art, then let us be grateful! [...] Just imagine if these things were really facts — then everything around us would collapse, [...] then our dear Melchior would have been right. [...] I repeat, let's shield ourselves from facts! Facts are mean! Let's believe in the spirit that is harmless! Let us be knights of the spirit!"

623   They others all cheer. Melchior and von Spät look at one another and smile. It seemed to Melchior that a thin veil spread itself over the image, and everything seemed to be

further away and stranger. Only to von Spät did he feel deeply connected.

624 In the next chapter we find the situation has calmed down a little.

The people are full of expectation; Mr. von Spät has left the room. When he returns, he is surrounded by blue, luminous veils of mist; his eyes are closed. His arms are stretched out in front of him and in one hand he has a strange-looking bottle, and in the other, a small knife. Stiffly, he passes by everyone present with dancelike steps and goes to one corner that is opposite the door. People's eyes are filled with hatred. Trümpelsteg and Mrs. Cux, who had been communicating through signs, creep bent over behind him. Von Spät climbs the steps to the bay window and puts the bottle on a table; then he turns, and his face resembles that of a person asleep. A pistol flashes in Trümpelsteg's hand, and he cries out in a voice that is hoarse with fear that it is no longer funny, and he is about to shoot. Von Spät, however, quickly cuts his index finger with the knife and lets a drop of blood fall into the bottle. Instantly, Trümpelsteg is also in the bottle, thumb-sized, and Frau Cux, who had wanted to stab Von Spät with a knife, soon follows. The group panics and protests, threatening to call the police, but one member of the group tells them to hush, saying that that would be too dangerous — von Spät would use his magic to put them all into the bottle. All the while, Melchior is leaning against the wall, quiet and in a good mood. Sophie goes up to him and asks him to speak to von Spät, but he declines, saying he no longer has anything to do with her for she has long since chosen the others over him. Parson Silferharnisk raises his voice, calling them all to prayer. This is God's punishment for their enlightened arrogance that doubts God's omnipotence. Everyone falls to their knees. Von Spät picks up the bottle from the table and holds it aloft. Everyone sees how

Trümpelsteg undresses himself and begins to make love to Frau Cux, and the tiny couple sink to the floor in a passionate embrace. A few begin to laugh at the sight and soon everyone is laughing uproariously, falling into each other's arms, kissing, laughing, and crying. Only Professor Cux is furious and wants to throw himself at von Spät but finds himself tied to a heavy armchair with thick rope.

625 With his eyes still closed, von Spät now places the bottle back on the table and claps his hands together. "A light mist gathered in the room. And when it parted, seven maidens in white appeared and bowed before Mr. von Spät. From deep within the earth came the sound of wild dance music with muffled drumbeats. Mr. von Spät seized the hand of one of the girls and only then does he open his eyes that glow silver blue. And when he opened his eyes, he appeared sevenfold, and danced with each girl simultaneously. Once the dance was over, he closed them again, and again he was one person." All at once, in the outer wall, a door that was not previously there, opens, and a room with a table covered with food appears. "And a voice called out three times, 'Come and eat! Come and eat! Come and eat!' Melchior thought he recognized the voice. In the doorway stood the old apple-woman from the station, throwing apples to the guests." Everybody pairs up with someone, next to every man a naked woman. Von Spät pairs up with one of the girls in white. The remaining six seat themselves so that next to each one of them is an empty chair. The old apple-woman serves the guests, speaking to them invitingly. When she fills Melchior's wine glass, she whispers to him, "Clever boy. You knew me at once, clever boy. But you are not clever enough. Be careful!" Melchior asks what he should be careful of, but the old woman may not tell him. He grabs her by the wrist and wants to force her to tell him everything. But the old woman pulls away and murmurs as she leaves, "Ring on the finger. Faces at the window. Ways cross. Winds blow southwards.

Soon it will be time. They're waiting! They're waiting!"
Melchior quietly repeats her words. A great longing and
restlessness fill him, and he feels tears rising. Only Sophie
had noticed this short exchange. The guests eat and drink
eagerly. The seven girls sit as if they are asleep, and von Spät's
eyes are also closed. Melchior looks at him and asks himself
why he hates and loves him at the same time. "What is his
power? What made him demonstrate his power to these
people? [...] Did he want to show me who these people are?
[...] I know them. I have forced them long ago to be naked
in front of me. But I want to leave. What I hoped for and yet
never expected has happened. A different type of company
is beckoning me. Why do I hesitate? The stranger keeps me
bound. What does he want from me?" He thinks he sees Fo's
face at the window, whose eyes look at him unwaveringly.

626   The meal is drawing to a close. The teacher, Schulze, stands
up to make a speech. "Honoured guests, even the most
amazing miracles seem quite natural when one has grown
used to them. [...] Today, for a minute, we were shaken by
unusual things which seemed miraculous to us. But now [...
] we are sitting quietly in a room that, as it were, rose up from
out of the ground in a few minutes; we are enjoying food and
drink that it seems to us has appeared out of thin air, and we
are no longer particularly surprised when one amongst us
becomes sevenfold by opening his eyes, not to mention that
two of us, trapped inside a tiny bottle, are making audacious
love. [...] All of these things seem natural to us. And what is
the result of all of this, ladies and gentlemen? Nothing is
supernatural! There are no miracles! There are only facts.
And facts in themselves are always reasonable. [...] We can
include it all in how we see the world. We can just remain
ourselves! [...]"

627   A terrible shriek interrupts him. The seven forms of Mr. von
Spät moan and shut their eyes and the seven girls dissolve
into mist. The room disappears and everyone finds them-

selves back in Melchior's sitting-room. Von Spät is lying unconscious on the floor. Fo is standing by the bay window, laughing. Von Spät lies writhing in pain. "Do you feel it now? Do you feel it now?" yells Fo. "It went beyond your power. You wanted to rest for a minute and play, eh? For a minute your power was not awake. Do you now feel that you may never sleep? Do you now feel that we are the masters?" He dances round von Spät with great leaps. Melchior sees the distorted, noble face of the man lying on the floor. He is overcome by horror and love, and wants to throw himself at Fo, but he is whirling toward the window. "Take him away, Melchior," he cries. "[…] We give him to you now!" he cries, and then adds softly, urgently, "We are waiting for you!"

628 When Fo has gone, von Spät's cramps slowly subside. He is lying naked on the floor, and Melchior studies his well-proportioned body. Without paying any attention to the others, he carries him to his study and waits for him to wake up. Melchior now sees von Spät's real facial features. "It is the face of a beautiful god, slightly distorted in length and by illness." Von Spät gradually wakes up and says to Melchior that he had come to his home to warn him about Fo and to take the ring from him once again. He asks him why he protected him while he slept. Melchior replies that he has realized von Spät is his brother. Von Spät cries out that he shall never sleep again because the boys, his enemies, overwhelm him every time he does so. He is their master. In response to Melchior's question, he says that no one knows the boys' true form. "They approach you as wandering boys, as fleeting girls, as animals. They lure you away into chaos and darkness. Somewhere they have a kingdom, the entrance to which I cannot find. But they are never there. They are always here. Perhaps they are here and there at the same time. … I must discover the way to them. I must destroy their kingdom. Those unbridled, free people must be brought into my service. […] No darkness may surround them, no night,

no refuge. They must no longer change, must not be transformed from one form into another. All around, there must be light. Their indiscriminate, wild love must die. […] Nobody may sleep any longer!"

629   Von Spät stood up. His body appeared to be transparent, with a shimmering glow around it, and he began to grow infinitely tall. The ceiling of the room disappeared, "and out of the darkness a face resembling his own, looking down and dimly lit, bowed to him. 'Who are you? Who are you?' cries Melchior, trembling. 'Make a choice, Melchior,' Mr. von Spät calls out, and his voice sounds like distant glass bells, 'if you want to go to the boys, you need only call for them, and they will take you with them into the sweet night; you will become one of them and forget all that you were and are. If you want to come with us, just knock on the wall of this room — […] and a way will open for you to reign in the light. […] The way to us is full of danger. You must pass through all the horrors of the world. […]'" As he speaks, Mr. von Spät's form dissolves into nothing. The ceiling closes again and Melchior is alone.

630   The discussion between Melchior and his wife shows that their marriage is past repair: There is a complete split between the two; they do not understand each other, and their love has been extinguished. Obviously, a terrific bitterness of disappointed love has piled up in Sophie, who feels that Melchior never takes part in her world and has never loved her. Like so many women who feel unloved, in her bitterness she has sold herself completely to the animus. Instead of trying to work on their relationship, she tries to connect to him by playing tricks on him. Their love has turned into a fight for power. Eros has disappeared from their relationship. She also hates her husband because of his spiritual searching that drives him into a restless conflict with the bourgeois world. He is searching for something that upsets her need for peace and security. She wants to be the professor's wife, to have a nice circle around her in which

she plays a role. But he destroys the security of this little world that she has built. She accuses him of dissolving everything, while he tries to show that the security of this bourgeois world is deceptive, that only the people who can give themselves to the irrational adventure of life have genuine security. But the talk gets them nowhere, and with von Spät's appearance, Melchior finally joins the party.

631 It also turns out that Mr. von Spät had been one of Sophie's friends when she was young, whom she had lost sight of. Von Spät had already described himself as the father-spirit, the spirit of tradition that comes from the paternal world. For a man, the father-figure represents cultural tradition. Von Spät therefore personifies cultural tradition that always comes too late. It is the opposite of renewal; it is knowledge with its poisonous "we know it all." Every cultural condition contains a secret poison which consists of the pretension of knowing all the answers. On a primitive level, you see this in the initiation of young men when the old men of the tribe tell them the history of the universe: how the world was made, the origin of evil, of life after death, of the purpose of life, and so on. On this level, for instance, all such questions are answered by the mythological tribal or religious knowledge conveyed by the old to the young, and on that level, except for perhaps a few creative personalities, this is just swallowed wholesale. From then on, the young men know everything too; everything is settled, all questions are answered, so that if a missionary comes and tries to talk to these people, he is just informed how things are: "Oh yes, we know, the world was made in such a way; evil comes from this and that; the purpose of life is so and so." We do the same thing, except that in our case it is a bit more complex; basically, however, it is the same.

632 Ulrich von Spät represents the archetypal principle of handed-down traditional knowledge, and this contends eternally with the principle of the puer aeternus — the spirit of creating everything anew, again and again. Sophie is secretly linked up with von Spät, who turns out to be the boyfriend of her youth. Seen from the standpoint of her psychology, he would therefore represent the father-animus. The pretension of knowing all the answers is exactly

what the father-animus produces in a woman: the assumption that everything is self-evident — the illusion of knowing it all. This is the attitude Jung is attacking when he speaks negatively about the animus: "Everyone does that" and "everybody knows this" — the absolute conviction with which women hand out "wisdom." When one examines it closely, however, one sees that they have just picked up what the father (or someone else) said, without assimilating it themselves. The daughter tends just to reproduce the knowledge of the past in the way she picked it up from her father. To hand on traditional knowledge without it being worked on by the woman's individual consciousness and then assimilated is dangerous and tends to be demonic.

633   It is also clear that von Spät's outstanding characteristic is a tremendous power complex. Sophie says that even as a child he suffocated all creativity in the other children and that they had to play the way he wanted. The basis of von Spät is power, and power, in a wider sense, corresponds to the instinct of self-preservation of the individual.

634   As discussed earlier, on the level of animals, there are two basic, natural tendencies which, to a certain extent, contradict each other: the sexual drive with all its functions, including, the bearing of children and rearing of the young, and the drive toward self-preservation. These two drives are in opposition to each other for procreation often means the death of the older generation. In many animal species, the male dies after propagation has taken place. There are spiders, for example, that are eaten by the female once they have fulfilled their function. He is no longer useful except in helping to feed the young by being eaten by the mother. That is an extreme case, but frequently older animals completely exhaust themselves for the sake of their young, even to the point of destruction. As hunters well know, the sexual drive causes animals to forget self-protection entirely. They become blind to danger. A roebuck pursuing a hind may run right into a man. If a buck is in that state, the hunter must hide behind a tree for the shyest animal will be oblivious of his own security when sex is the important thing. Sex means preservation of

the species, and therefore preservation of the individual is sacrificed to it. It is the species that is important — life must go on. In the usual state, when sexuality is not constellated, the drive to self-preservation (which takes the form of either fighting or fleeing) is uppermost. The animal is occupied by eating and by keeping away from mortal danger, i.e., by keeping itself alive as an individual creature.

635   These two drives, sex and self-preservation, are the basic tendencies in animal life. In humans, they appear as two divine and contradictory forces, namely, as love and power. Love includes sexuality, and power includes self-preservation. Eros and power, therefore, as Jung always points out, are opposed to each other. You cannot have them together; they exclude each other. The marriage of Melchior and Sophie, for instance, has become a power game in which each tries to save his or her own world from the dangerous world of the other. The possibility of giving of oneself, the generosity of letting the other's world penetrate one's own, has been lost. Both partners fight for their lives against each other. Since the wife has lost her capacity for love, she falls for the power-drive and for von Spät. That is the back door by which von Spät gets into the house. But he is just as much the power-drive of Melchior himself. How does the power-drive react toward the other drive of eros? Here, he ridicules it by putting eros in a bottle — a classic illustration of how the power-drive deals with eros, the other drive: he imprisons it! People imprison love and sex by behaving as though they were the owners, for example, the woman who uses her beauty and charm to catch a rich husband. She does not love him; she uses love, or what is supposed to be love, to get what she may want: men, wealth, career. She behaves as if she were the owner of her love, as if she were able to direct it. A woman who has fallen for Mr. von Spät would repress any spontaneous feeling of love. If she noticed that she was falling in love with a chimney sweep, she would repress her feeling in statu nascendi (nip it in the bud) because it would not suit her to love a social nobody. On the other hand, she would deceive herself into believing that she loved the great Mr. X who had a lot of money. She

would try to convince herself that she loved a man who would fit in with her ego and power plans, and any kind of spontaneous eruption of eros would be repressed. Thus, love generally degenerates into its most basic fact, namely sexuality. It is reduced to its prima materia, so to speak, to physical sexuality, which is imprisoned in intellectual planning. Sexuality is used to catch a suitable partner for suitable reasons, and all real love, which generally dissolves the fetters and boundary lines and creates new life situations, is anxiously repressed.

636   The whole episode with the bottle naturally reminds one of the alchemical retort in which the naked couple is together, but with a quite different meaning. Here, obviously, it is misused; it is a kind of cynical abuse of the alchemical mystery by using the sight to reduce it to an intellectual system. The alchemical idea is used with a "nothing but" nuance: It is "nothing but sexual liberty" or "nothing but the body" or "nothing but me with Mr. So-and-So," thereby excluding any of the mystery. Glass is a substance which can be seen through, but it is a very bad conductor of warmth. One could say that it has to do with the intellect, that it represents a system which makes one able to see through something, but which cuts off the feeling relationship. For instance, when Snow White is imprisoned in a glass coffin, she is cut off from life as far as feeling and certain perceptions are concerned. If you are in a glass house, you can see everything that goes on outside, but you are cut off from the smells, the temperature, the wind and so on, and you are therefore cut off from the feeling relationship to the outer world or to the inner world. It is interesting that we put some animals in the zoo in glass cages thus avoiding all the reality impact with danger. We are then able to study their behavior from an intellectual distance. In alchemy, on the other hand, the glass retort is even regarded as being identical with the philosopher's stone. The vessel is the feminine aspect of the philosopher's stone, which is, in turn, the masculine aspect of the self, but both are the same thing. In the present story, the glass is a mystical factor which is now in the hands of von Spät. Psychologically speaking, there is a big difference between the glass as a positive alchemical symbol and this misused glass vessel. In

alchemy, the retort is a place of transformation. However, it is the precondition for any kind of psychological transformation to look at oneself, to look carefully within: Instead of looking at the outer facts, at other people, I must look only at my own psyche. That would be putting it into a glass. Suppose I am angry with somebody. If I turn away from that person and say, "Now let me look at my anger and what that means, and at what is behind it," that would be putting my anger into the retort. Thus, the retort represents an attitude that aims at self-knowledge — an attempt to become conscious of oneself instead of looking at other people. As far as the will is concerned, it requires determination; as far as intellectual activities are concerned, it means introversion, the search for inner self-knowledge at all costs, and objectively, not subjectively, musing about one's problems; making the effort to really see oneself objectively. Nobody can find this attitude except by what one could call an act of grace. For instance, if somebody is either madly in love, or madly angry over some problem, one always tries to get the person for once to look away from that question, whatever it may be, to try to be objective. One tries to get them to look at the dream, to see how it looks from within, from the objective psyche, using the dream life as a mirror for the objective psychological situation. Very often, people cannot do this even if they want to, unless some miraculous turnaround happens. They begin again with the specific problem: "Yes, but you see tomorrow I have to decide with my banker whether to sell the stock or not." Then it is better to turn for a minute to the inner world, to see what the objective psyche has to say about it. "No, you see, I have to decide!" And then it is like a miracle if that person suddenly becomes quiet and objective and makes that turn and looks inside and says, "I will just abstain from looking at the emotions which flow toward this problem and try to be objective." That is a miracle, and it needs the intervention of the self. Something must happen in the person for him to be able to do it. We are often cut off from self-knowledge and cannot do it, and then suddenly this strange peace comes up within, usually when we have suffered enough. Then we become quiet and silent, and our ego becomes more objective and turns to look at the facts within, objectively, and stops the monkey-dance of thinking about the situation. Our ego's self-assurance stops, and a kind of objectivity comes over us. Then it is possible to look at ourselves and be open to the experience of the unconscious.

637   It can therefore be said that in a way the alchemical vessel is a mysterious event in the psyche, an occurrence — something which takes place suddenly and which enables people to look at themselves objectively using dreams and other products of the unconscious as mirrors. Without the latter, one has no Archimedean point outside the ego by which to do it. That is why an awareness of the Self is necessary before one can look at oneself, and that is why very often people are touched in the beginning of their analysis by an experience of the self. Only that enables them afterward to strive toward looking at themselves in this objective way. That is precisely what the alchemists meant by the vessel. It could also be said that the vessel symbolizes an attitude which is, for example, the prerequisite for doing active imagination, for you can only do it with the help of the vessel. You can call active imagination itself a sort of vessel, for if I sit down and try to objectify my psychological situation in active imagination, that would be having it in a vessel. Once again, this presupposes an attitude of ethical detachment, honesty, and objectivity, which is necessary to be able to look at oneself. That would be the vessel in a positive form.

638   If I judge the unconscious with my ego, I put it in a vessel too. But then it is the glass prison, the "nothing but" attitude, which gives this prison a negative aspect. Then it is an intellectual system, and the living phenomenon of the psyche is imprisoned in an intellectual system. The owner of it is power. This is very subtle. There are even people willing to look at themselves, but only to be stronger than the other person, or to master a situation. They still retain an ego-power purpose, and they even use the techniques of Jungian psychology — active imagination, for instance — to overcome their difficulty, or to be the big stag who did it. Their eye is fixed on power. This gives the whole thing the wrong twist, and nothing comes out of it. There are others who work for a certain time honestly analyzing

themselves — but to become analysts and to have power over others. That is another snare of the same kind: not looking within for its own sake, or because one has the need to be more conscious. Thus, power sneaks into everything again and again, and turns what has been a living spiritual manifestation into a technical trick in the possession of the ego. Ulrich von Spät is the demon of misusing everything, of making everything — even the highest spiritual power — degenerate into such a technical trick.

639   If we see von Spät as Sophie's animus, then he would be a father image. The father-animus in a woman produces not only opinions but also magic tricks. I am reminded of the case of a woman who had a schizoid father, a rather cold, sadistic man who perpetually criticized his children, constantly telling them that they were nobodies and that they would never get anywhere. If they tried in school, he said that they would never succeed, or if they wanted to take up art, he told them they had no talent and would not make a success of it. He always had a negative attitude. He also had the habit of cutting off the heads of flowers with a stick when they walked along the fields, which drove his daughters mad. It was a nervous habit and was done in revenge, or out of bitterness over his own disappointed and destroyed feeling life.

640   Now this daughter had a series of lovers — old men, young men, artists, businessmen — apparently all different kinds of people. After she had known them for more than a fortnight, they would always start to torture her in a sadistic way by telling her that she was nobody and that she would never get anywhere. It was the same old tune her father had sung. I have never found out whether she made them do it, or, if by some divination of instinct, she always picked such men. It was like black magic. In primitive language, I would say that there was a curse on that girl, compelling her to choose critical, unloving, sadistic men who trampled on her feelings, which were already nearly destroyed. Her dreams revealed that it really was the father working within her. The night after one such quarrel with a lover who told her that she was no good and everything was wrong with her, and so on, she dreamt that her father waited for her and

beat her on her shin bone with a stick, making her fall. It is a well-known fact that the father-animus, or the mother-demon in a man, does not only act as an inner wrong fate, a distortion of the instincts in the choice of the partner, for example, but also is really like an outer fate, and can appear in synchronicities, in synchronistic miracles outside the personal life, in events for which we cannot hold the individual responsible. I think it would be wrong feeling-wise to tell such a girl that she always fell for sadistic lovers because she had not overcome the sadistic father-animus within her. There is quite a bit of truth in that, but it is not the whole truth. Later, when she is further along, one may encourage her to see that she has such a father-demon and sadist within her and that it attracts sadistic men. Sometimes, however, when one tries to deal with such a dark fate, one feels that one is up against a divine destructive power, so much so that one cannot make the individual responsible. Thus, we could say that in a woman, von Spät is the demon of her secret thoughts who determines her fate.

641 When von Spät performs this magic, however, he becomes untrue to himself which is why Fo catches him. It is very important to remember that if von Spät had not performed this magical trick, Fo would not have overcome him. "I'll never sleep again," von Spät says afterward. "When I sleep, my enemies tear me apart. Sleep is always lying in wait for me. I played." We see, then, that he became untrue to himself because he played for a minute: He forgot his power-drive and amused himself with his magical performance. For a moment, he behaved like Fo, like the boys. He played — "and there he got me for the last time. But I am his master. Our body is not earth. Our body is music, mirroring the stars." It is a true enantiodromia, and we must see von Spät as the spirit of intellectualism, the power of thought, that is valid only as long as he does not play. As soon as he begins to produce magic, he begins to turn toward the Fo-principle. If you look at it as though there were two poles, one pole would be Fo and the other von Spät. When von Spät is at his best and is completely himself, then he is awake; he does not sleep, he does not play, and he does not perform magic tricks. But he got

drunk on his power and displayed it more and more. He wanted to show off his magic and forgot himself. And then Fo got him! We could just as well say that he fell into Fo's pole, for these two powers always fall into each other's pole through an enantiodromia, as do all unconscious opposites because they are gods, which means they are basic archetypal drives in the psyche. It is a play of opposites in which Melchior is the suffering human, in the middle of the two, for both von Spät and Fo want his soul. When von Spät goes too far in his power-play, he snaps into Fo, and we shall see that when Fo goes too far into his power-play, he snaps into von Spät. When von Spät begins to perform magic by using his own blood, he is really leaning toward the Fo side and going over to the other pole. They are secretly linked. We could say that they were two aspects of life, for both belong to life and you cannot live without either. But each one claims to be the only one. Both make a total claim on the human being. Fo asks Melchior to give himself totally to him, and von Spät asks the same thing, and the tragedy is, as we shall see at the end of the book, that Melchior cannot hold his own standpoint. Seen from the personal angle, this is the weakness of the ego: It is torn between the opposites and is their plaything. Melchior is between two gods or demons who both claim to be his unique owner, and he is unable to keep his feet on the ground and say, "I will not obey either of you, but will live my human life." And that is why he is caught up in this constant demonic game.

642   It is interesting that "Fo" is one of the designations for Buddha. This makes sense here because it is said that Melchior had traveled in China and India, and Fo is the ruler of an invisible kingdom, which would be Nirvana, as we shall see later. On the cover of this book is something like a Japanese torii, which has a mystical meaning in the East — the door through which you go into the beyond — and on the back of the book there is an eightfold star. These two symbols were probably chosen consciously. Obviously, the author knew Eastern material and was fascinated by it, as will become much more evident later, and he projects the puer aeternus — the creative eros-demon — into the East. Von Spät, on the other

hand, represents late Christianity. The latter has long since lost its powerful élan vital of its first centuries. In its now old and worn-out form, the Christian culture no longer serves us. We, the tired Western civilization, pretend that we know all the answers, but we are longing for a new genuine inner experience and are largely turning to the East, expecting a renewal from there. But this is obviously a projection. That would be another aspect of von Spät, whose slightly morbid face suggests a beautiful divine image, slightly oblong and sickly. Which god in many paintings looks like that? Christ! But von Spät is not Christ: He is only one of the images we have of him — a suffering, dying god — divine, but no longer capable of living.

643   Much of the book at this point does not need any comment. There is the journalist who just talks any kind of rot he thinks fitting, and the parson who pretends that he is studying the disorientation of modern life and then, while praying, just stops to stare at the sexual intercourse taking place in the bottle. The irony in all these things is transparent and comes out of the conscious layers of the author. No further psychological interpretation is therefore needed.

644   But the still unsolved problem is the role of the feminine. Women are described with the utmost scorn. There is not a single positive feminine figure in the book. The author ridicules them completely. There is no eros in the book, and the only positive woman in the chapters we have discussed so far is the apple-woman, who is a positive mother figure. She brings a message to Melchior when von Spät's power is at its height. She whispers to him that he is expected and that he should be true to Fo and the boys. She is the only feminine figure on the side of the boys, and this makes a cluster which consists of a group of mother-bound boys whose feminine ruler is archetypal mother nature and, at the same time, is the fat old woman who sells apples at the station.

645   That there is no young anima figure is typical of the German mentality. As Jung points out, on "the other side of the Rhine" the anima has not been differentiated but has remained for the most part within the mother complex. A man belonging to the Secret Service

told me that when he wanted to loosen up young Nazi prisoners to get military information out of them, the leading — and practically always successful — question to put when they were determined not to tell the enemy anything was, "Is your mother still alive?" He was almost always successful with this question. They would usually then start to cry, and their tongues were loosened. He discovered that this was the key question with which to penetrate the armor of the hostile attitude in German youths. Naturally generalizations must be taken as such: They are only half-truths in individual cases. But if we may characterize national differences, there is still a lack of differentiation of the anima in Germans compared with the more Latin-influenced peoples. The south of Germany, where there was a Roman occupation, is different to the north, so the statement has to be taken with a grain of salt. This novel, however, shows clearly the state of complete lack of differentiation of the anima.

646   Sophia means wisdom. It is meaningful that Melchior's wife's name is Sophie, but she appears as a bitter, animus-possessed, socially ambitious, petty, unloving woman — the typical disappointed wife. Nevertheless, her name means wisdom, which shows how greatly the unloving attitude of the man has altered the feminine principle. Sophie could be Wisdom; she could incarnate the love of humanity — she could be all that her name implies — but instead she is changed into this destructive, small figure because Melchior has not known how to turn toward her and make her blossom with his love. She is negative wisdom, and she is bitter because her husband does not love human beings. She likes human contact, and he hates it; she wants to force him to make human contact, but he remains in inhuman isolation. This is what they fight about. In the Old Testament, Sophie is called philanthropos, "the one who loves man." She is an attitude of love toward mankind, which naturally means being human among other human beings and loving them. That is the highest form of eros. As Jung sketches it in his paper on the transference, Sophie is even higher than the highest love symbolized by the Virgin Mary because, as he says, very meaningfully, "less sometimes means more." This means that if I

have an idealistic love for mankind, wanting to do only good, that is less than just being human among human beings.

647 But that kind of love is lacking at this party in which a completely barbaric animality breaks through with its egoism, vulgarity, and dishonesty. This shows what happens if love for the human being is not present. It also shows what neglecting the eros side of life produces, namely a conventional surface layer of so-called spiritual civilization and, underneath, the old animal ape-circus which may break loose at any minute. As soon as the conventions are gone and the women have undressed, there is just the ape-circus left, with a complete lack of differentiation of anything human. This is what people look like when they have not developed the feeling function; as a rule, they do not have the courage to reveal the animality lurking underneath. It takes a revolution, a Nazi movement, or something of that sort, to bring it into the open, and then one is just amazed at what comes out. When the conventions are swept away, then this ape-circus appears. Von Spät hates sleep. He is the enemy of sleep and says that when he has completely overcome his enemies, there will be no sleep, and his way to overcome the boys will be to cut them off from the source of sleep. In sleep, the power drive is knocked out, and we are completely helpless in our surroundings. It is a state in which power is knocked out. In this state, the unconscious comes up. At first, then, one thinks von Spät must represent consciousness and Fo, the principle of unconsciousness. But if we look more closely, it is a bit different. Von Spät is something unconscious too, namely, the unconscious demonic aspect of consciousness that "has all the answers." Consciousness consists of something we think we know; it is an immediate awareness — a knowing. Even if we do not know quite what it is, we have a subjective feeling that what consciousness is is intimately known to us. But behind this conscious awareness, behind the I and the whole phenomenon of consciousness, lies an unconsciousness: the shadow, the power-drive, and something demonic. We must never forget that consciousness has a demonic aspect. We are slowly becoming aware that the achievements of our consciousness — our technical

achievements, for example — also have destructive aspects. We are waking up to the fact that consciousness can be a disadvantage and that it is based on unconsciousness. That which makes me so passionately want knowledge in order to deal with life is something unconscious, and we do not know what that is. The need, the urge and passion for consciousness is something unconscious, as is what we know as conscious tradition. We could say that Christian teaching is a content of our collective consciousness. If we look more closely, however, we see that it is based on symbols such as the crucified god, the Virgin Mary, and so on, and if we think about these, about what they mean and how to link them up with our actual life, we discover that we do not know because they are full of unconsciousness. We find that precisely those known aspects of our spiritual tradition are completely mysterious to us in many ways, and that we can say little about them. Thus, consciousness contains a secret reverse side — the unconscious. And it is precisely this that is the demonic thing about von Spät, namely, that conscious views always behave as if they were the whole answer. One might say that perhaps it is now the task of psychology to uncover this secret, destructive aspect of consciousness.

648   I hope that we may sometime get to the point where consciousness can function without the pretension of knowing everything and of having said the last word. If consciousness could be reduced to a function, a descriptive function, then people would cease to make final statements. Instead, one would say that from the known facts, it appears at the present time as if one could explain it in such and such a way. That would mean giving up the secret power premise that claims to have said all there is to be said, so that now we know all about it and it is so. If that false pretension could be eliminated, that would be a big step. But that presupposes the integration of consciousness by our becoming aware of its relativity and its specific relation to the individual (I must know that I know and that I have that view in particular). It is not enough to have a conscious viewpoint. One must know why one has it and what one's individual reasons for having it are. The average person is still

possessed by collective consciousness and, under its influence, talks as if he knew all the answers. For example, people tend to regard a humanitarian attitude as being their own, forgetting that it is derived from the Christian Weltanschauung. They fail to realize that it is collective and that it is part of a Weltanschauung they no longer share. Power is the hidden motivation behind such behavior. Knowledge is one of the greatest means of getting power. Man has obtained power over nature and other human beings either by brute force or by knowledge and intelligence. It is uncertain which is the stronger, for strength and intelligence are two aspects of the power drive, and they account for the many primitive animal stories in which the witty, clever one outwits the strong one: The hyena outwits the lion, and in South America, the little dwarf stag outwits even the tiger. This shows up in the power drive of the individual; for instance, in the animus of women — either they trick their husbands, or they make brutal scenes. Emotional brutality and cunning are two manifestations of the power drive.

649   Our consciousness is still secretly coupled with these two tendencies for domination, and knowledge is generally combined with them. You see this most irritatingly in the prestige drive of the academic world. It is a rare event in university life that a scientist is interested in truth for its own sake; usually he is more interested in his position and in being the first to have said something. Power which is contained in knowledge is a demonic drive to dominate through knowledge, and it is stronger than the objective interest in finding out any kind of truth. Ulrich von Spät symbolizes all the positive and negative aspects of an ossified conscious tradition.

650   We must now turn our attention to the symbolism of the number seven, for after von Spät has conjured up his magic trick on the bottle, he appears at the dinner with seven girls dressed in white, and, as the companion of each one, he appears in seven-fold form.

651   In alchemy, especially in the later alchemical texts, which are probably the ones that our author knows, there are often representations of seven women sitting in an earth cave. They embody the seven planets or the seven metals. The idea was that

every metal corresponds to a planet: gold-sun, silver-moon, copper-Venus, lead-Saturn, iron-Mars, tin-Jupiter, quicksilver-Mercury. The eighth figure among the seven women would represent the ruler of them all and that would be either the sun-god or Saturn — Saturn was the old form of the sun. From his name (Spät=Late) one can also conclude that von Spät probably represents the old sun-god surrounded by the seven planets. We have interpreted von Spät as representing the principle of Christianity because he appears as an aristocratic but rather morbid looking god. Now he appears as the old sun-god, which would mean that it is not Christianity in itself, whatever that is, but the old tired Weltanschauung of Christianity: that which has been realized and is therefore a habit of thought that is no longer vital — a kind of principle at the base of our social and religious institutions. In fairytales, this corresponds to the old king who has lost the water of life and who needs to be renewed or must be dethroned or give up the throne to a follower. The Weltanschauung has grown old and has become an aged ruler who is sterile and needs renewal.

652   At the end of this chapter that I have presented in a summarized form here, von Spät has a double of himself, and he disappears into the sky like mist. This means that von Spät is an incarnation of a divine principle and now unites with his eternal form. If Melchior were able to draw conclusions from what he has experienced, this doubling would have practical consequences for him. The condition sine qua non of realizing consciously what a content means is the realization of its inner opposite, that is, that it is this and not that. This is a table, which means that it is not a chair or something else. You cannot make a conscious statement without excluding all the other aspects. Thus, if a dream figure doubles, it always means that it wants to become conscious — that it touches the threshold of consciousness and thereby reveals its double aspect. We have interpreted von Spät as the Christian Weltanschauung. Do we, who are born into the Christian civilization, really know at bottom what it means? What archetype is behind the Christian civilization? Could we honestly claim that we know what we mean when we say we

believe in a Trinitarian God and in Christ? Even the greatest theologian has never claimed to do so. Catholic theologians, for instance, speak of the mystery of each dogma. Some aspects can be put into words, but the nucleus is unknown to us. We would say that there is an archetypal content or an archetype behind it which, by definition, we do not know. One could therefore say that von Spät is that part which has entered human consciousness, which sounds familiar to us, and gives us that strange feeling of knowing what it means because we are to some extent aware and conscious of it. And then there is a whole other half which is completely unknown to us: its other side. One might say that only after having realized the pagan opposite pole — which would be the world of Fo and the pagan mother-goddess — could we become aware of the double aspect of Christianity — its conscious and unconscious aspects. While we are in it, we cannot become aware of it, for we are wrapped up in it. We would need an Archimedean point outside to realize the specific nature of our own civilization. The pagan pole is projected onto the East, for the boy Fo has a name which points to Buddha, which means that the capacity for looking at our own cultural and religious background is only possible for us when we get into closer contact with other civilizations and their religions. If, with a certain equanimity, you can accept the fact that the other person's religion contains some truth too, then you are able to become aware, objectively, of the specific character of your own culture. Detached awareness such as this is, of course, a modern development, and it has increased to such an extent that it is no longer possible for us to get stuck in the medieval prejudice that ours is the only true religion. Now that the world has shrunk and we are confronted with many other cultures, we must ask ourselves what is specific and different in our attitudes and in our civilization compared to other cultures. This question introduces a certain relativity which makes us realize how in some ways von Spät represents something we consciously know and which we attempt to convey to others (for instance, in foreign missionary work) and how much there is an archetypal, unknown background, namely, the eternal aspect of von Spät, which is the image of something divine behind any specific form in which it may appear.

653   In a certain way, we find this development in the writings of Arnold Toynbee, who, with a kind of extraverted approach, tries to say that now that we are in closer contact with the East and other civilizations, we should simply adopt a kind of mixed religion. He proposes a new form of prayer which would begin, "Oh Thou, who art Buddha, Christ, Dionysus…." We should just pray to a savior figure to whom one would ascribe all the names and make a nice cocktail of all the essentials of all the religions, slightly blurring the not too important differences, to have a kind of generalized world religion where Buddhists and indigenous South Africans, and everybody, can join in and think what they like about these contents. This is the same reaction that we already had on a smaller scale in the late Roman Empire. There, too, there were all those little nations with their local creeds and folklore and religious teaching — the Celts and the Syrians and the Israelites, and so on — and then the Romans tried to do the same thing. They said that you just had to pray to Jupiter-Zeus-Amun, which was the highest god, and the underworld god, Hades-Osiris. This is an example of a new cocktail religion in which the attributes of the gods are mixed. This would be as if we would now have new images of Christ in which he would be represented as sitting in a Buddha-position, with the mudra of pity and the cross somewhere behind him in a decorative way. All that is possible — human naïvety is boundless!

654   This attempt at relativity — the typical development of von Spät, the late development of a tired civilization, of a worn-out and decaying Weltanschauung — has no chance of success because the very essence of religious experience is that it has an absolute character. If I say that my experience could, but just as well could not, be, or that I believe such-and-such, but I can quite understand if another believes something different, this indicates that my so-called religious experience is not genuine because religious experience has a compelling and absolute character. One could say that this is the criterion of a religious experience. If someone asserts

that his experience has changed his whole life and will now pervade everything and if it really does apply to everything, being a total experience, applicable to every field of activity, then you know that whatever it may seem, it is a truly religious experience. Otherwise, it is merely an intellectual experience, or a mood, which passes away or which is kept in one drawer for Sundays — taken out and put away again.

655   Thus, we are in a terribly contradictory situation: In order to have a religious experience, one needs some kind of absolute obligation, yet this is irreconcilable with the reasonable fact that there are many religions and many religious experiences, and that intolerance is really outdated and barbaric. The possible solution would be for everyone to keep to his own experience and take it as absolute, accepting the fact that others have different experiences, thus relating the necessary absoluteness only to oneself — to me this is absolute (there is no relativity and no other possibility), but I must not extend the borders into the other person's field. And this is what we try to do. We try to let people keep a religious experience without collectivizing it and wrongly insisting that it must be valid for others too. It must be valid for me, but it is an error for me to think that the experience which is absolute for me has to be applied to others. We shall see that this shortly becomes a crucial point in our novel. Here, however, we see that the breaking in of a new religious experience, which is represented by Fo, makes it possible to realize the two layers of the late Weltanschauung of von Spät, who says, "If you want to follow us towards the kingdom of light, then just knock on this wall and a door will open."

Chapter Eight
Conflict and Madness

656   The next part of the book is called "The Open Door," and it shows that Melchior chooses the way of von Spät and makes up his mind to leave Fo.

657   When Melchior is alone again, he becomes very excited, just as though he heard a storm bell ringing inside of him. Finally, he cries, "I must be certain!" and he hammers his fists on the wall. He hears a whooshing sound and sees columns rising upward, and a large gate opens in front of him. He sees the nocturnal sea and a sailing boat silently approaches the shore. An evil, deathly stillness settles over everything, and it is as if Melchior is paralyzed. The clock in his rooms strikes, his paralysis disappears, and with widespread arms he passes through the gateway. Dark figures storm down upon him, and a hand of iron clasps him by the throat and strangles him. Then a black cloth is put on him and he faints. When he comes to, he finds himself lying bound on the deck of the ship with a hooded figure beside him. The ship is full of hooded figures; the sea is stormy; no one speaks. After many hours, a torch is lit which a giant of a man in the bow of the ship is swinging above his head in fiery circles. Answering signals come from the opposite shore, which seem to Melchior to be the first sign of a new world. "He drank the strange flaming writing of the unknown land into himself; his heart gave a flaming response to every sign from over there. […]" A small boat pulls up next to the sailing ship, and hooded figures come on board and seize him, tie him up in a black cloth

again and carry him away. When he reawakens from his swoon, he senses he is being taken through darkness, and he hears the shuffling of many feet all around him. They pass through endless passages and many splendid rooms of a huge palace, until finally they stop. Someone bangs resoundingly on metal, and everything becomes still and silent. In that moment, life returns to Melchior, and he tries to fight off his guards, but he comes up against nothing but empty air. He is alone. Suddenly a blaze of light reaches him and stabs his eyes. He is in a big hall, decorated with red velvet, and behind a large table are enthroned three veiled people dressed in red. Along the walls sit all the men and women whom he has known during his lifetime who look at him severely, whispering among themselves.

658 In the next chapter, "The Judgment," Melchior protests loudly at how he is being treated. But there is no answer. Angrily, he approaches the table and pounds his fist on it. Then he hears a stern voice say, "You stand before your judges, Melchior!" Shocked, he falls to his knees. The voice says that his accusers should come forward. There is a lot of whispering and murmuring in the hall, and one after the other, people approach the table and look at Melchior with their empty eyes. He recognizes them all, his friends and enemies, neighbors, and comrades. Their faces are gray, as though covered with dust; their faces are distorted and their mouths wide open and black, their lips bluish. Melchior's wife is standing in the front row, and she laughs at him in a crazy and lustful way. Cux and his wife, as well as Trumpelsteg, are there. All of them reproach him for not having bothered himself with them, for not loving them, or for not having been interested in them. Forgotten school comrades poke their tongues out at him, and Henriette is there. New figures keep swarming around him, mumbling unceasingly to themselves, and even the old apple-lady wheezingly reproaches him. The mumbling of the accusers becomes

louder and louder, until finally the judge's voice rings out, "You have heard the accusations. Do you admit your guilt?" Melchior's head drops onto his chest, and he says quietly, "Yes, I am guilty. Every step I took has made me guilty. We kill while we live. But who wants to be the judge?" The judge's voice breaks the silence: "You deserve the death penalty!" "There is no one here who can judge me," Melchior replies and stands up. "I know no one who may judge me other than myself. Who accuses me? I heard nothing but the mad cursing and mumbling of bodiless shadows."

659   His accusers begin to whine at his words, but the three hooded figures look at neither them nor Melchior, and together they repeat the death sentence of the invisible judge. Two wooden figures approach Melchior and lead him away, once again through endless dark corridors, and finally they lock him into a small glistening room, one wall of which is made of glass through which "the hot blue of the sky" penetrates. Suffocating heat flows through the floor and the walls that mirror the blue of the sky. Melchior cannot escape. Finally, the two wooden men return with a black, blood-stained cloak which they nail onto his shoulders, with blood streaming down him. Then they lead him out to a place by the sea on which there is a scaffolding. Melchior recognizes the houses that surround it for they are places in which he had once lived. The throng of people are also the shadows of his accusers who await his execution. The executioner with a sword follows him up onto the scaffolding. A large white bird flies over the crowd. "A bell began to ring within Melchior's breast. […] Laughing gleefully, he swiftly grabbed the sword off the executioner, swung it high and chopped off his head." In the same instant, a huge wave forms in the sea and rushes toward land, but ahead of it is a horse that halts in front of Melchior. Laughing, he swings himself into the saddle, and the horse gallops away with him while the wave engulfs the town and stifles the cries of the people.

660   In the following chapter, "The Call," Melchior rides on until he comes to the foot of a forested mountain. Then he dismounts and drinks from a stream. He becomes quieter, the nightmare of his accusers slipping away. When he turns back toward his horse, it has disappeared, but once more the white bird is circling above him. Melchior follows it into the woods and climbs up a small path. He senses how with each step he takes a chasm opens behind him. The path he follows through the woods therefore sinks into nothingness. A cold night descends as he reaches a barren high plain. A wolf barks at him and hundreds of wolves around him respond.

661   The court gives the events a fateful turn. We see quite clearly that from a literary standpoint this is judgment after death. It equates to what we think will happen after death. People appear who are still living, like Melchior's wife and Mrs. Cux, but there are also several dead people. The living and the dead are together, and they look like half-decayed corpses. Psychologically speaking, the unconscious catches up with him and generally reproaches him for his unrelatedness. He is reproached, for example, for not wearing the slippers his wife embroidered, for not looking at his colleagues' work, and so on. It is complete, cold narcissism which, from the very beginning, has been Melchior's disease — his absolute unrelatedness. We have already said that with the lack of differentiation of the anima and without any relationship to the feminine principle there can be no eros and no relatedness. The essence of the whole reproach is unrelatedness, and everyone is dead because Melchior did not keep them alive by nourishing them with feelings. It is relatedness which gives life to things. If I am not related to someone, it is irrelevant if that person is dead or alive. A person to whom I do not relate is as good as dead to me. All the people in Melchior's surroundings are dead. It is an entirely dead world. These people, then, represent his unlived life, for he escaped into complete intellectualism and did not suffer in life. He did not live a normal, human life, so his unlived life catches up with him. Going through the door is like going into the

unconscious, and the first thing that comes up is this revelation of his unlived life because he had no feeling. But Melchior escapes his punishment by chopping off his executioner's head — a punishment that, in fact, was his to endure. Psychologically — or symbolically — speaking, being beheaded means losing one's intellect, and in the moment that Melchior was going to be forced to make this sacrifice, the white bird appears above him. It, too, is a spiritual symbol, the embodiment of a spiritual attitude, and therein lies the typical trick of the intellectual onto whom all the unlived life and all the betrayed feeling-relationships fasten, giving him a terrific sense of guilt: He makes a clever twist with a spiritual or intellectual explanation — and escapes again. For example, he may say that these are mere feelings of inferiority or of neurotic feelings of guilt which he must overcome. In fact, this is the explanation that Mr. von Spät gives. Melchior falls into the clutches of von Spät, who says, "Thank God you did not fall for those judges! Thank God you freed yourself from those wrong feelings of guilt." That is what the intellect calls it. We know that there are pathological and morbid feelings of guilt that sometimes one must fend off. There is a kind of wrong conscience which tortures people to death. In women, it is generally the animus, and in men, the anima or the mother that initiates such feelings. It is therefore a very mixed problem, because having the apple-woman in it and all these feelings of guilt, there is also a little bit of the mother-anima poison in it. In practical terms, this means that the anima wants no further development of consciousness. She wants to keep the man at the same level of consciousness that he already has, and she does this through a terribly exaggerated emotional upsurge, bathing him in feelings of guilt. This is also illustrated by the red velvet hangings and the childishly dramatic performance in which he is guilty of God knows what. That is the wrong kind of mea culpa (my guilt) combined with true guilt, making a mix-up of genuine guilt and a hysterical, exaggerated guilt-realization, which is just another kind of inflation — an inflation of evil. "I am the greatest sinner. Nobody is as abject as I. I have done everything wrong in my life," and so on. That is inflation; it is simply swinging over into the opposite. The cloak which is nailed onto him is a nice indication of this inflated guilt. It suggests the Crucifixion. Before Christ was crucified, a royal red garment was put on him because he was accused of pretending to be the King of the Jews. Thus, they put a scarlet robe on him and a crown of thorns and mocked him. That is the parallel. Only here the garment is black, and the execution is that of beheading, which is symbolic of him being "deintellectualized." The garment is not the realization of his royal nature, but of his black nature. It is a kind of reversed crucifixion. But the destructive or poisonous aspect of it is the exaggeration, namely, the idea of feeling like a negative Christ: "I am the greatest sinner in the world and am now suffering for my sins." The royal garment of sin! That is the inflation. The nails, too, that are driven into his flesh are an allusion to the Crucifixion of Christ, but with the difference that it is the wrong kind of identification.

662　　I would like to draw an interesting parallel here from the dream of a woman who had tremendously impressive visions and because of that was very much estranged from reality. She had an urge to exteriorize all this inner material by telling it, but afterward she had the experience, common to many people after telling their great inner experiences, of being empty, deflated — now I have told it all and am empty. Because by telling the inner experience, one stops identifying with it, and just a miserable human being is left who says, "Yes, and now what?" As long as it remains an inner secret, one is filled with it. According to her dream, it was right for her to tell and be separated from her vision, but then she dreamed that a monument was shown to her — the figure of a naked man with an enormous nail going through his shoulder and coming out at the hip, and a voice said, "Lazarus was dead, and Lazarus is alive again." She asked me what this nail meant, and I could not figure it out. I remembered vaguely something about the thorn in the flesh of St. Paul, but my knowledge of the Bible was not good enough to get it at once. Thus, I merely said to her that in St. Paul there is something about a thorn in the flesh. I thought it a strange motif and looked it up in the Bible, and in Corinthians 12:7, St. Paul says:

663　And by reason of the exceeding greatness of the revelations, that I should not be exalted overmuch, there was given to me a thorn in the flesh, a messenger of Satan to buffet me, that I should not be exalted overmuch.

664　Thus, we see that the thorn in the flesh would be the reverse experience of being inflated. If I have great visions, if I have inner revelations and identify with them, then I get a thorn in the flesh, something which should remind me constantly of my inferiority and meanness and human incompleteness. That is how St. Paul put it. And now with this woman it was the same thing. Through her inner experience she got a tremendous inflation, and this last dream was an effort to show her that the great inner experiences she had were, in another way, also a wound, a constant torture — something that made her incomplete and wounded. You could even say that those revelations are the thorn in her flesh.

665　We have the same motif in our story, which again indicates that there is a tremendous inflation of the feeling of guilt. From schizophrenics, we know that they say, for example, that they are Christ, while others say that they caused the First World War. There is not much difference between the two. It is megalomania, this way or that, and sometimes it switches, and one minute they will say that they caused the First World War and two minutes later, that they are the savior of the world. Once they have crossed the threshold, those two inflations are one and the same thing, and that is only the extreme case of something you always find on a minor scale when people have committed some sin. Either they pooh-pooh it intellectually, or they bathe in their sin in an emotional, childish way with such hysterical pleasure and feeling so awful that everyone must comfort them. That is a pathological reaction which is just an escape from the realization of their real guilt. This typical reaction of an intellectual is a further sign of the weakness in Melchior's feeling function: He is hit in his inferior feeling function, and because that becomes too painful and too insufferable, the white bird carries him suddenly out of himself in a kind of spiritual elation.

666   We will see later that Melchior circles between the two worlds: the spirit world of von Spät and that of Fo — the feeling world of the mother and the boys. This does not give the picture of a mandala but of an ellipse because it is unbalanced, for the anima, who would make it round, is lacking. The mother would be an old figure like von Spät and the anima would be a young figure like Fo, and these two would make the circle complete. But these two poles are not there. Sometimes the apple-woman turns up at one masculine pole and sometimes at the other, and the anima is not there at all. Taken together with his lack of relatedness, this shows the complete deficiency of the feminine principle. Von Spät is always connected with the idea of stars, the firmament, music, spirituality, order, and power. Fo is connected to the mother, trees, animals, and boys.

667   When Melchior knocks on the wall, he comes to the von Spät pole. He is then attacked, accused, and judged, but, with the help of the white bird, he escapes. Only then does he come to von Spät, who praises him for having broken through his feelings of guilt. Thus, we see that the white bird is von Spät's messenger, and the trick is to get out of feeling guilty through a kind of false spirituality. You have just to do some yoga exercises or rebirthing, and then you are free again. Using tricks like this, von Spät enables Melchior to escape and compliments him on doing so.

668   Sophie, for example, says that it took her a whole year to embroider his slippers, so she invested a great deal of libido into them and worked on them with a great deal of love. To simply kick them away as he does would mean being unrelated. If he had looked at the slippers more closely, he would have had to have said to himself that he must give some kind of response to that feeling, without getting under her slippers, as it were. That would have created a conflict because women always add a little power-trap to their genuine love. That is exactly what the feminine problem is for the man: In women there is usually a mixture of genuine love and devotion, and then a little left-handed power trick to put him in his box. His mistake is that he simply casts away the whole thing, and that is just what the puer aeternus man often does. Because there is

always a little power trick in the woman's love, he takes that as an excuse to reject the whole thing: All women are rotten — their love is nothing but putting one under their slippers.

669   Cheap sweeping statements such as these save the man the difficulty of asking every minute of the day, "Is this a trick or is it love?" Such statements show that the man is not up to that problem with women. If he is not conscious of his anima and his own eros, he will always fall for tricks. For instance, he wants to go out, and his wife thinks that he might meet Mrs. So-and-so, in whom he is interested, so she pretends to have a headache and suggests that they spend the evening at home. If he has a differentiated feeling function, he will sense that today this is a trick, and he therefore will say that he is going out and that if she has a headache, she can stay at home. The next evening, she has a real headache, and it is very unrelated if he says, "No, to hell with you. I am going out!" Only if a man has a differentiated eros-development can he find out whether a woman is playing a trick or whether it is the real thing. This is too difficult for him, for if a man takes a feeling problem seriously, he has, from minute to minute, to relate to what the woman does, and on top of that, he always must be aware of whether it is power or real feeling. In an unconscious woman, both aspects are very close to each other.

670   In analysis, it is the same problem: An analysand may bring you a tremendous amount of feeling, but, as Virgil says, there is always a snake in the grass, which means that you are never quite sure what she is up to. If, however, you reject the whole transference on account of that, then you destroy the patient's feeling. If you cannot accept the real feeling in a transference, you are destructive to the analysand. If, however, you fall for the transference, then she will nicely put you in her pocket and make a fool of you. When a man is confronted with the problem of relating to a woman, he must perceive the difference between snake-in-the-grass tricks and genuine love, and he cannot discover that difference without possessing differentiated feeling. If he has that, he will just smell a rat and know from the woman's voice that she is up to something, or from her eyes and her voice he will learn that it is a feeling to

which he must respond. But a man can learn that only by differentiating his anima for a long time, by dealing with her and with the problems of relationship. If he makes a principle of yes or no, then he is not capable of relating to women or of being an analyst.

671   Here there is the either-or attitude. Melchior rejects women together with their slippers. Clearly, he is not a man who falls under the domination of his wife's slippers. He fought against that, and we remember the trick Sophie played by not having his room heated so that he should be forced to come to her party. That is a typical feminine trick, but Melchior does not fall for it. But he does not see that Sophie also loves him. For a woman, the one does not exclude the other. For her, the two go together — she can love a man and yet play such tricks — and it is the man's task to discover from minute to minute which is which.

672   Melchior is now surrounded by wolves and may not move, or they begin to snarl. Finally, the sun rises. He stretches his arms out toward the ever-brightening light and passes through the ring of wolves, without being aware of them. They vanish like clouds. Toward midday, the air becomes foggy, and a foul-smelling wind blows from afar. Eventually Melchior comes to a high wooden fence and enters a courtyard at the center of which is a tumble-down stone hut with empty holes where the windows once were. The place is teeming with haggard people wearing high fur caps over their birdlike faces. On long stands, and with loud voices, they are selling large yellow mushrooms with green flecks from which streams of yellow mist are rising. "Buy mushrooms! These are the last ones! The earth is dissolving into mist! The sun is rotting! Buy mushrooms before they are all gone! The woods are dying! The world is exploding! Bargains! […]" Melchior staggers in the flaccid air. The wounds on his shoulders upon which the black cloak hung, send shivers down his spine. The mushrooms on the table blow up and burst and become new

mushrooms, and the mist rising from them and circling overhead turns into shapes that dissolve, rising and falling to the earth where they mix with the softened earth to become a bubbling mud.

673 Uproarious laughing can be heard in the background. The old apple-woman approaches Melchior and dances around him with indecent leaps, naked, with loose, stringy hair that falls over her decaying body. She, too, shouts with the sellers to buy the bargains. Suddenly she is holding a young woman's hand who is swaying her hips. The mushrooms fall from the tables, sinking into the muddy earth and grow again into a forest of fleshy trees. Melchior seeks a way out and draws his pocketknife, stabbing at the old apple-woman and her young and vulgar companion. Their blood changes into red mist; their wounds immediately close. Laughing, the old woman tries to seize him. Melchior closes his eyes and sees "a blue light lighting up within himself, and on the cold sky of circling stars an enormous figure starts to take form." He pulls himself out of the embrace of the women and begins to sing with a reverberating voice. His song is echoed a thousandfold and a new dawn breaks. He sees green glaciers out of which a crystalline building rises in the distance. Von Spät is standing in front of Melchior and says to him, "You have found the way. Now you are one of us. You have escaped the judgment of human beings. You have overcome the greed of the animals, and you have banished the vengeance of the decaying earth. Now you serve the stars, and you are master over human beings, animals, and the earth. Come, and allow yourself to be crowned as one of our brothers."

674 A deadly cold spreads through Melchior's body, as von Spät leads him toward the crystal castle, where sleep has no power and it is always daytime, as he tells Melchior. Everything within the palace is made of ice. Melchior takes a rod that is lying on a table, and instantly his clothes fall from his body, and the nail wounds on his shoulders heal. With the sound

of bells ringing, a door opens and in front of him is a place that is filled with bright figures. Their bodies are like glass; their eyes like blue stones. Beneath him is von Spät, who points toward a glass shrine in the middle of the place upon which a glistening crown lies. To one side is a group of petrified, immobilized boys who stare at the ground. As Melchior slowly makes his way down the steps to the place, he becomes increasingly stiff, and his gaze more immobile. He reaches the middle of the place and the two crown-bearers stare at him. Melchior is greatly startled for they have Fo's eyes. Shocked, he realizes that he has betrayed Fo's band of boys, for whom he has been longing with all his heart. He is filled with horror when he looks at the petrified group of boys and the tortured faces of the two crown-bearers who are trying to remember in vain. They kneel before him, but his hands have not yet touched the crown when he hears a soft voice above him say, "Don't you want to go away from here?" Melchior's deathly stare melts as it is Fo's voice. Von Spät's eyes glitter threateningly, but Melchior spreads his arms and cries, "I want to go away!" At the same moment, he is lifted, cool lips are pressed to his forehead, and a gentle wind carries him away, while everything sinks into a blue mist. There is then a sense of gently sinking down, and Melchior finds himself again on a moonlit meadow, with Fo's face looking down at him, and he sinks into a deep sleep.

675 After having fallen into the half-right, half-wrong feelings of guilt and then having pulled away from them into a kind of wrong spiritualization, he falls into the pack of wolves. How would you interpret this psychologically? In some variations of the fairytale, Mother Holle has a wolf's head. Mother goddesses and witches have a wolf's head of iron, and it does sometimes denote the devouring mother. It is the problem of the negative mother that Melchior is being confronted with here. Whenever a man escapes the whole problem of relationship by a wrong kind of spiritualization, he is still

in the clutches of the devouring mother, and what is much worse, he turns all the women in his environment into devouring mothers. If he does not relate, he is eaten up by the women! That is naturally the wrong thing, but it is a kind of involuntary and automatic reaction in a woman. The more the man refuses to accept related-ness, the more she feels that she must imprison him, eat him up, forbid him to move around. Thus, he calls up the devouring mother in every woman, and then it is a vicious circle. He is disappointed because every woman turns out to be a devouring wolf. Then he says, "There you are! That is what I always said!" and walks out on the woman. His "flightiness" has constellated her devouring side, and that is the vicious circle. Because he has no love, he summons her wolf — her power complex.

676   Furthermore, the wolf in mythology does not have only feminine witch qualities. There are other aspects. In the Etruscan tombs, the god of death has a wolf's head or a wolf's cap. The Greek Hades was also often represented with a cap on which was the head of a wolf, so it is also the abyss of death, thought of as being a kind of devouring jaw, eating people up. The wolf stands — not only in women but also in men — for this kind of covetousness of wanting to have things without any further purpose. Jung says that often among the strongest drives with which we are confronted when we open the door of the unconscious are the power drive, the sex drive, and then something like a hunger which just wants to eat and assimilate everything without any reason or meaning. It is that which always wants more. If you invite such people to supper, they are not pleased but simply furious when you do not invite them again next week. If you give a tip, they are not grateful, for the next time if you do not give them more, they say, "What? Only a franc?" The worst are those who were starved of love in early childhood. They go about pale and bitter with a "nobody loves me" expression, but if one makes a kind gesture, there is no appreciation. There is only the desire for more, and if you do not give more, then they are furious. You could pour the whole world into such an open mouth, and it would not be enough. It is like the abyss of death; the mouth

never shuts and there is only the demand for more. It is a kind of driven passion of eating and eating, and it generally is the result of an early childhood experience where the child was starved and deprived of love or of some other vital need on the psychological or physical level. One can only say no to such greed because there is no end to it. It is a divine-demonic quality. It is that thing which says, "More! Still more! Always more!"

677   The wolf in Germanic mythology also belongs to Wotan. One of his names is Isengrim, which means "iron head," but it has also been interpreted in folklore as "grim, cold rage," and therefore the wolf very often stands for a kind of cold, hidden hatred. Most people who have had a very unhappy childhood have something like this at the bottom of their souls. It never comes up. It is something frozen and cold, a form of petrified rage that is also behind the demand for more and more: "The others owe me everything." If one works with orphans or children who have grown up in some kind of home and have been beaten a lot, one can generally see the wolf very clearly. Many others have this kind of wolf quality in them. Melchior has been frustrated from early childhood. We know that his mother was a weak, sickly woman who did not look after him, that he had to play alone and that out of loneliness he saw his double at the window. We know that he did not grow up in a warm, instinctually healthy atmosphere. This, then, is just such a situation that leads Melchior to this greed and the longing to always have more.

678   After having overcome his half-right and half-wrong hysterical feeling of guilt, he now falls into this new trap, and here again he gets out of it by longing for the light. When he stretches out his arms for the light, the wolves disappear. He does not really deal with the problem; he falls into it, and then, by an enantiodromia, comes out of it when the night turns again into day. He falls into this state without realizing what it means. He comes out of it again by the grace of God. Naturally, in such a case, nothing is worked out at all. The problem sinks again into the night, and the next situation in life will bring it up again. Some people who have this wolf problem realize that this kind of greedy wanting more and more and eating

everybody and everything up is mad and unreasonable, so they do not let it out. They behave very correctly and never ask for more, but you always suspect that it is just politeness behind which is caged the starving wolf. Such people then suddenly fall into the wolf complex and come out with terrific and impossible demands. If you want to discuss it analytically, they instead tell you a very interesting dream and the wolf side is just gone again. I may say, "Listen, I am sure you are furious because I could not do what you wanted when you rang me up, and I think we ought to talk about that." But they reply that that is quite all right, they quite understand. The wolf has gone into the woods again and nothing has been solved. It would be much better for that person to make a terrific scene, so that one can deal with it and discuss it. But it has all crumbled away, and if you then say that they should come out with it because of a dream, you will get the reply, "But I know it is unreasonable. I know you have no time. I know I should not have asked it of you." Thus, the wolf has disappeared again without being transformed. That is exactly what happens in the story. Melchior sits in this problem and then comes out with it, and then the same thing happens with those moldy mushrooms and those sensuous women dancing around, saying that the earth is now being destroyed. This is an image of a morbid Mother Nature who is about to perish.

679   There is an area where the mushroom now plays a role that is invading our world, namely, in the new drugs, some of which are made from some kind of fungus. It is now hoped that a chemical cure for schizophrenia will be found, and quite possibly this can be done because any kind of overemotional state causes intoxication. It seems that, according to Jung, in schizophrenia there is a certain condition of intoxication, which means it can be treated with chemicals. The snag is, however, that the psychological problem which brought about the schizophrenic episode is not removed. All the morbid emanations of the problem — the craziness and the mad behavior of the people and other symptoms — can be stopped with these drugs, but later analysis shows that the basic problem remains unchanged. If at this point the patient does not engage in

psychotherapy, he is simply heading for another episode, and the drug will have to be given again. This process can continue endlessly. After such a partial cure with drugs, a series of dreams will point out the danger of a countertendency, namely, that the patient can now say, "I can continue with my wrong attitude, and the next time I go off my head, I will just ask for another pill." The worst thing about these drugs is that it can have a demoralizing effect as it is easier for people with a weak character to simply continue using them, rather than changing their attitude. This results in constant relapses that require more and more drugs. Certain dangerous conditions can be short cut, but one will pay for these shortcuts for they undermine the confidence of the patient in being able to pull out through his own moral effort. They make one forever dependent on the doctor who will give one the right pill in the right moment. If the drug has not been used over a long period of time, there is no loss of soul. But one loses one's belief and confidence and this is the real danger. If today there is a move to refrain from using psychopharmacology, it is a matter of one's Weltanschauung, for one has to decide if it is preferable to let people remain in their madness, thereby maintaining a certain degree of the own inner life, or force them into what appears to be a state of health with pills. That kind of existence is like a whitewashed tomb, for those people can at least live in a socially adapted manner. Their social behavior is more socially tolerable, even if nothing else has changed and they are as crazy as they were before. I heard the confession of such a person. She had been changed into such a white persona, but later when her madness came back, and with it her better part, she said, "I was mad all the time. It was only covered up. I had a pseudo-adapted behavior." That is not a cure; it is only beating people into socially adapted behavior, so that they may be less disturbing, which is naturally useful for the doctor. It is really a self-defense mechanism on the part of the doctor.

680   If drugs are not used for a too long a period, the effect is reversible. What seems to be a loss of soul is really an abaissement of the emotional level. The patients say that the hallucinations and

other experiences of the psychotic stage are still there, but that they do not experience the emotional part so strongly. After a lobotomy, a patient said to me that she could still feel that her madness was there. She used an image to describe it: "It was in the cellar but it could no longer come up the stairs." She was carefully living in the upper story. The emotional problem is not solved; it is only removed. There is a certain distance between the problem and the person. The operation here had the same effect: The too strong emotion was simply cut off. If people fall into too strong an emotion, they afterward generally switch to the opposite pole of being too reasonable. They then have a secret homesickness for their former emotional madness because to be emotional and mad is to experience the plenitude of life. They are never as fully alive as when they are mad. It is a kind of life peak! If you are not mad enough to have experienced that, then just remember some time when you were madly in love, or in a mad rage. What a wonderful state of affairs that is! Instead of being this broken human being, always fighting between emotions and reason, you are for once whole! What a pleasure it is to once give in to your rage! You feel so honest, and whole; for once, you have not been polite, and you just said everything! That is a divine state, and it is a divine state to love in that way, where there is no doubt anymore. She — or he — is everything! Divine, complete trust! None of that mistrust that everybody has toward everybody else, and no safeguards against the faults of the other fellow human! Instead, we are completely one with the other and the stars dance around us! It is a state of totality. And the next morning she or he has a pimple on their nose, and the whole thing collapses! But emotion creates the experience of being totally in something, whatever the emotion is. This is why people secretly long to return to their madness, for they are too normal and adapted and they no longer feel whole.

⁶⁸¹ Medication is therefore no solution. The emotions must recede, and the two poles brought together. Reason and emotionality must both be reduced. Thank heavens some leading psychiatrists today — Stanislav Grof and John Perry, for example, among others — are

encouraging schizophrenics to view their illness as a process of rebirth, which has probably been the meaning behind this illness all along.

682   The opposites must unite, like the opposites in our book where pure emotion is represented by the boy Fo, and order and reason by von Spät. The author of the book is torn between these two. At one end everything is in order, but rigid; it is the overadaptation you get from drugs. The excess of reasonableness that people have after an episode is a form of madness. It is mad to be as coldly reasonable as that, and its opposite is another form of madness. If you cannot keep in the middle between the two, you are lost, which is exactly the tragedy of the book. On a political level, you see the same thing everywhere: mad mass-psychotic, emotional movements where people go around with either a Celtic cross or a Swastika, raving in emotion and feeling whole. It is wonderful to walk howling through the streets in thousands, for then you feel whole and human. But then there are the police and order, business order, the law, and all the rest, which is von Spät. Then you regress into what is called the restitution after the revolution, in which everything is in order, but power dominates. People are deadly bored and think how nice it would be if they could go back into the chaos of revolution, where at least life flowed. One sees more and more how nations now switch between those two poles, just as individuals do. Groups do the same everywhere, and that is why we must deal with the problem. I am sure most of those young people who are behind the barricades just enjoy the plenitude of life, feeling whole and heroic. They look as though they were moved by a total emotion of some kind, and then that switches back to the boredom of order. And what can you do with that? The order of von Spät is cold!

683   We recall that Mr. von Spät nearly won: Melchior was already in his glass and ice kingdom and was on the point of being crowned when he suddenly realized he was in a prison. With the cry, "I want to go away," he broke the spell, thereby freeing Fo, too, who took him away with him.

684 The boys now dance on a moonlit meadow and one of them aims a spear, made of moon rays bundled together, at Fo's heart. He pulls it out of his chest and a pale stream shoots out of the wound and runs along the ground where it grows into a stream. The boys kneel and drink from it. Meanwhile, Fo becomes smaller and thinner until he collapses, and his whole body turns into waves. The stream dries up, the boys grow tired and fall asleep on the grass with their eyes open. From their foreheads comes a glowing mist which turns into spheres which float higher and higher. "Flowing in and out of each other a hundredfold, they form one great ball of mist which whirls round the moon in one great swoop in ever-narrowing circles and finally melts into it. The moon grows lop-sided. A faint pause. And then it sinks to the earth, splitting up into dust-like rays of light."

685 Fo appears out of the rays, and floats over the meadow, touching lightly all who are sleeping. The boys spring up and burst out laughing. Melchior joins in with their laughing, and the boys surround him and welcome him; he had been so far away from them. Slowly, he starts to recall what had happened, thinking it had all happened only yesterday. Fo leads him to a small lake. Melchior looks into the water where he catches a glimpse of his reflection and is greatly shocked for his hair is white, his skin is wrinkled, and his eyes are sunken. Fo tells him not to be afraid, that he is among his own people again, and when he is crucified, he will belong entirely to them. Whilst being kissed by Fo, his past again recedes within him, and Fo leads him to an enormous cross in the middle of the meadow. The boys take a hold of him, and one approaches with a crown of thorns bound together by light and places it upon Melchior's head. The rays cut his forehead and blood flows over his face. Then he is nailed to the cross, but the nails feel like cold shadows, and his whole body like a light shadow. "He hangs . . . a shadow on the shadow of a cross, high between heaven and earth, his face

turned toward the slowly rising sun. But he sees nothing, for heaven and earth disappear."

686   The first rays of the sun strike his chest and tear open his body. His blood rushes out in a mighty stream. He sees how it divides itself and disappears into the earth, where it rises again, weaving its way between boulders, flowing on until it loses itself in the infinite. He has become one with the cross, and out of the earth comes a swelling sap that rises up in him. His outstretched arms have become many branches; his green hair waves in the wind. Fo is sitting in his shade, playing the flute, while the boys dance around him, the shapes transforming back and forth into large birds flying. Other animals come: lions, tigers, snakes that lay themselves down at his trunk, cattle, stags, bears, wolves, and foxes. A cry breaks from Melchior, and while he is crying out, he becomes a boy like the others. While Fo plays his flute, the others sing, "All animals return to the Garden of Eden." Fo asks him if he still knows his name. Melchior cannot recall it. Fo says that they all had other names before they were crucified, but they have forgotten them. When one is taken into their group, he is given a new name, but it is not his true name. One only gets that when one comes to the "kingdom." Melchior asks which kingdom he is referring to and Fo tells him he is referring to the kingdom where they are at home. "There we play round the old fountains and drink of their holy waters, and there in black mirrors we see everything we have lived. There, we are again all that we have lived. From the dark surfaces arise thousands of forms which we leave behind when we enter the kingdom and which we must resume when we begin to wander again." Melchior asks why they must wander again. "Don't you want to be everywhere?" Fo replies, "To be the wind and the rain? Do you not want to be the trees and the grass? Don't you want to be a part of the sunset and to melt into the moon? Don't you want to be every animal, and every human? […] We escape into and out of

every figure. Wherever we appear everything changes into a whirlwind, and nothing is durable."

687 In response to Melchior's question, Fo replies that time means nothing to them, that they will get to the kingdom at some point in time, and that one touches its borders everywhere, quite unexpectedly. But until then, they must wander, they may not rest, for otherwise they will not get there. But Melchior needs a name; he will be given one by one of his companions, and this companion will remain with him when the group scatters in the tumult that is caused by their transformation. Melchior looks at Fo and asks him if he would like to be his companion. "We have saved each other," says Fo, "so we will stay together." And within the circle of boys, he is given the name of Li, which is passed on joyously, from one boy to the other.

688 Through a tremendous enantiodromia, a turning into its opposite, a kind of anticlimax, Melchior has now arrived in Fo's kingdom — Ulrich von Spät's archenemy. The first part of this chapter reveals who Fo is. As the leader of the boys and as the bearer of one of Buddha's names, he represents eternal wandering in karmic incarnations, whereas Buddha himself teaches escape from the karma of incarnation, from the wheel of rebirth. Fo, on the other hand, considers endless incarnations a pleasure. Moreover, since he turns into the moon and then returns to earth after having been wounded, he is also a moon-god — a moon-god and the god of running water. When his chest is cut open, blood does not flow but a spring of life; it is specifically stated that a white stream comes forth and that this water revivifies all those who drink it.

689 Earlier, we saw that von Spät is associated with the old sun — Sol Niger or Saturn. In old sun-god mythology, he would correspond to the Greek Kronos and to Saturn in medieval alchemical mythology. This we deduced from the fact that he danced with the seven girls who would represent the seven planets. Logically, as the opposite principle to the sun, Fo is the moon-god, the god of night,

of sleep, of the irrational, of eternal change, with naturally a latent feminine tinge. And it must not be forgotten that in German regions, the moon is masculine, while in Roman mythology, it was hermaphroditic and was worshipped as both a male and a female figure. This hermaphroditic aspect of the soul shows that the symbol of the Self and the anima are not yet separated. Fo represents the unconscious in its feminine and masculine personifications. He is the principle of the night, the other side of the light of consciousness.

690   It seems to me to be worth briefly comparing this book with Saint-Exupéry's The Little Prince to show the difference between German and French mentality. One characteristic would be that on the other side of the Rhine — in Germany — the anima is not as differentiated. The only feminine figures in this book are the apple-woman (the mother nature figure), Sophie, who is also more of a mother figure and is also very negative, and then the pale anima-girl, Henriette Karlsen, who dies almost before she appears on the scene. The powerful soul-figure is a hermaphroditic being — namely Fo, the moon-god. If you compare him with the soul-figure in Saint Exupéry's book — the couple on the asteroid, the rose and the little prince — there the hermaphroditic aspect is at least differentiated into a couple, and the anima is differentiated one step further, although she is still a rather negative feminine figure, both haughty and hysterical. She has not progressed much, but at least she is separated from the symbol of the Self and appears as an independent being. The German book gives the impression of a more archaic, more powerful symbolism and a much greater dynamism. The reader is pulled into an emotional, charged atmosphere with an exaggerated, hysterical undertone which is not entirely agreeable.

691   If we look at the negative factors, the French book is suffused with cruelty and childish sentimentality, in clear contrast to the dynamism and hysterical exaggeration of the German book. Two assumptions to account for this difference can be made: first, that the pagan layer in France is more Celtic, while in Germany, it is Germanic (the difference between the Celtic and the Germanic character has been described by Tacitus). Then — and perhaps this

is even more important — there is the fact that France was thoroughly Romanized before it became Christian (which is also true of southern Germany and Austria, and, to some degree, also Switzerland), whereas north of the Main River, Germanic heathendom was directly covered over by Christian conversion. In the Mediterranean realm, Christianity was the end-product of a long civilizing development and therefore became a spiritual and differentiated religious form. In ancient Rome, it was possible for people to understand Christian symbolism. Wherever Christianity was superimposed on a Romanized background, there was the possibility of a transition, whereas in areas where Romanization was lacking, the historical continuity of evolution was interrupted, and Christianity superseded something very different. Using a metaphor, you could say that north of the Main, people have "a hole in the staircase" — there is a lower story and an upper story and in the middle is an open space. This situation is not only typical of Germany. It will soon arise in Christianized Africa, where it is already creating a terrific tension and restlessness, and it will possibly be a much greater problem there, quite apart from the other cultural and economic problems. The problem exists also among the Americans who fell, when they went West as pioneers, into a primitive civilization. Survival in that primitive environment could only be achieved by becoming as tough and as primitive as the indigenous population. On the other hand, the pioneers had a Victorian Christian past, and this explains why the North Americans have, in many ways, a similar hole in the stairs.

692   Such a hole is not only a disadvantage, however: It gives the personality a powerful dynamism and great perseverance. The inner polarity and tension which such a cultural situation creates makes people dynamic and active, rather like electrical tension that increases with the distance between the plus and minus poles. Of course, such a tension-charged population is also more susceptible to hysterical dissociation, and to dissolving more easily into mass movements as the inner balance is more readily disturbed. It is well-known that those Africans who converted to Christianity are

partially very mistrustful, unreliable, and unpredictable, because the polarity between the culturally highly-developed consciousness and the archaic, unconscious part of the personality is very strong.

693   Returning to our comparison of the French and German mentalities, this hole between the upper and lower levels is, of course, only relative, for, on a lower level, the French have the same problem. When one makes such sweeping statements about nations, one must also be aware of the many exceptions: This is simply an attempt to characterize the differences in a general way.

694   The crucifixion of Melchior is very revealing. One sees that Fo really represents the return of the archetypal figure, which is also behind the figure of Christ, in an older form. If we compare Fo with other gods, we could say that he was closer to Dionysus. Whenever Fo appears in the book, roses and grapes are mentioned. This crucifixion in which the crucified person turns into a tree reminds us of Attis, who was changed into the maternal tree. One could therefore say that in giving himself to Fo, Melchior becomes "Attified" — he becomes an Attis. This appears to have happened to all the boys, who first lived an earthly life and, after being crucified, became those eternally wandering boys. The myth of Attis is repeated in each one of them. As we know, Dionysus and Attis represented the early-dying son-god, the son of the mother, who dies in the spring. The date of the Feast of Easter has been taken over from the Feast of Attis, and, in ancient Rome, the Jewish-Christians were executed on crosses around which grapevines were entwined, with the invocation, "O thou, Dionysus, Jesus Christ!" Thus, at least at the beginning of Christianity there was considerable doubt as to whether Christ was not a rebirth of Dionysus — or of Attis — in another form. The Church Fathers tried to make a definite break to establish Christianity, hoping in this way to prevent the new symbol from being sucked back into the past (which would have implied a victory for von Spät!). To make sure of its creative élan, the newly converted Christians were emphatic in contending that Christianity was entirely different from the cult of Dionysus, but the similarity of the archetypal figure was so striking that everyone felt very

doubtful, which accounts for such stress being laid upon the fact that Jesus Christ was a historical personality, in contrast to the archetypal god figure of Dionysus.

695   When Fo, therefore, returns in the form of Attis or Dionysus, he could be said to represent an attempt by the unconscious to create an archetypal experience which would bridge the gulf created by this sudden Christianization. One might think that after having passed through this experience the author might now really understand what the figure of Christ means. If you sweep away all the accumulated historical dust, you see that this is a return to the original experience of what it means to take the cross upon oneself, to carry it and be crucified with Christ, only here, there is a different shade of something more ecstatic and more dynamic and, in an archaic way, vital. It is an attempt of the unconscious to recreate the Christian symbol and revive it in a form in which it is linked again with the deeper layers of the personality. How widespread and how vital this problem is can be seen by the fact that one finds the same attempt of the unconscious in other times and in other areas. Christ appears to Niklaus von Flüe, for example, in a bearskin — as a Berserk — and here, too, it is an attempt not to abolish the symbol of Christ but to reinterpret it, linking it with the archaic layers of the instinctive psyche. Only if we understand it in this more complete form can the symbol of Christ survive, for if it is not anchored in the depths of the soul, it will be cast off and there will be a return to atheism and neopaganism in some form.

696   The same thing can be seen in the African-American spirituals in which a pagan layer of the psyche with its symbolic expressions and religious emotions appears. Over this is layered a Christian doctrine, which is just a lacquer that any kind of movement or antipropaganda would remove unless the main archetype of this Christian doctrine, which in our civilization is called Christ, constellates a similar archetypal symbol and links it up with the whole emotional personality. Only then does it become a living faith in which people can understand from underneath what Christ means to them personally. Otherwise, it is purely intellectual and

there is the hole in the staircase: Below, one still prays to Dionysus, or as it is here, to Wotan, for he is the one who is speared and who hangs on the World Tree.

697   In this book the archetype constellated below is Wotan, as is naturally the case in a Germanic civilization. In France and those countries where there is a Celtic background, the archetype called up in this form is not Wotan but Mercurius-Kerunnus, a stag god. This is a god who is transformed, who is crucified, and who is the sacrificed sun god — the spring god who resurrects. In medieval legends, in the legend of the Holy Grail and in Celtic material in England, Ireland, and Wales, it is the archetype of Mercurius-Kerennus, there is an attempt to link these superimposed Christian figures of God with the roots of the archaic and genuine inner experience of these people.

698   There are other motifs in the description of the kingdom of Fo, for example when he says "We play around old fountains [which brings to mind the Germanic Fountain of Urd at the base of the World Tree] and we drink of the holy water. [If you drink from the Fountain of Urd, you become a seer. The shamans and the medicine men drink from that fountain.] In black mirrors, we see what we were." Here an Eastern influence is introduced which we have already noticed before — the idea that in this kingdom you can mirror all former incarnations. We shall see later that the author believes in reincarnation, something he has derived from his Eastern studies and blended into this German material. Since the Germanic races were, in general, on the introverted side, pre-Christian Germanic civilization was introverted and had an affinity with the Chinese and Eastern spiritual life. The Germanic runes (which were believed to be the letters of the Germanic alphabet) were originally used as an oracle, as are the sticks of the Chinese oracle, the I Ching. They were still used in this way later, too. Thus, when the Germans took prisoners, a certain number were slaughtered in honor of Wotan, for which purpose the captors "threw" the runes, that is, they took sticks on which they had carved different runes, and if the specifically marked death-rune lay on top, then that prisoner was

sacrificed, while the others were kept as slaves. According to the myth, this technique of divination was invented by Wotan when he was pierced by a spear — we do not know whether by himself or by another, but we must also remember the spear of Longinus in the case of Christ — and here Fo is speared. Wotan then hung nine days and nine nights on the World Tree, Yggdrasil, after which in bowing down, he discovered the runes at his feet. Therefore, one could say that the creative product of the long crucifixion was the discovery of the runes — a new manifestation of cultural consciousness which originally consisted in reading the moment of fate. This also underlies the ideas behind the I Ching, which is a way of exploring the Tao, a method of divination based on the principle of synchronicity.

699   Even nowadays many people who have a Germanic racial background display a great affinity for the Eastern world, and since the war, there has been quite a widespread tendency in Germany to seek the healing of their western cultural problem by turning to Eastern philosophy. This would mean again finding a sufficiently introverted attitude with which to work out the problem from within, instead of from without. I once suggested to one of my analysands from North Germany, who was in the habit of consulting the I Ching, to look at this problem in this way. That night he dreamed that he was in front of a Prussian military barracks. At the entrance was a shield with writing on it in Chinese signs and Germanic runes. This shows that the unconscious at once picked up the suggestion as something very important. I would say that people north of the river Main are more introverted and are more interested in synchronistic phenomena, rather than in rational causality. In the north, and particularly in Russia, there is a tendency toward uniting the Eastern and Western minds in a middle attitude. It is well-known that in the so-called Pan-Slavonic movement, to which Dostoyevski belonged, it was claimed that Russia was the chosen country which one day would be able to unite the introversion of the East with the efficiency and extraversion of the West. Today, the Russians have departed from that idea by becoming markedly extraverted.

700 Fo's kingdom is characterized here in a strange way, for it is partly the Garden of Eden, to which all the animals return, and partly the old paradise of the Germans, the Fountain of Urd under the World Tree. But it is also clearly influenced by Eastern ideas of Nirvana, where one finally escapes the eternal wandering from one reincarnation to another. Fo and his band, however, have not reached the kingdom — which is interesting. The boys see a meaning in wandering, which is the opposite of the Buddhist teaching that one should escape the karmic wheel of reincarnation. This is a more Western tendency, and a rather fatal one, namely, the glorification of dynamic movement, even if it has no goal. But the exaltation of feeling psychologically alive and being in a creative movement with neither result nor goal is a dangerous and demonic aspect of this tendency.

701 As mentioned earlier, von Spät is at one end of the pole and Fo at the other, with Melchior in the center. At first, von Spät was successful and then came the reversal with Fo and the crucifixion, and Fo's victory. Later it turns the other way once more. Von Spät is fatal because at his end of the pole things are absolutely static; once you are in the glass palace, in the spirit kingdom, nothing happens anymore. Everything becomes clear, glasslike, transparent, and rigid. At Fo's end there is an absolute glorification of the creative movement and ecstasy, with the idea of creative ecstasy having a meaning, irrespective of whether there is any result. Here, constant emotion and creative ecstasy are taught. We find this expressed in rock-'n-'roll dancing, which represents the enjoyment of psychic and physical dynamism, with no further goal. When it is over, you are tired, and the next evening you start again, and that is satisfactory. On von Spät's side there is result without life movement and at Fo's end, eternal movement without result. It is another example of extreme one-sidedness, with no union of opposites. One is simply being torn between them.

702 | Von Spät | Melchior | Fo |
Reason without life	Ego	Eternal Movement
		without result
Ice – North	Li	South
	(Consciousness)	

703 There could only be healing if two other (feminine) poles had developed, because in a man's psychology, the feminine, the anima principle, is the principle of reality and also realization. That is lacking in this constellation.

704 After Melchior has been given the name Li — which means pattern, order, principle, consciousness — and the band moves to the town that is ahead of them, we enter the third part of the book that includes the chapters, "Stuhlbrestenburg," "The Buck in the Church," "The Great Trial," and "The Uprising," in which the trouble-making activities of Fo's band are described. Melchior plays no special part here: He has apparently become a part of a general happening.

705 Firstly, the historical background of the town "Stuhlbrestenburg" is described. Apparently, it once burnt down to the ground and it was upon these ruins that an airy, more spacious town was once again built. Every house had a visible old, blackened part that was not disguised in any way, and a new part painted white or pink. Deeper down below ground there were extensive, interconnected cellars that had been built at a time when Stuhlbrestenburg had been a stronghold. In these rooms, crime ruled, and the rest of the story is concerned with the effects of this layer on the life of the town. The real denouement only comes about when Fo and his band appear who, in a manner similar to the beginning of the story where, in Melchior's house and under von Spät's influence, they broke down the bourgeois façade of the citizens invested with civic authority. A general madness spread that revealed itself on different levels, firstly at the

school, then in the church and in the law courts at the trial of a sex murderer — in his madness, the Crown prosecutor reveals that he is a sex murderer himself — and finally, in the theater of the lascivious king. The already dissolving bourgeois decency of the townspeople that is founded upon darkness and crime provides the opening for Fo's band to attack, who now appear at every corner to ensure the escalation of the situation. Relentlessly, the whitewash of the middle class is scratched away: "one" goes to the city-run pleasure-houses to meet up, and there one surrenders to one's sexual, raw desires, which are suddenly interrupted when Fo's boys summon the young girls who were about to be the victim of some perversion or other. The men who want to hold them back are suddenly turned into fat rats, while the girls and the boys fly away as glowing moths into the clear night sky.

706 In the theater, too, the game the boys are playing is interrupted. This happens just when there is an important dialogue taking place between the hero of the play, the director of the electrical works, and his stepbrother, who has been out of the country for many years and who is a member of a literary-anarchistic society. The director is sermonizing to his stepbrother that he and people like him are a cancerous tumor on the country who would destroy everything that he, the director, and the people of his own class had sown. "I do not deny that not everything is as it should be. Modern consumerism has mechanized the spiritual life, has robbed life of its soul. But do not believe that by turning everything on its head, you will be able to bring back to life the souls of the dead. If life today is more materialistic, at least it represents ordered materialism." In a faint voice, he goes on to say that the soul only appears to be dead — that something exists that could reawaken it. Then he points at his money safe. He and those who guard the money with him are the guardians of progress, and their task is more important than

the "small happiness of the hordes," on whose behalf they have already made so many concessions. When he asks his brother the final question, whether he still wants to stand in his way, a door opens that leads onto the stage and two boys dressed in white enter. While they stand there motionlessly, the stage is turned into a flourishing garden. The director of the electrical works begins to shrink, then fills with air and turns into a ball that the boys play football with and kick into the box where the king is sitting. The king throws the ball back, and it bursts and rains money and blood down upon the audience. The boys then carry off the laughing king across a bridge made of flowers. A general pandemonium ensues. The doors to the outside are flung open and the "subterranean" people rush in, armed with axes, pistols, and swords. A carnage between the criminals and the audience follows which, once the theater has caved in upon itself, spreads throughout the entire town. At the marketplace where the fighting is the heaviest and the air is filled with the screams of a thousand voices, one clear voice suddenly rings out above the crowd. A figure has swung itself up onto the roof of a tram wagon and has brought it to a halt. More and more people begin to listen, and soon silence falls upon the crowd. "Friends!" the voice calls out. "Be reasonable! It is only because you are afraid of each other that you are murdering each other. The old order makes enemies out of you. Create a new order! Do not forget who your real enemies are — the boys! […] They hide everywhere and in every form. Citizens, people of the underworld! You hate each other, but you know each other. But who are these boys? Who knows them? Where have they come from? What do they want?" They want to destroy all order, the speaker tells them, and nothing will remain. Insanity will draw everybody into horror, desire, and disgust.

707 The crowd again grows unsettled; curses and questions interrupt him. Some call out for the boys, while others insult

the speaker who begins anew, "You want your life to have a new form. You want a holy order, the holy order of your work. It lies within you, in your longing and in your work. I will show it to you. [...] I will teach you about what you want. I will give you the laws you impose on yourselves. I and those like me want to be your brother, your helper, your redeemer... We were the secret order and now we want to serve you!" A beam of moonlight falls upon the sharp features of the speaker's withered face. It is as if his eyes are made from some light, transparent stones. A group of his followers swirls around him and shines in an unearthly light, twinkling like glass. "Suffer no darkness!" cries the figure. "Dive no more into the old, dark well! Then your sleep will be broken and there will be no more fleeing into another realm [...]! Do not hunger for an eternity that does not exist! This is how the boys who exterminate and destroy you are enticing you. Forget them — and they will lose their power and be at your service; they will become like you and their reign will be over!"

708   Once again, the crowd calls out for the boys to be killed, for the madness to end. No one listens to the glass figure's warning not to touch the boys. In the middle of the square a flame shoots up, and a group of naked boys appears in its light. One steps forward and says, "Come to us, those of you who want to be free. Let the others force heaven down to earth! Let them petrify in their order, work, and happiness! Let those who love the flame and eternal transformation come to us!" The naked band starts a wild song, and a shudder goes through the crowd. Out of the air, a new, wild song mixes in with the other song, trying to force it into the strict beat of the glass men. The crowd cries out, "To the Lord! To the Lord! To the new God! Pray to him! Kill the boys! Sacrifice!" Crazed, the people grab their weapons and throw themselves upon the boys. But a gust of wind inflates the flame into a sail, and a boat of fire rises with the boys

singing within it. Canons aim at it, and when the boat explodes into sparks of light, millions of roses float down onto the square and fill it with a stupefying scent.

709   This third part of the book speaks for itself. It is amazing to think that the book was written in the year 1919 and that we have passed through all that was predicted. This is how prophetic art can be. Even the burning of the Reichstag is hinted at. But the strange and uncanny thing is the motif of the burned town, upon which the light and more tenuous architecture is constructed. That shows that there is such a hole in the staircase — such a blatant contrast between the lower, emotional, archaic parts of the psyche, with its pagan outlook on life, and an upper layer of a higher civilization. If the problem is not made conscious and faced, it continually creates general catastrophes such as wars and revolutions, followed by a kind of repressive reconstruction on top of the old, unprocessed attitudes.

710   The new is built upon the debris of the old, as it was in Germany, without really becoming conscious of the past. The moment for reflection, of genuine inner processing was overlooked in the economic boom and the eager efforts to build a new life on the ruins of the Second World War. Instead, the subterranean world lives on, and once again it is beginning to seethe with revolution.

711   It is similar to taking drugs to get your old life started again after suffering a nervous breakdown, rather than turning to the unconscious and asking what was at the bottom of it. In a breakdown, there is always something positive which wants to come through. If the person does not turn and do as Cinderella did — discriminate between the good and the bad corn — that person loses their connection to the positive values of the unconscious. The same is true of National Socialism, which was a distorted impulse toward a creative renewal. If this symbolic figure of Fo — who is clearly a new form of the archetypal savior figure — had been realized by the Germans as a subjective, inner figure, rather than on the outside in the political "Führer" craze, it would have been the beginning of a great creative dynamism. Instead, this figure was externalized and

mixed up with political propaganda and a fatal power drive that we have all suffered from.

712   On the societal level, we see a development absolutely parallel to the development of the neurotic individual. What is constellated in a neurosis is really something creative which, if not recognized, will work toward a breakdown. If one turns toward it, the thing that makes one sick is also what heals one. It is clear from Goetz's novel that the romantic, religious élan vital of National Socialism might have brought about a tremendous cultural renewal of the German people and great progress in consciousness. But, through a wrong twist, the dynamic energy flowed into extraverted political aims instead, and the opposite came about — and the terrible catastrophe. I speak of the Germans because the book was published in Germany, but the problem is widespread. The same situation exists in America, especially among teenagers and young delinquents. Each country has its own tinge, but it is a modern problem that is not limited to Germany, even if Germany was the first, the locus minoris resistentiae (place of little resistance) where the disease showed itself. We all suffer from it in different variations.

713   If this breaking through of the new god had been recognized and realized inwardly, it would have led to the discovery of the unconscious and of the necessity of turning creatively toward it. But von Spät, who represents the eternal seduction to turn the unique inner experience into an outer collective order, got the Germans into this fatal vicious circle. And what is more terrifying is that right now they are again building a light rococo architecture, all rosy and white, on top of the burnt-out ruins. They are therefore moving toward another catastrophe — unless for once a few people notice what they (and we) are moving into. In Italy and in other Mediterranean countries, this hole in the staircase is less evident, as I mentioned earlier. It is, however, still there for this wind blows everywhere, also southwards of the Alps.

714   Before I give a short resumé of the rest of the book, I want to say something about the name "Li." With "Fo," it is clear that the author means Buddha, but "Li" is a very great problem because in the

Chinese dictionary there are innumerable "Lis," and it is not clear which "Li" the author means here. The most probable would seem to be "reason and reasonableness, order," because, as we recall, Melchior represents the ego-figure who is torn between those two opposites — of Fo and von Spät — so that Li — reason — would fit best with the ego. Moreover, Melchior is a chemist — a scientist, then — and until he became torn between those two powers, he might really have been called the cultivated, reasonable scientist. Thus, he represents reason, or consciousness, torn between the opposites. In this connection, it is interesting to note what one of the participants in my Puer seminar has found out about the original meaning of the word "Li" — that stands for "reason": It refers to the secret tracings which one finds in precious stones, the tracings and patterns that are to be found, for example, in an opal or an onyx, in which there are frequently dark interior patterns. To understand this, one must naturally think in Chinese terms. All the cultural patterns in China were obtained, according to the myth, from the meandering of the big Chinese rivers. These rivers were sketched onto a map, and their patterns stand for the cultivated surface of the Chinese earth. Thus, for the Chinese, consciousness means an awareness or perception of the hidden patterns in nature.

715   The Chinese, the Eastern peoples — and, strangely enough, to a certain extent, the Germanic people — are not interested in causal rationalism. Instead, the natural tendency is toward becoming aware of the patterns of Tao, an awareness created by divination, and, through that, an awareness of synchronicity and of image analogies. Within this mentality, the secret patterns in a stone correspond to reason. In the book, however, there is a fatal association because Fo and Li connect, and if you write them together, you arrive at "foli(e)" — folly or madness. Since the outbreak of an entire mass psychosis is predicted in this book, it is possible that the author thought of this connection.

716   The fourth part of the book begins with the chapter "The Transformations of Love." Melchior, who is now called Li,

walks over the sunburnt earth. He feels at one with nature. The path under his feet seems to him to be a living body. Wherever he turns he senses breathing flesh. The trees have turned into naked bodies. A radiant face bends down toward him from the sky. Voices call after him from all directions. He allows himself to fall with outstretched arms. The river that he was following now swells slowly beyond its banks and envelops him in soft waves, pulling him along with it. Li's body expands and fills the space. He is floating above the earth, until he is called back with a cry. Once again, he falls, and a passionate woman presses herself against his body, becomes bigger and bigger and more powerful, a hall grows around her with white columns and fills with small, flickering flames and smoky light. Gentle drumrolls can be heard, and Li's body turns into a woman's body. His partner turns into a giant pressing down upon him, and from this point onward, one transformation follows the other in quick succession. "In ever-changing embraces, he knows himself to be in new rooms with different bodies. Sometimes he is a slave, kissed by an emperor in a tent that is hot, sometimes a war whore, stretched over a drum, underneath the blood-smelling bodies of panting soldiers, sometimes a priest in the scented bed of a delicate woman." Finally, as a short, black-haired peasant, he finds himself in an embrace on an altar with his peasant woman partner, where they are sacrificed by priests. Once again, everything is transformed as his blood splatters. "A primeval forest with wavering trees of a thousand limbs rises; a panther digs his claws into Li's flesh. A final cry, and Li dissolves into emptiness. [...] Falling fast, he catches himself again. In one second, he falls through all the rooms through which he has passed." Li awakes on cushions of clouds, garlands of flowers surround him, and he finds Fo sleeping beside him; his body is so graceful, Li bursts into tears. Fo opens his eyes, and simultaneously his followers also wake up and stretch in their clouds in the morning.

717 Here we can see that the kingdom and the power of Fo are as dominating, strong, and absolute as was the power of von Spät, for Li is now drawn into the earth and into the principle of eternal transformation, whose main drive is eros, or even more, sexuality in all its different forms.

718 The next chapter, "The Downfall," is concerned with the approach of the kingdom and the death of the boys. The kingdom is heralded by a storm. Fo says, "We are home. We die into the kingdom. We dive into the black springs to blossom again in the world." Ceremoniously, he continues, "Time sinks, space disperses, gestalt is obliterated." The whole group shakes with pain and cramps. Their faces grow age-old and faded, their hair turns white, their eyes are blind, their hands are thin and aged. All look at Fo, who seems bent under a heavy burden. "And, as in a fog, a figure streams out of him, a second and a third one follow, and then more and more are released out of him. [...] A long line of airy figures come out of every boy, who are twisting in pain: girls with fixed smiles, old people looking crazed, some wearing armour with black seams, angels with heavy, blood-seamed wings." All that they have been, loved, and feared now stream out of the boys. Their bodies become increasingly ethereal, their movements weaker, and their cries of pain softer. But the procession of forms goes on and on, and powerless, they surrender themselves to the fleeting flood. They do not see how the distant glow of their kingdom becomes enveloped in mist and disappears, or how hostile air swirls around them. The clouds on which they floated sink down to the earth and they find themselves in a rotting copse of trees. In a whisper and dying, Fo gasps, "This...is...not...our...kingdom." Strangers have crept up to them and embrace them, but with the little strength they have left, the boys push them away, while a few who have no more strength surrender to the kisses of the strangers. Fo can no longer hold them back, and

they are carried away by them. Their bodies become as transparent as glass. Li then finds himself on a wide, icy surface, and he asks himself what has happened. The band disperses and they no longer recognize each other.

719   Here we have a further enantiodromia, exactly as we did when Melchior was crowned, and the boys carried him away when he cried out to them. Now, when they are near the kingdom and are detaching from all projections — in the Eastern sense of the word, getting free from karmic projections, from involvement in the world, to turn to Self, to their kingdom — the other pole then enters, and the pendulum swings back again. They have missed the turning point and are once again the victims of a meaningless reversal.

720   In practice, this is best illustrated in the alternating states of schizophrenics. There are times when they are filled with the collective unconscious in the form of constant transformation. They might say that they are God, or Jesus, or the Tree of Life, or the gold and silver island, and then they are "Naples" and they "have to give macaroni to the whole world." This is an expression of the eternally transforming nature of collective unconscious. But if it is a schizophrenic episode that has something fatal in it, there is fragmented rationalism in the material, for just as they say, "I am Jesus Christ. I am the World Tree," which is understandable, they go on, "I and Naples must provide the world with macaroni," which brings in absolute banality, a fragmented part of the outer-ordinary, which disturbs the harmony of this manifestation of the collective unconscious. Schizophrenic material can at once be recognized, for fragments of intellectual banalities are inseminated into very important material. One could say that there are von Spät-like fragments in such archetypal material: The glass kingdom has shattered, and it has been ground up within the collective unconscious. To say, "I and Naples must provide the world with macaroni" is complete nonsense, but to say, "I am Christ and the World Tree" is quite meaningful because in the Self, we have a divine source, and every Christian mystic must accept that with a grain of

salt. If one could sort out the material, the illness would not be fatal, but if one pulls out of it with drugs, without sorting the grains, he falls into a rigid normality typical of the postpsychotic state. People become rigid, normal, and highly intellectual, and they totally condemn everything they experienced, saying that they do not want to talk about it. They repress it completely and carry on in the rigid normality of established reason, which is generally the standard of the collective conscious and intellectually something very cheap.

721   In both states, two things are lacking: The first is that the schizophrenic person is unable to see the reality of the psyche, for in this state he takes the archetypes and the inner world as being completely real, which is why he thinks he is Jesus Christ. But he does not say that with the nuance of the mystic; he means it quite literally, for he will say that he is Jesus Christ and therefore is unable to go to his office tomorrow. This shows that he does not understand it as an inner content, but instead he takes it concretely and literally. In my experience, the greatest difficulty one has in helping a schizophrenic to come out of his episode is getting him to understand the symbolic level of interpretation, for he insists on everything being quite concrete, which brings a strange rationalism and materialism into his madness. He does not see that there is a reality of the psyche. He cannot accept the hypothesis of psychic reality as opposed to outer physical reality. He mixes the two up, which accounts for the nonsense. When such people snap into the "normal," rational von Spät state, they once again do not recognize the reality of the psyche.

722   The second thing which is lacking here is the feeling function, that is, the possibility of assessing values correctly. Jung tells the story of a schizophrenic patient of his who from time to time stopped listening to him. He had great difficulty in finding out what she was doing when she broke off like that, but after a long time, she confessed that at such times she was telephoning the Virgin Mary, to just quickly get her opinion! At such times the patient was inaccessible because there was someone else on the line, so to speak! Now if you had a mystical experience of the Virgin Mary, as the

Christian mystics sometimes did, you would be completely overwhelmed. People who have had such inner experiences remain shaken for days afterward, which is an appropriate reaction after such an overwhelming religious experience. But it is typical for a schizophrenic to say, "Hello! Oh yes! The Virgin Mary? OK." Either you believe nothing of it, or you are horribly shocked. When a person is having a psychotic episode, everything is said in the same tone, whether they are Jesus Christ or delivering macaroni. The cheapest banalities and the deepest religious material are interspersed without evaluation.

723   That is why the theme of discriminating between the different grains, separating the good from the bad, as Cinderella does in the fairytale Cinderella, and Psyche does in the age-old, famous story of Amor and Psyche, is very meaningful, for this theme shows it is a function of the psyche to discriminate values. If the anima is lost, feeling is lost, and that happens often in schizophrenia. As soon as feeling and contact with the anima has gone in a man, there is this picture, and then many people get into such a state, which in turn induces a mass psychosis, as we have already had and may possibly have again.

724   Now Li is caught in the ice and finds himself among the ghosts of the dead. He sees his dead father, Henriette Karlsen, and Otto von Lobe once more. He wanders about, and we see that he is slowly moving back again to the north and to the ice pole of Ulrich von Spät. Von Spät is associated with the north, and when the wind blows southward, Fo is approaching. The cold here naturally belongs to the land of the dead. Suddenly, the dead turn into black birds that screech with human voices that they will always return. Li is standing on the quay of a large harbor at which an enormous sailing boat is docking with many people on board. Fo is standing at the bow of the boat and waves at him, and all at once he is riding with him across a broad plain. Fo picks up the pace, and the ride gets faster and faster. The horses get

closer and closer and Fo and Li embrace. For the first time, Li is gripped with fear when they touch. Their boat is at the seashore. They push it quickly into the water. At the same moment, after having ridden through a starry night, the sun rises with no preceding dawn. Li sees that the steersman who paddles them away, is not Fo, but is rather the glassy figure of von Spät.

725 Here, we have a further enantiodromia, but this time one factor comes near consciousness, namely, that von Spät and Fo are two aspects of the same thing — each is secretly also the other. This is something one always finds in extreme psychological opposites, for at the turning point, the two are one. It is the Tai-gi-tu of Chinese philosophy: The germ of the opposite is always in the black or in the white.

726 The next chapter that is called "The Return" opens in a lunatic asylum. Among the madmen is a sad-looking old man whom we can recognize as Melchior, who is soon to be released. Prior to this, a dialogue takes place between him and a bald old man who feels he is being followed by Melchior and who wants to convince Melchior to cooperate with him. He explains to Melchior what his plan is once the two of them are its two great rulers; how they will divide it up to stamp out humankind. Earth should once again become a paradise, with only a few women surviving with whom they can propagate the earth with new beings. The approach of a doctor interrupts the crazy speech of the bald man, which Melchior finds strange. Melchior again asks to be released, and the doctor explains he has come to discuss it. "I cannot bear living here any longer, Doctor. Everything here is too true. Out there, it is hidden under a false level of deeper meaning. Here, life plays out naked in front of us. I want to return to work. I believe I shall not be a burden to anyone." The doctor takes a moment to consider this, and then he

responds by saying that Melchior is completely cured. The chemical experiments he has performed in the asylum which the doctors followed have established this. The only thing he has been unable to talk him out of is his fixed idea that he is Dr. Melchior von Lindenhuis who disappeared a hundred years ago. But the wild fantasies that he had a year earlier when he was found drifting in a fishing boat have all disappeared, and there is no longer anything to prevent him from being released. As he is unable to recall his real name, the doctor shall recommend to the authorities that from now on he shall be known as Melchior van Lindenhuis. The state university that is very interested in his research will take care of him.

727 This is a fatal turn, because, under the veil of madness, the other half, the shadow — the bald old man — has tried to unite the opposites. It is a last-minute attempt in the lunatic asylum to bring the two sides — the southern and the northern half of the world, Fo and von Spät — together, to recognize the opposites, and to realize that they are two aspects of one and the same thing. But this attempt is mixed up with megalomaniacal ideas of destroying the whole world and creating a new race. The so-called Herrenrasse was one of the fantasies of the Nazi regime: All other people were to be destroyed quickly because of overpopulation (a part of the trouble that we are confronted at present) and a new race created. The proposition of the bald man shows a strange mixture of constructive tendencies (the union of the opposites) and of megalomaniacal, destructive fantasies. The union of the opposites fails, and Melchior regresses into rational normality once more. If we relate it to the author, he must have been near complete madness, in which he could have realized the problem of the opposites, but instead, he switches into the one-sidedness of his conscious standpoint. So, Melchior is released from the asylum, becomes a professor at the University, and is once more successful in a boring way, just as at the beginning of the book.

728   There follows an eerie description of an encounter with a student whom Melchior believes he knows from earlier times. He introduces himself as Walter Mare — a name that reminds one of "night-mare" and "mare" — a female horse. In Melchior's apartment, Mare confesses that when he was young, he often dreamt of a face that resembles Melchior's face, though much younger. This face had looked in at him through a window, and it had called out to him that he should follow him and let himself be crucified. Melchior becomes increasingly unsettled as dark memories start to stir within him. "The cross will be raised… the morning dawns…the body is torn apart…Blood streams through the world….one is caught up in the monstrousness…When was that?... When did this happen?... We must roam, dear Mare, always roaming… We must be free. We may not rush. I, too, must become a wanderer again… I want to leave… Will you come with me?"

729   Mare kisses Melchoir's hand and says he wants to go with him. They agree to meet the next day. Then Melchior stands in front of the mirror and undresses himself, as if he were under some compulsion. His body is without any imperfection, without a trace of aging or decay. Only his pale, fear-filled expression seems like a petrified mask, with unmoving, lusterless eyes. "What is this old head doing on this young body? I am still strong. I can still leave. […] Where have I seen his face, his manner of walking, his form? Is he luring me to leave, or am I luring him?" He puts his clothes back on and works at his desk, but he cannot stay in the apartment. For the first time, he sets out for the café. There he meets a colleague who wants to discuss the 100th anniversary of Stuhlbrestenburg that is taking place that day. The great revolution, in which the king was killed at the theater, a mad, dark time of mythical intoxication is now one hundred years ago. One was less content and more unsettled in those times. Nowadays, we do not know this longing for

the limitless, that was so much talked about back then. There is talk of mysterious boys who caused great confusion at the time. Melchior takes his leave and finds his way home through endlessly long streets. With every step he takes, he feels lighter and freer, and he feels he could go on forever, and gradually loses his sense of the present. "The streets grew wider. The houses grew. The sky circled deeper and more sweepingly. The clouds were torn apart. Great, yellow stars glowed hot and close." He thought he heard footsteps behind him, but he could not see anyone. Melchior is filled with dread. Once again, he heard footsteps that walked in unison with his own. He seemed to be surrounded by invisible wanderers. New strength swept through him, and when he sang loudly into the night, invisible choirs responded from all around. In a vision, he sees himself on a white horse riding into an illuminated tow. Naked youths wearing wreaths on their heads and holding torches high at arm's length, seamed the streets that led into a square. A high door opened in front of Melchior. He climbs down from his horse and is suddenly standing alone in front of his own front door. Desperate, Melchior sinks to the ground where he lies for a long time. When he finally wants to open his front door, it seems to him to be threatening, and his apartment seems foreign to him and frightening. Someone must be in it. He hears deep breathing and finally discovers von Spät, sleeping in an armchair. At that moment, the fog in his memory leaves him.

730 The next chapter, "The Snow Wanderer" describes how Melchior struggles, with the help of the boys, to get von Spät into his power. But he shakes off this temptation and cries out as he did in the past, "I want to leave!" but nothing stirs. He tries it again, and when he gets no response after his third attempt, he realizes that the boys are in the power of the "master." Resigned, he lies down to sleep without having woken up von Spät. In his dream, he finds himself again in the kingdom of the glass lords whose bodies move like the dead, empty and in time with each other. While roaming, he

comes to the meadow in which there stand an empty cross, which resembles a dead tree. Then the marble palace rises up once more in front of him, with dilapidated columns and withered flowers. He enters the rotting forest and hears his name being called from afar. He runs faster and finally leaves the forest behind him and finds himself on the seashore. There, von Spät comes toward him, bleeding from a thousand wounds. Melchior ducks and takes out his knife, then he falls upon him and as quick as lightning, he cuts a cross into his chest. Von Spät cries out, "Melchior!" and Melchior wakes up to find him standing next to his bed with a lit candle in his hand. "The earth is mine," says von Spät, "and you have called for the boys in vain. They cannot hear you. They are only reflections now. They are going into the light." "I am not yours!" Melchior cries out. "I will pull them back into my world, into the world of longing and confusion, into the transformation from one form to another. My willpower is free." "I will break your will, as I have broken the will of the others," said von Spät quietly. "Form is illusion. I destroy the deception. I tear the veil. I resolve the game into truth!" Melchior stands up and replies, he will weave a new veil, for he wants the game to go on forever. "Come with me," says von Spät, "and I will show you the end of the game." They go out onto the street where heavy snow is falling, and they walk for some time until they reach an unknown area with narrow, dark streets. Above the entrance of a dilapidated house, they see a sign illuminated by the glow of an oil lamp that reads in pale, golden letters "World-Stage Radium."

731   "We have arrived," says von Spät and raps on the door with his stick. An aged dwarf opens the door and informs them that they have come in time to see the final act of the play, but the audience is no longer there. They follow him into the auditorium and sit down upon the ripped, upholstered chairs that are in a loge by the stage. The wallpaper is torn and its tatters rattle in the cold draft. Melchior shivers. "Good seats," says von Spät. "One can observe the actors from an angle that

prevents one from taking the play all too tragically." A long, piercing bell rings, and the curtain flies up. On the stage is the same city that Melchior had seen a few hours earlier in his dream. "Once again, the same transparent inhabitants with the same immovable faces are dancing the circular dance in line with each other. And this time, Melchior knows who they are: He recognizes the boys. In the middle of the performance, he catches sight of Ulrich [von Spät] for the second time. The entire dance seems to revolve around him." Von Spät stands up and sits down on a stool behind Melchior, pulls out a pair of opera glasses and, with his elbows resting upon Melchior's shoulders, he watches the play. On the stage, one of the dancers begins to move toward von Spät and calls out, "Time sinks away. Space vanishes. Form disappears." It is Fo's voice. Melchior wants to jump up, but von Spät's elbows weigh him down. Beneath him, the dancers line up in pairs, and they stand expectantly in front of an enormous door, with light pouring through its closed wings. Their eyes are closed, as if they are deeply asleep. The eyelids of von Spät's double slowly close. Melchior feels how the pressure of von Spät's elbows grows lighter, and he sees that he, too, has fallen asleep. Free now, he stands up, victorious over the sleep that is trying to overcome him. He shouts strange words into the room that echo around him. Then he sees a new form on the stage and recognizes it as he, himself. He hurries toward Fo and shakes him sharply until he wakes up. He hears someone calling out, "He sleeps. Now is the time!" And they throw themselves upon von Spät's double with their knives. In that instant, von Spät falls from his chair onto the floor. On the stage, Melchior leaves with Fo. Melchior gets caught in a snowstorm. A pale light is dawning. He is alone on the snowy streets. The town is far off in the mist. Melchior feels his strength leaving him, and he drops down onto the snow and looks into the distance. "The circles are closing," he whispers to himself. "My shadow has freed your shadow. The enemy is destroyed… Where on the wide earth are you?

Beyond the great seas which divide us, my secret calls have awoken you from your glassy sleep. […] Over wild roads you come nearer and nearer. In time it will be morning. […] And you will appear before me naked and glowing, stars in your hair […] and your cool lips will kiss my beating heart. The earth will no longer be dumb. Your words will call to all life; your breath comes from every body; your love blossoms from every heart. The cross will be raised. The newly risen will shed their blood into the veins of the world and will transform from one form into another. The new play begins. […] Come to us in the foliage of night in naked conflagration, young flame, singing flame, Master and Child!"

732 Melchior rises once again and stumblingly stamps his way through the snow until he reaches a path that gently leads upward. There in the snow he sees a drop of blood. But when he gets closer, he sees it is a rose petal. A few steps further on there is another, indeed, the whole path is strewn with rose petals, and next to them are the tracks of delicate, bare feet. Melchior cannot help but follow the tracks into the white mist, following the trail of the blood-red alluring rose petals. Ahead of him, he sees a distant figure surrounded by a silver light that slowly becomes golden. The sun breaks through, and Fo is standing there on the peak in a glow of light, with roses in his hair and around his loins, his flaming arms spread wide. The tired wanderer falls to his knees. "The kingdom," he stammers, "the kingdom without space…" His pulse ceases. His heart has burst.

733 Again, there is an enantiodromia at the end of the novel. Von Spät has won again by luring Melchior in the form of Fo into the boat. A hundred years later, we find Melchior in the lunatic asylum, for as soon as you are in the kingdom of intellectual reason, anything experienced at the opposite end — in Fo's realm — seems to be sheer madness. On the stage, Fo again gets the upper hand. He finds the kingdom at last, but he leaves his body behind, and von Spät gets it. He himself is a dead old man, which means that the problem is not

solved but is again postponed, because if a solution is described as taking place after death, it means that the conscious means for realization have not yet been found in this reality. That is why in Christianity victory over evil and the union of the opposites is projected into the time after the Day of Judgment. Paradise comes after death. Here, as in Faust, the solution is projected onto the afterlife. In The Kingdom without Space, the bridge to realization has not yet been found because in this fight, the reality of the psyche is not realized. It is all fought in the projection — intellect versus the archaic reality of the unconscious. Having no name for it and not seeing its reality, the author mixes psychic reality with concrete reality.

734   This is also the ominous background of our present-day problem, in connection with which I would like to quote a saying of Rabelais to which Jung drew my attention: La verite dans sa matière brute est plus fausse que la faux (truth in its prima materia — in its first appearance — is falser than falseness itself). And that is very true of this last summarized section of the novel. But despite it all, these are attempts to bring forth a new creative religious attitude and a renewal of cultural creativity — which can only manifest in a psychological and individual form. But it comes up with such a disgustingly false political twist, it is falser than falseness itself. Despite this, however, we must turn toward it and discriminate the seeds in it. Otherwise, we are stuck, forever building light, rose-colored buildings upon burnt-out ruins.

735   In his life and work, Bruno Goetz himself went beyond this unsolved problem. In the poem "The God and the Snake," he describes the divine puer as a symbol that at first overcomes the snake (similar to the boa with Saint-Exupéry), then cleanses it in order to finally unite with it. Its destructive aspect is overcome, and the opposites unite in a sacred marriage. We would like to hope that this will also take place in the experience of the collective.

736   If we compare the two puer figures — the little prince and Fo — we see that they share a romantic view of life, and both must face the aged figure — the king and the vain man in Saint-Exupéry's story and von Spät in Goetz's story. In both instances, they represent the

possibility of creative inner renewal, a first perception of the self. But because of a weakness of ego, and a missing or insufficient differentiation of the anima, these two figures are lured into death or madness, or both.

737   An American version of this same puer figure would be Richard Bach's Jonathan Livingstone Seagull. Bach's story, however, has a positive ending: It is his love of his friends that draws Jonathan back to the flock to teach the gulls how to fly. Further, Jonathan is a bird, not a human being, so it is natural for him to stay airborne. The danger remains, however, for the puer to identify with Jonathan and to become a "misunderstood genius." The image may nevertheless be understood correctly, in which case it delivers the healing message of love, freedom, and submission to one's task in life.

In Bruno Goetz's novel, the problem of the puer aeternus is not only a personal one but is a problem of our time. The senex, the old man, is an image of a worn-out god and world principle. The puer figure of Fo is an image of a new god-image which, in the novel, is unable to incarnate in human form — in Melchior. If a new god-image is unable to be born within the psyche of a human being, it remains an unconscious, archetypal figure that has a disintegrative and destructive effect. We are heading toward a "fatherless society," but the "son" has not yet been born, i.e., it has not yet been consciously realized within our psyche. This inner birth can only take place with the help of the feminine principle. For this reason, this principle now has the general public's attention. If embittered and scheming Sophie were once again able to become what she once was — Sophia, divine wisdom — the new birth could occur. Then, the puer would become what he should be — a symbol of renewal and of the whole inner person, which is what the neurotic pueri aeterni of our time are unconsciously seeking.

Appendix

Bibliography

Apuleius. *The Golden Ass*. Translated by P. G. Walsh. Oxford: Oxford University Press, 2008.

Bach, Richard. *Jonathan Livingston Seagull: A Story*. New York: Thorsons, 2011.

Baynes, H. G. *Analytical Psychology and the English Mind and other Papers*. London: Methuen, 1950.

Berthelot, Marcelin. "Codex Marcianus." In *Collection des anciens Alchimistes Grecs*. 2 vols. Paris: Steinheil, 1887–88.

Bruno Goetz. *Der Gott und die Schlange: Balladen*. Zürich: Bellerive-Verlag, 1949.

_____. *Das Reich ohne Raum: Eine Vision der Archetypen. Eine Chronik wunderlicher Begebenheiten*. 4th ed. Introduction by Walter R. Corti. Comment by Marie-Louise von Franz. Bern: Origo-Verlag, 1995.

Cate, Curtis. *Antoine de Saint-Exupéry: His Life and Times*. London: Heinemann, 1970.

Eaton, Frank. "Der Dichter Bruno Goetz." *Rice University Studies* 57, no. 4 (1972): 33–38.

Eliade, Mircea. *Shamanism: Archaic Techniques of Ecstasy*. Princeton, NJ: Princeton University Press, 2004.

Fromm, Erich and Rainer Funk. *Zum Gefühl der Ohnmacht*. 1st ed. Munich: Edition Erich Fromm. https://nbn-resolving.org/urn:nbn:de:101:1-20160205348.

Goethe, Johann Wolfgang von. *The Sorrows of Werther*. New ed. Richmond Surrey: Alma Classics, 2015.

_____. *Torquato Tasso: A Dramatic Poem from the German of Goethe with other German poetry*. Translated by Charles des Voeux. 4 vols. Stuttgart: Belser, 1987-1990.

Grof, Stanislav. *The Adventure of Self-Discovery: Dimensions of Consciousness and New Perspectives in Psychotherapy and Inner Exploration*. Albany, NY: SUNY Press, 1988.

_____. *Beyond the Brain: Birth, Death, and Transcendence in Psychotherapy*. Albany, NY: SUNY Press, 1985.

Hoffmann, E. T. A. *The Golden Pot and other Tales*. Translated by Ritchie Robertson. Oxford: Oxford University Press, 2008.

Jaffé, Aniela. *Bilder und Symbole aus E. T. A. Hoffmanns Märchen "Der goldene Topf"*. 5th ed. Einsiedeln: Daimon Verlag, 2010.

Kerényi, Karl. *Heros Iatros: Über Wandlungen und Symbole des ärztlichen Genius in Griechenland*. Zürich: Rhein, 1945.

Kubin, Alfred. *The Other Side*. New ed. Translated by Mike Mitchell. Sawtry Cambs, England: Dedalus, 2014.

Lönnrot, Elias. *The Kalevala: An Epic Poem after Oral Tradition*. Translated by Keith Bosley. Oxford: Oxford University Press, 1999.

Löwis of Menar, August von. *Russische Volksmärchen*, edited by Reinhold Olesch. *Die Märchen der Weltliteratur*, no. 41. Dusseldorf: Diederichs, 1955.

Magee, John Gillespie. "High Flight." In *The Family Album of Favorite Poems*, edited by P. Edward Ernest. New York: G. P. Putnam's Sons, [1983] 1959.

Pauli, Wolfgang. *Atom and Archetype: The Pauli/Jung Letters, 1932–1958*, edited by C. A. Meier. London: Routledge, 2001.

Mitscherlich, Alexander. *Auf dem Weg zur vaterlosen Gesellschaft: Ideen zur Sozialpsychologie*. Munich: Piper & Co, 1969.

Nerval, Gérard de. "Aurelia." In *Œuvres*, 357–414. Paris: Éditions Gallimard, 1974.

Jung, C. G. *Bollingen Series XX: The Collected Works of C. G. Jung*, edited by Herbert Read, Michael Fordham, Gerhard Adler and William McGuire. Translated by R. F. C. Hull. 20 vols.

_____. *Aion: Researches into the Phenomenology of the Self*. 2nd. ed. Vol. 9/II. Princeton, NJ: Princeton University Press, 1978.

_____. *Alchemical Studies*. Vol. 13. Princeton, NJ: Princeton University Press, 1983.

_____. *Archetypes and the Collective Unconscious.* 2nd ed. Vol. 9/I. Princeton, NJ: Princeton University Press, 1980.

_____. "On the Nature of the Psyche." In *The Structure and Dynamics of the Psyche*, §§ 343–442. 2nd ed. Vol 8. Princeton, NJ: Princeton University Press, 1981.

_____. *The Practice of Psychotherapy.* 2nd ed. Vol. 16. Princeton, NJ: Princeton University Press, 1985.

_____. *Psychiatric Studies.* Vol. 1. Princeton, NJ: Princeton University Press, 1970.

_____. *Psychological Types.* Vol. 6. Princeton, NJ: Princeton University Press, 1990.

_____. *Psychology and Alchemy.* Vol. 12. Princeton, NJ: Princeton University Press, 1993.

_____. *Psychology and Religion: West and East.* 2nd ed. Vol. 11. Princeton, NJ: Princeton University Press, 1989.

_____. *Symbols of Transformation: An Analysis of the Prelude to a Case of Schizophrenia.* 2nd ed. Vol. 5. Princeton, NJ: Princeton University Press, 1990.

_____. "Synchronicity: An Acausal Connecting Principle." In *Structure and Dynamics of the Psyche*, §§ 816–958. 2nd ed. Vol. 8. Princeton, NJ: Princeton University Press, 1970.

_____. *Two Essays on Analytical Psychology.* Vol. 7. Princeton, NJ: Princeton University Press, 1967.

Jung, C. G. *Letters*, edited by Gerhard Adler in collaboration with Aniela Jaffé. Translated by R. F. C. Hull. Vol. 1, 1906–1950. Princeton, NJ: Princeton University Press, 1973.

_____. *Visions: Notes of the Seminar Given in 1930–1940 by C. G. Jung*, edited by Claire Douglas. 2 vols. London: Routledge, 1998.

_____. and Karl Kerényi. *The Science of Mythology: Essays on the Myth of the Divine Child and the Mysteries of Eleusis.* London: Ark Paperbacks, 1985.

Perry, John. *The Far Side of Madness.* Washington, DC: Spring Publications 2020.

Picinelli, Fillippo. *Mundus Symbolucus.* Hildesheim: Olms, 1979.

Poe, Edgar Allan. *Collected Works of Edgar Allan Poe*, edited by Thomas Ollive Mabbott with the assistance of Eleanor D. Kewer and Maureen C. Mabbott. 3 vols. Cambridge, Mass.: The Belknap Press of Harvard University Press, 1969–1978.

Radloff, W. *Proben der Volksliteratur der türkischen Stämme Südsibiriens.* 10 vols. St. Petersburg: Kais. Akad. d. Wiss., 1872.

Rousseau, Jean-Jacques. *Confessions.* London: Dent, 1964.

Ruska, Julius. *Tabula Smaragdina: Ein Beitrag zur Geschichte der Hermetischen Literatur.* Heidelberg: Carl Winter's Universitätsbuchhandlung, 1926.

Saint-Exupéry, de Antoine. *Flight to Arras.* New York: Houghton Mifflin Harcourt, 1969.

_____. *Le Petit Prince.* Paris: Gallimard, 1945.

_____. *Night Flight.* New York: Mariner Books, 1974.

_____. *Terre des Hommes.* Paris: Gallimard, 1953.

_____. *The Wisdom of the Sands.* Mattituck, NY: Amereon House, 2007.

Seton, Ernest Thompson. *Wild Animals I Have Known.* Toronto: McClelland and Stewart, 1977.

Tacitus, Cornelius. *Germania*, edited by Alfons Städele. Dusseldorf: Artemis & Winkler, 2001.

Von Franz, Marie-Louise. *On Divination and Synchronicity: The Psychology of Meaningful Chance.* Toronto: Inner City Books, 1980.

Index

www.ingramcontent.com/pod-product-compliance
Lightning Source LLC
Chambersburg PA
CBHW021123270326
41929CB00009B/1013